A First Course in

EXPERIMENTAL PSYCHOLOGY

A Letter to Young Scientists
from Ivan Petrovich Pavlov

(Written just before the death of the famous scientist at the age of eighty-seven years, on February 27, 1936. As printed in SCIENCE, April 17 [1939], p. 369. Used with permission.)

WHAT can I wish to . . . youth . . . who devote themselves to science? *Firstly*, gradualness. About this most important condition of fruitful scientific work I never can speak without emotion. Gradualness, gradualness, and gradualness. From the very beginning of your work, school yourselves to severe gradualness in the accumulation of knowledge.

Learn the ABC of science before you try to ascend to its summit. Never begin the subsequent without mastering the preceding. Never attempt to screen an insufficiency of knowledge even by the most audacious surmise and hypothesis. Howsoever this soap-bubble will rejoice your eyes by its play, it inevitably will burst and you will have nothing except shame.

School yourselves to demureness and patience. Learn to inure yourselves to drudgery in science. Learn, compare, collect the facts! Perfect as is the wing of a bird, it never could raise the bird up without resting on air. Facts are the air of a scientist. Without them you can never fly. Without them your "theories" are vain efforts.

But learning, experimenting, observing, try not to stay on the surface of the facts. Do not become the archivists of facts. Try to penetrate to the secret of their occurrence, persistently search for the laws which govern them.

Secondly, modesty. Never think that you already know all. However highly you are appraised, always have the courage to say of yourself—I am ignorant.

Do not allow haughtiness to take you in possession. Due to that you will be obstinate where it is necessary to agree, you will refuse useful advice and friendly help, you will lose the standard of objectiveness.

Thirdly, passion. Remember that science demands from a man all his life. If you had two lives that would not be enough for you. Be passionate in your work and your searchings.

IVAN PETROVICH PAVLOV

A First Course in

EXPERIMENTAL
PSYCHOLOGY

B. R. BUGELSKI

Professor of Psychology, University of Buffalo

NEW YORK: HENRY HOLT AND COMPANY

To my wife

Preface

IN THE LEISURELY DAYS before the war, the small numbers of psychology students could obtain a proper scientific orientation through personal association with an instructor trained in the experimental traditions of psychology. The postwar increase in numbers of students has made it impossible to retain the old practices, and now new methods, more suitable to handling larger groups, have had to be developed. This book represents an attempt at solving the problem of providing a scientific orientation for large groups of students. The writer has aimed at a practical solution of the laboratory instructor's problems. This solution consists of, first, providing a background in the nature of science, and, second, locating psychology within that background through the process of acquainting the student with the tools, techniques, and assumptions of the psychologist.

Among the writer's many biases, which the text makes no attempt to conceal, is the belief that all psychology must be based on experiment, and that it is quite improper to set aside an area of study labeled "experimental" as if to suggest that other areas of psychology exist which are not experimental. At the present time, when interest in applications is growing strongly, the vitally important component in the training of the future psychologists is the development of an experimental attitude with all that implies of scepticism, restraint, and a thorough appreciation of the complexities that must be investigated before even modest generalizations are in order. The student who faithfully works through the included experiments should acquire an appreciation of what must be done to establish psychology among the sciences.

The attempt at providing a scientific orientation for the beginning student of experimental psychology is the chief justification of the present text in view of the fact that since the war a number of admirable volumes entitled *Experimental Psychology* have appeared. These new texts, with all their merits, have different aims and have not tried to provide a solution to what the writer considers the real need of the student, which is that of allowing him to find a realistic framework from which to evaluate his own efforts and those of others working in the widespread problem areas now included in the psychologists' domains. It is because the writer believes that his own effort is a step in that direction that he has the temerity to offer this book to the student public.

In the attempt to provide a text that can be practical, the writer has developed his course, experiments, and apparatus in such a manner that any instructor with access to a small shop and a Mimeograph can either duplicate or improve upon the course as described in this text. Practically all the apparatus can be locally manufactured by the students themselves at ridiculously low costs compared with the prices of supply houses. A drill press, small power saw, and a few hand tools were used to make the apparatus described in the text. To facilitate local manufacture, schematic drawings and photographs of the apparatus have been provided. The construction talents of an average class are more than adequate to the tasks involved, and the opportunity to make their own equipment is one which should not be denied to students. By making his own equipment, the student makes the experiment his own, and begins his progress on the road to psychological experimentation. Psychologists traditionally have built their own equipment because of the nature of their problems, and it is well for the beginning student to learn the relation of apparatus to the solution of a problem.

Current practices in teaching experimental psychology differ widely in hours and credits at different institutions. Some schools offer only one semester of laboratory work, others two. The author does not presume to dictate standards and believes that the course as described in this text can be adapted to a variety of circumstances. At the University of Buffalo the text is used in a two-semester course, meeting for five hours per week, for three credits per semester. The five hours are divided roughly into two hours of lecture and discussion and three hours of laboratory work. A satisfactory approximation of the work is covered in an evening course for adults meeting for two and one-half hours per week. In the latter course demonstrations are substituted for some of the experiments, and other short-cuts are employed. In both instances the following practice is adopted: an experiment is designed by the class in free discussion, the data are then collected and statistically treated where necessary, and finally the results are evaluated in group discussion. The usual prerequisite for the course is a course in elementary psychology. There appears to be no good reason, however, why the laboratory work should be delayed until such a course is completed, and the laboratory work might readily be introduced to accompany the general course just as it is in the other sciences.

If there is any merit to this text, it must be attributed to the efforts, suggestions, and criticisms offered by the writer's students, assistants, and colleagues, who have generously contributed their time, energy, and enthusiasm to the development of the experiments included in the text and to the invention and manufacture of the apparatus that is described. Special mention must be made of the services of W. A. Rogers, R. A. Coyer, and R. T. White in the matter of design and construction of apparatus. David Abel, Donald Bullock, and Walter Cohen tested the text "experimentally" in their classes at the University of Buffalo and contributed energetic criticisms of impractical ventures and impossible apparatus. Through their cooperation a course has been developed that the writer believes to "work."

My greatest personal debt is to Professor Carleton F. Scofield, who was my first instructor in laboratory methods and, as it turns out, my latest. Professor Scofield must have literally "found" time, since he had none available in the ordinary twenty-four-hour day, to read the text with a teacher's critical eye, and he seemed intent on "flunking" the writer outright. If I had taken his advice on all the suggestions he made, the text might have rated "passable" with him, but I fear it would never have been finished. Wherever signs of restraint or temperance appear, the reader should suspect the hand of the critic. I am glad to absolve Professor Scofield of all responsibility for what I have included, but somebody ought to take the blame for all the really good ideas and inspirational insights that were dropped because of a firm red-pencil mark.

Donald Cook, an artist with a scientific attitude, prepared most of the illustrative material, did all the photographic work, and supervised the drawings which were executed by Robert H. Walsh.

Final mention should be made of the services of three brave girls who refused to surrender in the face of illegible copy made up largely of hints and suggestions of words. These more than admirable young women are Irene Kohsmann, Grace Enright, and Beverly Kurtz.

Buffalo, New York
December, 1950
                                                      B. R. B.

Contents

Appendixes   399

Index   411

Experiments

Illustrations

Introduction

PSYCHOLOGY as we know it today is generally acknowledged to have started as a laboratory science in Leipzig in 1879 in the laboratory of Wilhelm Wundt. For many years, psychologists from various countries, including the United States, took their professional training with Wundt or his students in Germany and returned to their own countries to originate formal laboratories of their own.

Notable among Wundt's students was E. B. Titchener who began experimental work after the German pattern at Cornell University. The influence of Titchener spread broadly, and for the first decades of the twentieth century, American laboratories were reasonable facsimiles of the German, with strong interests in the type of psychological experimentation that interested Wundt in the analysis of mental content.

Meanwhile, a variety of independent psychological enterprises and revolts against the Wundtian tradition arose in France, England, Germany, and the United States. In France, Itard, Janet, Le Bon, and Binet introduced educational, abnormal, and social psychology, and mental testing. In England, Galton fostered the study of individual differences, and the British tradition of associationism left the armchair for the laboratory. In Germany, Ebbinghaus studied memory as a psychological process rather than for its Wundtian atomic content. Animal psychology and practical applications of psychological findings became interesting to American psychologists. In Russia, Pavlov studied "conditioned reflexes of dogs. All of these trends were destined to occupy a major share of psychology and of experimental and other types of research work, while the Wundtian tradition slowly declined.

In academic circles it rapidly became recognized that the young science of psychology could grow only on a firm foundation of experimental data and that information must be discovered before it could be taught. The entangling apron strings of tradition, common sense, and folklore also made it plain that psychology could not make progress unless its students were trained as rigidly as were those in the more established sciences. To foster such training for scientific thinking, laboratory courses were established in the fond belief that working with apparatus and performing "actual experiments" would teach the student respect for the facts, inculcate scientific habits of critical appraisal and caution, and provide a host of new discoveries.

The content of laboratory courses has never been standardized throughout the country in a degree comparable with courses in physics and chemistry. No single authority or text has been commonly recognized. The experimental psychology course at any given university has been a function of the facilities, space, equipment, course-credit time, and interest of the instructor. Course content varied so widely that students at different schools might complete courses which bore practically no resemblance to each other. Such a state of affairs might have been justified on the grounds that after all it was *method* and *not content* that counted, and that the method would be the same regardless of the content.

Such a justification is largely a dream. One does not learn method by *going through* a miscellaneous assortment of experiments selected on an opportunistic basis of feasibility and practicality. In some experimental courses, for example, students take a series of vocational, intelligence, and aptitude tests gratuitously labeled "experiments." What they learned from these adventures about experimental procedure is a mystery. In one recent text, the experiment on "reaction time" was omitted because the author found that it was boring to the students and did not prove anything important to them. From the author's viewpoint, the student of experimental psychology ought to be bored, and bored often, if he is ever to acquire the patience to outwait an experimental animal or to plough through the extensive tabulations of data often required by experiments. "Reaction time," boring or not, is one of the few measuring sticks available to the psychologist in his researches. It will be the subject of the first experiment in this text.

Experiments which teach method must be selected for that purpose, and the selection must not be limited by "practical considerations." There must be a basis of organization that determines the content and limits of a course. Such an organizational basis must, inevitably, reflect the bias of the instructor and his interpretation of what is meant by "Experimental Psychology." Some authors, like Boring, regard the subject as an area of investigation where sensation and perception are treated almost to the exclusion of other areas. Personal interest often determines inclusion and exclusion. Bills, for example, devotes five chapters to "fatigue." Woodworth, in his outstanding sourcebook, does not even mention the term in connection with experimentation.

From the viewpoint of this text, there is no content, as such, specific to "experimental psychology." Taking "psychology" to mean a subdivision of science in which certain tools and techniques are employed which are not the commonly used tools of other investigators, it becomes the business of "experimental psychology" to teach students the use of these tools and techniques. Since the apparatus and procedures used by psychologists are best employed in the study of "behavior" or "interaction between organisms and their environments," it becomes obvious that both environment and behavior are the content, if such there be, of psychology.

To study the environment and behavior of organisms, it is necessary to indicate the measurable aspects of each of these components. In this text we equate the environment with stimuli and the behavior with responses. The laboratory can deal with nothing else if it is to deal with measurables. This book, accordingly, tries to analyze the problems, difficulties, techniques, and controls involved in the presentation of stimuli and measurement of responses.

Before stimuli and responses can be studied, however, it appears desirable to the writer to prepare the student for his future work by a brief analysis of the nature and meaning of science and experimentation. Without such an introduction the student is hardly in a position to evaluate what he is doing. Precise answers to most psychological questions cannot be looked up in a book. There are no *right* answers to the questions raised in the experiments. Students with experience in courses in physics and chemistry often find psychological experiments unsatisfactory because there are no answers in the back of the book. Such an attitude simply indicates a lack of understanding of both science and psychology. The early chapters in this text represent an attempt to provide such an understanding. Later chapters offer an attempt to bring an operational viewpoint into the analysis of certain traditional categories of behavior.

In general, each experiment included in this text has been chosen to teach at least one new technique, control, or procedural feature. Some of the experiments are, in part or in whole, duplicates of experiments reported in psychological journals. These have been selected to serve as goads for reading journal literature as well as to provide bases for comparisons of data. Other experiments are included because they involve some commonly used device such as the Skinner Box. The latter device is an excellent one to introduce the student to animal experimentation, and in the experiment included here, such an introduction is made simple, safe, and pleasant.

Many readers will wonder why certain traditional experiments are not included in this text. There is no experiment dealing with taste, color zones, discrimination of overtones, etc. The reason is that no one can anticipate the special interests of all potential users of a text. The author has tried to select experiments which teach method and has included more than can be handled adequately in a year's work. Since the experiments are meant only as illustrations of methodology, it is anyone's privilege to pick and choose, and to substitute his own illustrations as he likes. It is assumed that much of the sensory material which is not emphasized in this text can be handled by demonstration.

How successful the current presentation is must be left to the reader and user of this book. The author can only hope that the student is sufficiently challenged by the problems raised to examine his foundations for psychological work. Whether he does so because he is pleased or because he is infuriated is of minor importance.

A First Course in
EXPERIMENTAL PSYCHOLOGY

Part 1

Psychology and Science—General Methodology

1

A Brief Historical Appreciation of

Experimental Psychology

IT IS generally conceded to be the policy of wisdom to know one's forebears and understands one's roots. For the experimental psychologist, it is more than wise; it is necessary. More often, perhaps, than in any other science it is brought to the psychologist's attention that there is nothing new under the sun. Whenever you read an experimental report, you will first be introduced to the subject through a brief historical preface. The psychological writer will indicate how he happened to arrive at his experimental hypothesis, what previous work had been done on the specific problem, and how closely other investigators had approximated his findings or speculations.

An article by O. H. Mowrer illustrates this nicely. He writes of a two-factor theory of learning, attempting to show that there are at least two separate types of learning. Modestly he admits that his views are not too new. They have been anticipated by many other psychologists, notably by B. F. Skinner, H. Schlosberg, and Hilgard and Marquis. He presents his own views as merely a refinement or crystallization of the suggestions of these predecessors. The same story is repeated in nearly every experimental report. The work of psychologists has spread unevenly into so many areas that one can rarely be certain that he is not repeating a study already reported. The literature is so vast that no one can know it all, and a special historical project must be embarked upon with every piece of research, not only to avoid unnecessary duplication, but for hints, explanations, interrelations with other phenomena, etc. The historically unindoctrinated psychologist is not prepared for research.

The above remarks are meant to be more than a plea for thorough bibliographical work on the part of an experimenter investigating a specific problem. The *problems* that preoccupy psychologists today are still the same old problems that once puzzled the early Greek philosophers, and the opening reference to Aristotle is still good form. The *methods* of psychology, however, have been continuously changing. By "method" we mean here the ways of thinking and working, the kinds of metaphysical assumptions that are made, and the types of scientific systems that are devised to cope with age-old problems. The psychologist, whether he likes it or not, is a philosopher, with his own metaphysics. To work effectively, he must be able to state his own biases, methods of inquiry, and then his justifications, as well as to understand the biases and logic of those who oppose his views. To recognize and appreciate them, the psychologist must turn to the history of thought and find out from where the various views come and to where they lead. Only through a historical review of his science can the psychologist gain the perspective he needs to establish his own position in relation to the problems of psychology and to see their interrelationships among the problems of science as a whole.

The more or less complete history of psychology is now being written as part of what is genuinely a monumental enterprise by E. G. Boring (1), (2). It is to be a three-volume work, two volumes of which have been published, and a third of which is in the writing. The first volume, already twenty-one years old, has just been revised. There is little hope that an up-to-date historical handbook will ever be available. The average psychologist will have to remain his own historian, at least for his own sphere of interest. We cannot pretend even to notice the high spots of the history of experimental psychology in this chapter, and no attempt will be made to do so. The interested student will already have visited the library for his copies of Boring. We can, however, attempt to get a feeling for the historical point of view, to find out where we came from, what we are doing, why and how, and perhaps get a perspective from which we can view the future.

Experimental psychology started in an astronomical observatory! And that by accident. An astronomer's assistant who was supposed to report the exact time at which a certain star passed the hairline in his telescope reported times which were at variance with the reports of others. It was only a matter of a fraction of a second, but that was too much for the astronomer to tolerate. The assistant was discharged, and the astronomer in trying to salvage the assistant's work found an amazing thing. The reports were *consistently* slower. The assistant was making a constant error, which could be measured and subtracted from the reading for an approximation of the true time. That astronomer had unwittingly discovered "reaction time." * That was in 1802. It was of little or no interest at that time to a slow-moving world. The information was buried like Mendel's later studies on the heredity of peas; and like Mendel's studies, "reaction time" refused to stay buried. It waited for a propitious moment to emerge from its sanctum. Let us pass it by for a while and turn our attention to another phase of our historical survey.

In the 1860's philosophers were busy trying to locate man and his purpose in the universe, but for some time they had begun to manifest interest in the original nature and equipment of man. Philosophers had to come to terms with physiologists. They had to locate their minds, innate ideas, *tabulas rasas,* somewhere within the human nervous system. Descartes had started the new trend with his anatomical studies on the nervous system. He had "located" the soul in the pineal gland.

The mind-body problem was a burning issue. The successful development of a philosophy might well depend upon the inter-

* Reaction time will be the subject of your first experiment. (see pages 14–21).

pretation of the role and function of the brain and nervous system. Without hard scientific facts about the nervous system, a philosopher might build his cosmological structures on shaky foundations which could be collapsed by the leverage of a single neural fact.

Some of the basic questions facing the philosophers were of this nature: Can the mind hold more than one idea at a time? Can the mind store ideas? What are the physiological correlates, if any, of ideas, images, etc.? Do thoughts occur instantaneously? Do they depend on physical structures and processes? What, for example, is the speed of mental activity? Is it like the speed of light, sound, electricity? Does it depend on the speed of nervous activity? How fast *is* nervous activity? It was this last question that perplexed philosophers and physiologists alike. The answer to this question could set definite limits on the speculations of some philosophers. But there was no answer. No method had been invented to study the speed of impulses. But hadn't there? How about the astronomer's assistant?

Can you bridge the gap between the error of the astronomer's assistant and the measurement of the speed of the nervous impulse? All that it takes is a little thought. At the University of Berlin there was an extremely able scientist. We cannot overrate his abilities, and his contributions to physics, physiology, and psychology are probably beyond compare. Boring thinks so highly of this now-dead physiologist that he dedicated the second volume of his history to this genius (on the grounds that he isn't really dead except in an ordinary mundane sense). This man decided to discover the speed of the nervous impulse, and he did it in a fashion that is amazingly simple. At least it was simple for Hermann von Helmholtz. No one else at the time thought of it. His procedure was that of every scientist: to find out all that is known about a problem and to put all of your information together. The answer may be staring you in the face.

Helmholtz knew that you could make an extirpated nerve-muscle preparation react by stimulating the nerve with a slight ics and to such problems as attitude measurement, and their broad application to many problems that at first glance have nothing to do with the rarefied atmosphere in which the methods were first developed.

A rather important recent application of psychophysics was made in an extensive conditioned-response research by C. I. Hovland, who found the methods of psychophysics excellent for selecting ranges of auditory stimuli in attempting to develop a mathematical analysis of the principle of "generalization of conditioned responses." Another important contribution has been made through psychophysical techniques to the basic problems of sound and audition. In fact, the very unit of auditory intensity, the decibel, is a psychophysical as well as a physical unit. We shall return to the decibel and psychophysics later.

Helmholtz is best known to psychology students for his theories of audition and color vision. These are only partial contributions, as an examination of his great works on physiological optics and on the science of sound will quickly show. But his direct contributions would not have made a science out of psychology. His indirect contribution was more instrumental in this latter respect. We have alluded to him as the grandfather of psychology. His scientific son was Wilhelm Wundt. Wundt was Helmholtz' favorite student, and it was primarily through Helmholtz' interest in Wundt that Wundt was enabled to take the first professional chair in psychology, with the title of Professor of Psychology, and with a building known as a Laboratory of Psychology. Before Wundt there were no psychologists known as such. There were no psychological laboratories, if we except a small room set aside at Harvard for the private researches of William James, the first American psychologist. In 1879, the date known to all students of experimental psychology, and now to you, Wundt opened his laboratory and began active research in what were at that time the problems which interested a group of men who were neither physiologists nor philosophers but something in between. One can almost consider psychology a child of a temporary and perhaps illegitimate union of philosophy and physiology which occurred sometime in the middle decades of the nineteenth century.

Wundt's mission was to analyze the mind into its structural elements. That was his problem just as the problem for chemists of that era was to analyze the content of the earth into its elements. Wundt considered psychology a purely mental science of a highly purified form, and was interested in little else. When shown a copy of William James's *Principles of Psychology,* he is reported to have read it in one night (a marvelous achievement, if true) and to have returned it the next morning with the comment: "Very interesting, but it is not Psychology." The more practical and pragmatic views of James did not appeal to the scientific rigor of Wilhelm Wundt. He felt his new science demanded a new method, and he produced it, the method of *introspection,* of which we shall speak more extensively later, and he set about the problem of training his students in the use of this method. His students came from all over the world and carried back the word, method, apparatus, and all, to their countries of origin.

The Wundtian system and its development by his followers are fully described by Boring, and it would be an affront to Boring's work to attempt to summarize it here. We can note, however, that although Wundt was able to create a strong school of supporters, he also had many dissenters. You had to be for or against him, and the opposition appears to have won out, at least along major lines. The pure introspective method was judged too vague and sterile and the emphasis on pure science too academic for some American viewpoints, which demanded that science be practical.

Even in Germany, the demand for results of some use to mankind gave impetus to the researches of Hermann Ebbinghaus, who introduced psychologists to the use of nonsense syllables as a tool for the study of memory. Ebbinghaus was interested in discovering efficient ways of memorizing. The practical problem of improving the German educational system was his main interest. For Wundt, memory hardly deserved attention from a genuine psychologist. But in laboratories all over the world, psychologists are using nonsense syllables today, still seeking the secrets of the principles of learning and forgetting, while Wundt's introspectors are declining steadily in number and influence.

Wundt's insistence on psychology as an analytical science prompted his opposition (the Functionalists and, later, Watson) to search for alternate elements or principles. They found these first in reflexes, then in habits, and finally, as a consequence of the extensive researches of Pavlov in Russia, in the conditioned reflex or, as it is more commonly known today, the conditioned response. Psychologists did not abandon the analytical method which Wundt fostered, although this method came to be attacked as meaningless and futile by later German psychologists who now are identified as Gestaltists. These later psychologists insist on the unity and wholeness of psychological processes and believe that to analyze them is to destroy them. They set about devising their own types of experimental procedures which are designed to demonstrate the inadvisability of analysis. Even though the Gestaltists are primarily interested in eliminating the old type of Watsonian behaviorist and even the new or modern behaviorist, they are still equally anxious to joust with any kind of analyzers, and we can attribute a good deal of their vigor to anti-Wundtism.

We need not go much further in this brief historical sketch to make our original promise good. There is no need to scan the contributions of psychologists in England, France, and the rest of the world to see that our present science, arising as a historical accident, as a misfit in an area of interest in which philosophers and physiologists were seeking eternal truths, came to independence in the figure of Wundt and reached whatever maturity it now possesses through his influence upon his supporters and attackers.

Although Wundt was the first professional psychologist, the average student in elementary psychology today rarely hears his name. Psychology, like all other sciences, has changed, and radically, since 1879. Whereas for Wundt, psychology consisted of attempts to analyze the content of the mind in terms of sensations, images, and feelings, the modern psychologist has little interest in these "elements." The easiest way to learn about the nature of modern psychology is to glance over the section headings in current copies of the *Psychological Abstracts*. If we can temporarily and "operationally" * define psychology as "that which psychologists do," we can find all manner of activities, ranging from studies of the behavior of cockroaches to the influences of electric shock on schizophrenics and the effect of ego-involvement on level of aspiration. Psychology has grown so rapidly that it is now estimated that by 1980 there will be 40,000 professionally trained psychologists in the United States. If the range of their interests and fields of activity continues to expand as it has in the past, it will be quite impossible for any individual to know what psychology is all about even in terms of the definition given above.

Despite the differences that exist among psychologists in their numerous spheres of operation, they are held together by a common tie. This unifying bond is a devotion to science and its methodology. The principles and practices of psychology rest on a base of experimentation. New and bold insights and flashes of genius may be presented to the psychological world for inspection and adoption, but the first question asked by the psychologist is: What is the evidence? The respect for evidence is the distinguishing mark of the scientist, and the source of this respect is easy to discover. Anyone who has ever performed an experiment and faced the difficulties hampering the search for the truth is not likely to accept the confident stranger's word, the glowingly described panacea, or the beautiful theory until the experimental evidence is fully detailed. To get acquainted with the difficulties and complexities in the study of human behavior is the privilege and responsibility of all psychologists, as it has been from the time of Wundt. It is to these difficulties that we now turn. As a suitable

---

* In general, "operational" definitions are attempts to define some concept in terms of the observations, manipulations, or measurements through which the concept is derived rather than through reasoning or empathy (see pages 72–76).

introduction to experimental work, we shall start with the problem that once intrigued Helmholtz: reaction time.

References *

1. Boring, E. G. *A history of experimental psychology*, 2d ed. New York: Appleton-Century-Crofts. 1950.
2. Boring, E. G. *Sensation and perception in the history of experimental psychology*. New York: Appleton-Century. 1942.
3. Woodworth, R. S. *Experimental psychology*. New York: Henry Holt. 1938.

* The references included in this book are meant to be read. For this reason, there will not be long lists of readings beyond any possible hope of coverage by even the most rapid readers. When entire books are cited, it is expected that the student will browse selectively, consulting the index frequently, *looking* for information rather than hoping to arrive at it in a page-after-page fashion.

Experiment 1. Reaction Time

NOTE: The first four experiments you will do are designed to illustrate the content of Part I of this text. They deal with widely differing subjects, which have nothing to do with each other. The first experiment, on reaction time, was chosen because it most nearly typifies what the student is likely to expect of an "experiment." It has everything in it, quite literally. A whole course could probably be taught around this one experiment. In later chapters, when you read about experimentation, you will have had the benefit of having carried out an experiment to strengthen your appreciation of experimental procedure.

There is no point in *talking* about experimentation without some such foundation. In view of the history of experimental psychology, it is fitting that we begin our work with "reaction time," not only for its classical glory, but because it so clearly exemplifies such a host of experimental features and procedures. Chapter 2, which deals with some elementary statistical procedures, should be studied carefully, so that the data in this and other experiments in the course can be handled by quantitative methods.

The Effect of Caffeine on Reaction Time

Introduction. This is a sample experiment to demonstrate the basic features of experimentation in general. It involves the isolation and control of numerous variables and the introduction into a controlled situation of an independent variable whose effect on a selected dependent variable can be observed. Although this experiment deals with the effect of a drug on a behavior sample, and can presumably serve as a model of method in the study of drug effects, the student in this course is expected to concentrate on the procedural features of the experiment rather than to concern himself about the content of the problem. The problem was chosen as an exercise in experimental design and not for any intrinsic interest.

Apparatus and Procedure. The general procedure in the psychologist's study of drugs is to compare the behavior of an organism before and after administration of a drug. In order to study the effect of a drug on behavior, however, there are many questions to consider before the experimenter can administer the drug and begin observing its effects. The major factors to take account of are: (1) the drug, (2) the subject, and (3) the behavior. Let us consider the problems that arise immediately in the order just mentioned.

1. *The drug.* (a) How much of a dose shall we use? To do a completely adequate study, we should have to employ all possible dosages, from the minimal amount that could be prepared to the highest amount tolerable. (The only way to arrive at even tentative tolerance data for human subjects is to use subhuman subjects and drug them into insensibility, some acute reaction, or death depending on the action of the drug.) For our purposes, we shall use $\frac{1}{2}$ grain of caffeine, an amount known to be physiologically harmless.

   b. How shall it be administered? Orally, subcutaneously, or intravenously (these are the common methods). All but the oral methods involve using the drug in liquid solution. We shall use the oral procedure, with the drug in tablet form.

   c. How long shall we wait for the drug to have its effect (if any)? Here again the correct answer is to wait a full range of time, from zero through an extensive range of different intervals, to determine the course of effect. Some drugs have an initial stimulating effect and then a depressive effect. Your findings would depend upon the time of the test if you did not study the temporal range. We shall use only one time interval, 15 minutes.

2. *The subjects.* Some people are not affected as much as others, because of a variety of factors. In connection with drugs, such variables as *body size* and *tolerance* (physiological adjustment) are most important. A good big man can always drink a good

little man "under the table," if their tolerances are equal. Other factors to consider are stomach content, allergy, and suggestion effects. The student can readily see that, before embarking upon the actual experiment, considerable library research should be done concerning the host of variables involved, so that he can take the proper steps to eliminate or account for those that will affect his results. For our purposes, we will ignore these variables except for the suggestion factor. This can be controlled by using an extra group of subjects who get no drug, but think they do. Consider this "suggestion factor" carefully. Do we control it fully by the placebo technique? How many subjects will we need? This is a question that will have to be postponed until we attempt a statistical analysis.

3. *The behavior*. Behavior is too loose a term to use in an experimental setting. We can't just study behavior in general. We must select a sample which we can prepare to watch and record, if possible, for more leisurely scrutiny and confirmation. It is difficult to choose a sample which will *necessarily* show effects of the drug. The sample we choose may be completely unaffected or, on the other hand, might be the only aspect of behavior that is affected. In either case, we could get into difficulty in generalizing from one sample. A variety of samples, then, should be studied, but we will work with only one for the present. Our choice will be a typical laboratory response, that of the simple reaction to a simple stimulus, where the speed of the reaction is the item of interest. Such a measurement is generally known as "reaction time," but, as previously noted, it is more appropriately designated "latency."

The procedure in measuring reaction time is to arrange the apparatus with appropriate keys or switches so that the experimenter can simultaneously present a stimulus (e.g., a light) and start a chronoscope (a clock or other timing device which is started by the experimenter and stopped by the subject). Figure 1 shows a simple chronoscope that can be made from readily available ma-

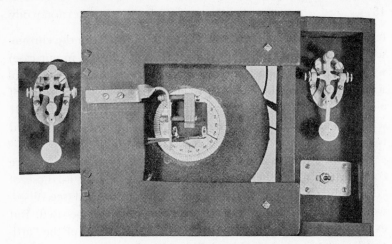

FIGURE 1. *AN EASILY CONSTRUCTED CHRONOSCOPE.* A phonograph motor is mounted on a suitable support. A paper dial divided into 100 units is glued to the phonograph turntable. (For mass production of dials, draw one and photograph it, making photographic prints.) A hole somewhat longer than the record spindle is drilled in a small wooden block with a pointer attached. This block rides on the spindle like a record. A piece of soft iron is attached to the wooden block. Slightly above the block a magnet is mounted. The magnet will lift the block when it operates. All that remains is to wire a key for the subject and the experimenter in series with the magnet. When the experimenter says "Ready," the subject presses his key. When the experimenter presses his key, the magnet raises the block while the dial spins freely under it. When the subject reacts to the sound of the magnet by raising his finger, the block drops. The distance covered by the dial between the stimulus and the response is a measure of the reaction time. This distance can be converted into time units by determining the speed of the motor (counting revolutions per minute before and after the experiment) and dividing the speed by 60 to obtain the revolutions per second. If the dial has 100 units, each unit will then equal $\frac{1}{100}$ of $\frac{1}{\text{speed}}$. Thus if the motor speed is 78 r.p.m., the speed per second is 1.3, and each unit equals .007 seconds. If 12 units pass the pointer during a reaction, the reaction time equals $12 \times .007$, or .084 seconds. Direct current is used to operate the magnet. This can be tapped from battery chargers, batteries, or other power-supply sources. If the power-supply unit is adequate, a large number of magnets can be operated by wiring them into the power line in a parallel circuit.

terials at a cost of under $10.00. The subject can stop the chrono-scope by making a simple movement (lifting a finger, in our case) which he does as soon as he can react to the stimulus. A chrono-scope records the elapsed time in hundredths or thousandths of a second, depending on its sensitivity. In the older literature, .001 seconds was abbreviated σ (sigma), but ms. (millisecond) is used today.

Both the stimulus and the required response can be made more complicated, and other kinds of reaction time, such as those of "discrimination" and "choice" reaction, can be studied (see Wood-worth, 3). In our case, "simple" reaction time will be used. But even "simple" reaction time is said to differ in terms of the "atti-tude" or "set" of the subject. The subject can be concentrating on the appearance of the stimulus; this leads to a "sensory" re-action time. On the other hand, he may get set to *act* as soon as the stimulus (almost any stimulus) appears; this type of response is called a "motor" reaction time. We shall take measurements of both.

We are now ready to detail our procedure in the following steps:

1. The instructor will brief the class on "sensory" and "motor" sets and issue appropriate instructions with regard to the appa-ratus to be used. The students will work in pairs, each serving alternately as experimenter and subject.
2. Each subject's reaction time is measured before the drug is supplied. The pre-drug results are recorded in the accompany-ing table (Table 1). The following details are to be *rigidly* ob-served:
    a. Before each stimulation, the experimenter will say, "Ready," and wait from ½ to 2 seconds in random order before pressing his key.
    b. The subject will function scrupulously in accordance with the required "sensory" or "motor" instruction.
    c. All accidental responses will be repeated.

3. After the pre-drug trials are completed, the students will be divided into "matched" groups by the instructor, and the drug will be given to one group, the placebo to another. The student subjects will not be told to which group they belong.
4. After a 15-minute wait, the post-drug reaction times are obtained and recorded in Table 1.
5. The results of pre- and post-drug trials are then compared for significance of any differences obtained.

Table 1. *Sensory and Motor Reaction Times of One Subject Before and After Consumption of ½ Grain of Caffeine or Similar Amount of Lactose*

	Before						After				
Trial	A Sensory	B Motor	Trial	B Motor	A Sensory	Trial	A Sensory	B Motor	Trial	B Motor	A Sensory
1		11				1		11			
2		12				2		12			
3		13				3		13			
4		14				4		14			
5		15				5		15			
6		16				6		16			
7		17				7		17			
8		18				8		18			
9		19				9		19			
10		20				10		20			
Total						Total					

Mean of 20 sensory R. T. _____   Mean of 20 sensory R. T. _____

Mean of 20 motor R. T. _____   Mean of 20 motor R. T. _____

Mean of both   _____   Mean of both   _____

Table 2. *Means and S.D.'s of the Pre- and Post-Drug Reaction Times of the Experimental and Control Groups*

	Experimental			Control		
	Sensory R.T.	Motor R.T.	Both	Sensory R.T.	Motor R.T.	Both
Mean						
S.D.						
S.E.						
N						
Diff (E and C)						
S.E. diff.						
Critical Ratio						

Results

The pre- and post-drug reaction times should be tabulated in Table 1 for one subject. The average times for the class should appear in Table 2. The student will submit a report * covering the following items:

1. A description of the chronoscope used, including a wiring diagram and an account of the mechanism adequate to enable a reader to construct a similar "reaction timer."
2. An interpretation of the results based on:
    a. "Sensory" and "motor" reaction times of his subject and of the entire group.
    b. The sources of error observed by himself and brought out in the class discussion.
3. The reasons for the ABBA order of trials where A refers to sensory and B to motor trials.
4. A statement on the effectiveness of the control of "suggestion."
5. A discussion of the significance of the "latency" concept for psychology.

    * The formal writing of a report is described in Appendix 1.

References

1. Hilgard, E., and Marquis, D. *Conditioning and learning.* New York: Appleton-Century. 1940.
2. Peak, H. An evaluation of the concepts of reflex and voluntary action. *Psychol. Rev.,* 1933, *40,* 71–89.
3. Woodworth, R. S. *Experimental psychology.* New York: Henry Holt. 1938.

2

A Bit of Statistics *

THE TRAINING of every psychologist involves a reasonable familiarity with statistics. Some students shudder at the very notion of statistics or any form of mathematical manipulation, possibly because of early unpleasant experiences with numbers, but more likely because they anticipate much more complexity than is actually involved. Just as there is more joy in the anticipation than in the event, so is there more dread. Statistics, as far as the experimental psychologist is usually concerned, is only a method for orderly handling of data. If you are orderly, or can learn to be so, you will welcome the assistance of statistical methods.

The student taking a course in experimental psychology will find that he spends a lot of time manipulating numbers—entirely too much, many will say. He may as well find out that experimental psychology is like that, right at the beginning. When the experimentalist is not obtaining data, he is working on it. The calculating machine, the book of tables, and the slide rule are part of the experimental psychologist's standard equipment just as they are of any other scientist.

Although handling data may be tedious and often dull, the experimental psychologist must have patience and a better-than-average capacity for applying the seat of his trousers to the seat

* The material on statistics is introduced at this point in order to get the greatest benefit from the first few experiments. Chapter 8 will deal with statistical problems encountered later in our work.

of a chair. The reason for all this is *individual differences*. If Human *A* were identical with Human *B*, or Rat *A* identical with Rat *B*, there would be no need for statistics, dullness, patience, hard work, uncertainty, speculation, or argument.

For the purposes of elementary experimental psychology, there is not much in the way of specialized statistics that the student must learn. Actually he must know the answers to only two questions: (1) How much of a difference must there be between the results of an experimental group and a control group or of any groups being compared to show that there is a true difference between them which can be attributed to the experimental variable? And (2) to what extent does a change in one variable reflect a change in the status of another variable? The second question is the question of correlation, which we will examine later. The first question is more immediate, experimentally speaking, and to it we now must turn our attention.

In order to answer the question of how much difference between two sets of results will be acceptable as indicating a true difference,* we must first answer many other questions. To help our discussion, let us take a question such as the one you face in your first experiment. The experiment deals with the effect of caffeine on reaction time. You will have a group of people whose reaction time is tested before and after they consume some of the drug. Another group, equated with the first, will also be tested before and after consuming a placebo. We can equate the two groups before they take the drug or placebo. In their second tests they may differ. Perhaps the drug will speed up those who take it, and their reaction times will be faster than before. How much faster must they be for you to be sure that you can attribute the difference in speed to the drug? Remember that you cannot expect huge differences to begin with; after all, you are using only a tiny amount of drug and working with a response that is rather automatic and unlikely to vary extremely during the short time you will be working. Also, remember that not all people are

* A "true" difference is one that could not have happened by chance.

equally sensitive to the effects; some may even slow down. Some of the "control" group may speed up on the basis of "suggestion." You can expect almost anything except consistency. Suppose that the average scores of the two groups after the drug are 0.13 seconds and 0.15 seconds for the experimental and control groups respectively. That makes a difference of 0.02 seconds. Is that a large enough difference to prove that the drug speeds up reaction time? What do you think? How would you go about finding out?

A similar experiment was performed in one of the writer's classes. The two groups took a test involving subtraction speed for simple numbers instead of simple reaction time. Let us see how the question was answered in that experiment, and then you can apply the same principles to your own data. The raw data of the writer's experiment are found in Table 3, page 25. You can see from the table that there were 16 subjects in each group. In the subtraction-speed experiment, the experimental group averaged 25, the control group 27. This seems to be contrary to our expectation that caffeine is a stimulant. Can we conclude that it is, on the contrary, a depressant? It looks that way. Still, the difference between the averages is not much. If you should repeat this experiment, would you be willing to bet that your own experiment would show the same results? Is it worth any risk at all? Before you bet any great amount of money, you will probably want to consider many factors. The groups are not large, are they? Just 16 cases in each? Is that an adequate sample? You'd feel more secure if there were 1600 cases in each, or 16,000. How about 16,000,-000? Would you bet then? How many subjects *should* you use in an experiment?

Well, then, the difference isn't very much. Only 2 points. Would you feel safer if it were 4, or 40? You see, we have immediately run into the problems of how many subjects we need and how much of a difference between two scores must exist before you are willing to risk a prediction of a future event. Maybe the difference you have is due to too small a sample and to the possibility of just random factors playing an influential part in determining

Table 3. *Speed-of-Subtraction Scores in the Post-Drug Test*

EXPERIMENTAL GROUP		CONTROL GROUP	
Subject	Score	Subject	Score
1	36	1	36
2	34	2	35
3	30	3	35
4	30	4	34
5	28	5	31
6	27	6	31
7	25	7	30
8	24	8	27
9	24	9	26
10	24	10	26
11	23	11	25
12	22	12	23
13	20	13	20
14	20	14	20
15	18	15	19
16	15	16	14

TOTAL	400	TOTAL	652
N = 16		N = 16	
Mean = 25.0		Mean = 27.0	

Difference between means = 2.0

the averages. Shall we quit right now and say the whole thing was a waste of time? But then, again, maybe we have something real here. After all, there is a difference. If we only had some way of finding out whether this difference is due to chance variations among the individual scores or not, we might, at least, be able to say that the experiment proved something to be true or not true. We should not just say that we do not know what it proves.

In practically every experiment you will do in psychological problems, you will face this same situation: you will have a score representing an experimental group and another score representing a control group. If there is a difference between the two groups, you must be able to say whether the difference is real, a true difference determined by your experimental manipulations, or a chance difference arising from the activity of chance factors of an unknown or at least unclassified nature.

Fortunately for us, there is a way to arrive at such a decision; statisticians have developed techniques for us which help us evaluate differences between groups. The statistics we will need are not difficult. If you can add, subtract, divide, multiply, and look up square roots in a table, you will not have the slightest trouble; all you have to do is work in an orderly fashion, and the answers work themselves out. (We are not going to teach you formal statistics in this text; you will have to take special work in statistics later if you ever hope to be able to get the most out of your data and, also, to design your experiments efficiently. There are, however, a few rudimentary ideas without which we cannot function even in elementary experimental work; these you will have to learn now.)

Let us begin with the averages. In statistical work we call these "means." Now you already know that averages are made up by a simple process of adding up the figures and dividing the sum by the number of cases (N). The sum of the scores is usually called "sigma" and is written as a capital Greek S or Σ. Nothing new so far except the terms. But averages, being arithmetical constructs, are apt to be very tricky and unreal things. The average of 0 and 100 is 50. So is the average of 25 and 75, of 49 and 51, and of many other combinations. When we average a number of scores, we may find that the arithmetical average is strongly affected by very extreme cases and bears no resemblance to what we usually think of as a representative score. Our average of 25 could be the result of 8 cases having scores of 50, and 8 of zero. In that case we should not think very highly of our average as a representative score or "central tendency."

If an average is to be considered representative, it should be a figure around which most of the population clusters, with relatively few extreme scores at either end of the distribution. That is the kind of average we get when we take a great number of cases, say, 10,000, and measure them on some biological or behavioral trait, such as height or weight or intelligence. If we graph the results of the measurement of some trait, we find, in many cases, that the graph takes a particular shape, somewhat like that of a bell, with the average score in the approximate center. Thus, in intelligence testing, we find an average score of 100, most people scoring around that figure, with fewer and fewer cases at scores higher and lower than a 100. If we look for the number of people with scores below 60 and above 140, we find somewhere around 2 percent in each of those areas. An average which represents a central point in such a bell-shaped or "normal" distribution is considered a representative figure. An average which is far from the center of a distribution is proportionately less representative.

Generally, in experimental work, you do not have 10,000 cases or anywhere near that number. You select cases as a sample of the total population and hope that your sample is a miniature normal population. If your sample is indeed such, then your average has a representative meaning; if your sample is loaded or biased in any way, little trust can be placed in your average. In order to evaluate your average, then, you must find out how your scores are distributed around your average, or, putting it otherwise, how much your scores differ from or "deviate" from the average. This procedure amounts to drawing a graph and seeing whether it looks "normal" or not. It is simpler and more "objective" to calculate the total amount of deviation of the scores from the average and in that way to obtain a numerical estimate of how good your average is.

In order to calculate the amount of deviation of the scores from the average, we can simply subtract each score from the average, or vice versa, and total these deviations. By dividing by the number of cases, we have a figure standing for the average deviation. This figure is of some help, since it tells us whether our average is from a population that deviates greatly in the individual scores or from one that differs only by small amounts. In a population where an average of 50 is obtained from 10 scores of 51 and 10 scores of 49, we see that the average deviation is only 1. If the average of 50 is obtained from 10 scores of 0 and 10 scores of 100, we see that the average deviation is 50. Which is the more meaningful average?

An average-deviation score has many uses which you will learn about in statistics courses. For our purposes it is less useful than a similar score which requires an additional step. You will note that the average deviation is obtained simply by subtracting the mean from the score, entering the difference in the D column in a work sheet (see Table 4), adding these deviations, and dividing by N. Sometimes we subtract the mean from a higher number, and

Table 4. *Speed-of-Subtraction Scores in the Post-Drug Test*

EXPERIMENTAL GROUP				CONTROL GROUP			
Subject	*Score*	*D*	*D²*	*Subject*	*Score*	*D*	*D²*
1	36	11	121	1	36	9	81
2	34	9	81	2	35	8	64
3	30	5	25	3	35	8	64
4	30	5	25	4	34	7	49
5	28	3	9	5	31	4	16
6	27	2	4	6	31	4	16
7	25	0	0	7	30	3	9
8	24	−1	1	8	27	0	0
9	24	−1	1	9	26	−1	1
10	24	−1	1	10	26	−1	1
11	23	−2	4	11	25	−2	4
12	22	−3	9	12	23	−4	16
13	20	−5	25	13	20	−7	49
14	20	−5	25	14	20	−7	49
15	18	−7	49	15	19	−8	64
16	15	−10	100	16	14	−13	169
N = 16	400		480	N = 16	432		652

M = 25   S.D. = 5.5   M = 27   S.D. = 6.3
            S.E. = 1.38   S.E. = 1.58

3 3 7 2 7

sometimes from a lower. In the latter case we preface the answer with a minus sign. In obtaining the total deviations, however, we ignore these signs—not an especially recommended procedure.

Suppose we make amends by squaring these deviations, sign included. That will automatically absolve us from our mathematical lapse, because all numbers become plus or positive numbers when squared. We then have figures to enter into our D^2 column. If we divide these squared deviations by N, we will have another average, the average of the squared deviations. Since we squared the original deviations before in order to get out of our difficulty with signs, we can now take the square root to get out of the further difficulty of working with artificial numbers, i.e., the squared figures.* Taking the square root of this average of the squared deviations leaves us with a figure which is a little larger than the average deviation, but has the same general meaning. It tells us something about how the individual scores are distributed about the average. If this figure is large, it means that the individual scores are widely dispersed; if it is small, the scores are clustered about the average. This figure has certain other advantages when we think of it in connection with the normal distribution we spoke of earlier. For purposes of convenience, we call this figure a "standard deviation," or "sigma" (it is sometimes abbreviated as *S.D.* and sometimes written as a small Greek *s* or σ).†

In a normal distribution (the bell-shaped curve) an *S.D.* has certain percentage values; thus, if we count all the cases between the "mean" and some point above it marked off by 1 *S.D.*, we will find 34 percent of our cases. If we subtract 1 *S.D.* from the "mean" and count the cases within the limits set by the "mean" and this

---

* "Squaring was resorted to for the purely mathematical reason of eliminating signs. The immediate objective being accomplished, one may now reverse the move by extracting the square root of m_2 so as to return to the original scale of measurement." (Treloar, A. E. *Elements of statistical reasoning.* New York: Wiley. 1939.)

† It is just an unfortunate fact that the word "sigma" is used for the Standard Deviation (σ) and also means "sum of" (Σ). The student must distinguish the written symbols.

lower figure, we would also find 34 percent of our cases. Thus, if we add and subtract 1 *S.D.* to and from the "mean," we will have marked off the middle 68 percent of our cases. Look at our example in Table 2. The "mean" is 25, the *S.D.* is 5.5. If we add and subtract 5.5 from 25, we get the numbers 30.5 and 19.5, respectively. Between these figures, we should find approximately 68 percent of our cases. Since there are 16 cases in the population, we should find 10.88 cases within these limits. If you count them, you will see that there are actually 12 cases within these limits. The 68 percent is arrived at from a study of probability laws, both practically, in terms of pitching pennies, and mathematically, in terms of the binomial expansion you learned about in algebra. It would take us out of our field to go into the derivation of these statistical procedures. The interested student is going to study statistics in separate courses before he learns much more psychology, anyhow, so that it is unnecessary to go beyond certain empirical facts.

For our present purpose it is enough to know that, by adding and subtracting 2 *S.D.*'s, our "mean" will include 95 percent of our cases, and 3 *S.D.*'s on both sides of the "mean" will include practically the whole population, or 99 percent. Having a measure such as the *S.D.*, we are in position to evaluate the averages we have found. Which is the "better" average? The *S.D.* of our control group is 6.3, while that of our experimental group is 5.5. The scores in the control group spread out farther from the average than do those in the experimental group; we can conclude that the experimental group's average is to that extent more representative, and therefore, "better."

We have a few more operations to perform on our data. They are no more difficult to perform than the calculation of the *S.D.* So far we have been talking about the averages and the individual scores. But since we have performed an experiment, we would like to know how good it is. How good are our "means"? Are they stable? Are they what we should expect to get from other similar groups? Suppose we did the experiment again. Would we get the same "means"? What if we do it 100 more times? Would our 100 new "means" be the same or nearly the same?

We don't have to do the experiment 100 times to find out. By making certain assumptions about our data, we can figure out in advance what we might expect. We already know that we can judge the value of a particular "mean" by its *S.D.* We also can assume that the value of an average depends on the number of cases. The more cases we have, the more likely it is that we have obtained an adequate sample. What we are interested in finding is some relationship between the number of cases we actually used, and the *S.D.* of the average that we found.

Just thinking it through logically, we can then say that our average is good if the *S.D.* is small and the number of cases large; the average is less reliable if the *S.D.* is large and the number of cases small. If we could find a ratio of *S.D.* to number of cases, then we could take account of both factors, the *N* and the *S.D.* in one figure. Suppose we set up the ratio in the form $\dfrac{S.D.}{N}$. If we divide *S.D.* by *N,* and the answer is large, we know that either the *S.D.* is too large or the *N* is too small. If the answer is small, we must have a relatively small *S.D.* or a large *N*. If we want to decrease our ratio, all we need to do is to increase the number of cases or decrease the *S.D.*

Increasing our number of cases will increase the reliability of our average, but the relationship is not a simple direct one. We do not double our reliability by doubling the *N*. If we want to double our reliability, we must get 4 times as many cases. To get 5 times as reliable a sample, we must increase the *N* 25 times. In other words, we must think of reliability in terms of the square root of *N*. We have to modify our formula for the ratio by changing the *N* factor to read $\sqrt{N}$, so that our formula becomes $\dfrac{S.D.}{\sqrt{N}}$.

Let's apply this formula to our own data: Our experimental *S.D.* is 5.5; our *N* is 16. Substituting in the formula, we have $\dfrac{5.5}{\sqrt{16}}$. The square root of 16 is 4. Dividing 5.5 by 4, we have 1.38.

The control group S.D. is 6.3; the N is 16. Dividing 6.3 by 4, we have 1.58. These ratios tell us roughly how reliable or dependable our "means" are. The smaller the ratio, the more reliable the "mean." These ratios are technically called "standard errors," or S.E. They have the same percentage meanings as do the S.D.'s, but in the case of S.E.'s we are talking about *means* of *groups of scores* and not about the distribution of scores in any one group.

Sound complicated? It isn't, really. Think of it this way. We go out and do our experiment 100 times with various college populations from all over the country. We expect that, 68 times out of the 100 new experiments, the "means" of the experimental group will fall between the limits we set by adding and subtracting our S.E. to and from our original "mean." Thus our "mean" was 25. If we add 1.38 to 25 and subtract 1.38 from 25, we have 26.38 and 23.62 as the limits of the middle "means" of the 100 new experiments. Had our S.E. been smaller, our middle 68 percent of new "means" would have been closer to our original "mean." Thus we have a way of estimating the sizes of future "means" without actually going out and doing the extra experiments.

Just as with the S.D., adding and subtracting 2 S.E.'s gives us the limits of the middle 95 percent of new "means"; 3 S.E.'s give us 99 percent limits. In effect, we can determine the lowest possible and the highest possible "means" we would get in 100 or 1000 new experiments without doing the work. Our experimental "mean," for example, can never be higher than 25 plus 3 times the S.E., or 29.14. We can expect it never to be lower than 25 minus 3 times the S.E., or 20.86. Our control group can be expected never to exceed 27 plus 3 times 1.58, or 31.74, and never to be lower than 27 minus 3 times 1.58, or 22.26. We now know how much faith we can place in our "means." We know that, just by chance, future "means" might range in such a way that the experimental group might be as high as 29.14, the control group might be as low as 22.26. What does this suggest to you? It looks as if, in some experiments, we might have the experimental group actually ex-

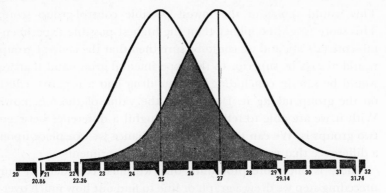

FIGURE 2. *OVERLAPPING NORMAL DISTRIBUTIONS.* The two means are at 25 and 27. For further explanation, see text.

ceeding the control group! If that is possible, we cannot be sure that our results are necessarily of any great worth or significance.

Let's take a closer look at our data. It always helps to draw pictures. Suppose that we represent our data in graphical form and draw the probable distributions of the future possible averages for 100 future experiments. Let's draw a line to represent the range of these averages (see Figure 2). Mark off the line at the lowest possible experimental score, the "mean" of our own experiment, the highest possible experimental score, and the same for the control group. If we draw bell-shaped curves over the two "means" we see at once that there is quite a bit of overlap under the two curves. This area of overlap represents the percentage of times we might expect the experimental group to be higher than the control group, contrary to the results of our original experiment. If the two curves overlapped completely, we could draw no conclusions whatever about our data except that there was no difference between the groups. If they did not overlap at all, we could conclude that there was a real and significant difference.

Suppose that the *S.E.*'s remained the same but that the control group had made an average score of 34.14 instead of its actual score of 27. If we plotted the "mean" of the control group at 34.14 and subtracted 3 *S.E.*'s (4.74), we would reach a point of 29.40.

This would represent the lowest possible control-group score. This score would be higher than the highest possible experimental score (29.14), and we could be sure then that the control group would always be superior to the experimental group and that we would be safe in concluding that the drug had a negative effect on the group taking it. Do you see the value of the *S.E.* now? With it we are able to tell how meaningful a difference between two groups is. We can tell how much reliance we can place upon a difference that we find as a result in our experiments.

There is one more procedure that we must consider. In our preceding step we drew a graph or line to find out how much overlap there would be in the distributions of the "means" from 100 or 1000 future "means." We can estimate from the graph whether the overlap is large or small. It would be convenient to be able to get a numerical estimate without bothering about graphs, so that we could express the percentage of overlap or freedom from overlap in objective numerical terms. We can get such a numerical expression by reducing what we have just done by pictures into numbers.

Let's see what we did. In effect we added plus 3 *S.E.* to the lower "mean" and subtracted 3 *S.E.* from the higher "mean." Thus we did something that we know is not mathematically permissible: we added positive and negative numbers and ignored the signs. We know we can get around such a difficulty by squaring the numbers. Suppose we do that, and for the moment deal with only one *S.E.* from each group. Thus we can add the $S.E.^2$ of the experimental group to the $S.E.^2$ of the control group and get a combined *S.E.* for the entire spread of the two "means" together. This we would get by obtaining the square root of the combination or, in terms of a formula, $SE_{diff} = \sqrt{SE^2_1 + SE^2_2}$.* This *S.E.* would represent the "standard error" of the sum or the difference be-

* This formula is not complete, but it will do for present purposes. Later you will learn to take account of any possible "correlation" between the variables. If such a correlation exists, the formula is corrected to read:

$$SE_{diff} = \sqrt{SE^2_1 + SE^2_2 - 2r\ (SE_1)\ (SE_2)}$$

where *r* stands for the degree of correlation.

tween two "means" because it includes the subtraction and addition of the separate "standard errors." Now, we know that we have to multiply this *S.E.* by 3 in order to get the complete range of probable "means." We also know that if there is to be no overlap between the "means," the two "means" have to be so far apart that the lower "mean" can never be as high as the lowest possible higher "mean." In short, the *difference* between the "means" has to be 3 times as big as the *S.E.* of the difference.

In formula form, a difference that is completely free of overlap, indicating a significant or true difference, can be expressed as $D = 3\ SE\ diff$. Another way—a more common one—of saying the same thing is that $\dfrac{D}{SE_{diff}} = 3$ or more. The ratio of the difference to the "standard error" of the difference is called the "critical ratio." If, as indicated, the "critical ratio" is 3 or more, it is assumed that the difference found in the experiment is reliable and dependable. In common terms, it means that the difference is so big that the lower score found will never be higher, by chance, than the higher score found, if the experiment is repeated.

We have been using the words *never* and *ever* in the above discussion; actually, we mean *hardly ever*. In terms of percentages, *ever* means 99.999 percent of the time. Actually, critical ratios of 3 or more are not found too frequently in psychological experiments. There are so many factors that may influence individual performances that significant differences of such a level are hard to obtain. Some degree of overlap is often found, but if this degree is minimal, we need not be too unhappy about not getting a "critical ratio" of 3. Lesser values have some predictive value in percentage terms. We can find out, for instance, how many times out of 100 we can expect a given group to score higher than another group. If, for example, a "critical ratio" of 2.5 is obtained, we know that, 98 times out of 100, the group that originally was higher will again be higher, the other two times the scores may be even, or the formerly lower group may be higher. If the "critical ratio" is 2, the same kind of prediction would be possible for 95 percent of the new "means," and so on down. The following table * gives us the prediction values of "critical ratios" in terms of the number of chances out of 100 that a given discovered difference in a particular direction will be maintained in future experiments.

Critical Ratio	Chances in 100
3.0	99.99
2.5	99.4
2.0	98
1.5	93
1.0	84
0.5	69
0.2	58

We have come a long way from our simple little experiment in drug effects. We have had to take an excursion into some statistics in order to evaluate our findings. Let us now apply what we know. Our own difference was only 2 points. Is that enough? We found our S.E.'s; we can calculate our S.E. of the difference easily enough. It is 2.09. Dividing this into the difference of 2, we get a "critical ratio" of 0.95. This means that there is considerable overlap between future possible "means," and that the chances are 83 in 100 that, in the future, the control group will exceed the experimental. We are now able to predict something about the future. We know how many times something will happen fairly certainly, and how many times it is unlikely to happen out of a given number of experiments or tests of the hypothesis. We can predict. If we can predict, we are fulfilling one of the steps of scientific method.

Suppose you go ahead and work out the results of your own experiment. What critical ratio do you find? It's a great deal of work? That's how it is in experimental psychology. Experiments are not just dashed off. Experiments involve considerable planning, careful performance, and careful evaluation with appropriate statistical treatments. You may as well learn the hard facts

* See any text on statistics for a complete table of such values.

now. We cannot be satisfied with *apparent* findings. Average scores mean practically nothing. Distributions are important. "Standard deviations" and "standard errors" must be obtained. Some kind of test of significance must be applied (there are others besides the "critical ratio"). Without a test of significance, no difference between scores is of any interest.

You have learned that this type of test depends upon the reliability of each "mean" besides the difference between two "means." The reliability of a "mean," in turn, depends upon the number of cases studied and their variability. The variability, in turn, may depend upon many factors, such as selection of subjects, instruction of subjects, uncontrolled experimental factors, and the number of subjects involved. To get results from which predictions are possible, you know that you have to select subjects carefully, get enough of them, do your experiment with utmost care, and control every possible source of error and variability. As we go through the other experiments to follow, apply the lessons of this sample. In the future, there will not be so many comments and hints to guide you. You have to learn to depend upon yourself. By the way, how many subjects do you need for an experiment?

References

1. Edwards, Allen L. *Statistical analysis for students in psychology and education*. New York: Rinehart. 1946.
2. Garret, H. E. *Statistics in psychology and education,* 2d ed. New York: Longmans, Green, 1937.

3

The Steps in Scientific Work

PSYCHOLOGY is gradually coming of age as a science and is now quietly taking its place along with older members of the scientific family. Not so long ago, psychologists, at least in their textbooks, engaged in fairly extensive debates, insisting, or trying to prove, that they were scientific; and often they gave the impression of *nouveaux-riches.* That tendency has all but disappeared, and it is no longer necessary to insist loudly and defensively that psychology is a science. But as we come to accept a status among "the 400," we are often prone to forget our origins; we forget what all the shooting was about, and without a thorough appreciation of our relationships with other members of the scientific family, we can often be led astray in scientific bypaths.

The student of physical science, as often as not, has little comprehension of the basic problems and nature of science and, although in his training he performs many experiments, he is often unfamiliar with the actual nature of his role in the experiment. As a test, ask one to define an experiment for you. The student of psychology, on the other hand, must learn something of the nature of science before he can begin the study of psychology. There is a simple reason for this, although it is not often recognized, and the beginning student frequently feels that time is being wasted by an instructor who lectures about science instead of getting on with psychology.

The reason for this preliminary orientation in science is that

38

every student starting a course in psychology has so many preconceptions, pet ideas, prejudices, superstitions, and assorted false and fantastic beliefs about people that he must be told the rules of the scientific game relating to the kinds of views that can be accepted and the kinds that must be rejected. Because every student is already a "psychologist," and legally, if not scientifically, entitled to an opinion, only endless arguments and differences of opinion would result if no restrictions were placed on admissible forms of evidence. Where the student of physics will listen attentively to his physics instructor lecturing about atoms, he will not extend the same receptive courtesy to his psychology instructor lecturing on "women" because *he* knows women. After all, he has lived with them all his life.

It will repay the student of psychology, especially the experimentally inclined student, to give some attention to the nature of science. Scientific psychology is not a matter of private opinion, common sense, or helpful hints on how to make friends and sway people. It is a serious attempt to understand problems whose very complexity is not even appreciated. It is not a simple matter of collecting facts or quoting sage philosophers or successful businessmen. Today, psychology is an eager, scientific enterprise, and its major aim is to produce a theory of behavior that will stand experimental test. The student of psychology must be a student of theory.

Psychology at present is greatly concerned with theories. To understand the nature of theory and to be able to contribute to the support or refutation of a theory, it is necessary to recognize the role of a theory in the scientific world. The understanding of a theory involves a conception of science, a philosophical position, and a recognition of the position of psychology among the sciences. To these problems we shall now turn.

We might start by asking ourselves: What is science? Before we try to answer this question, let us make an admission which may be generally recognized but which is rarely stated: Any definition of science must take cognizance of the fact that it is a definition based on the culture and tradition in which any particular scientist is operating. What was science in the Middle Ages and what will be science in the twenty-fifth century need bear no resemblance to science of the present day. The discussion to follow must be evaluated in terms of today's traditions. The student must recognize that there are no absolute standards by which science can be defined, and that all we can do is to consider the procedures used by scientists today as representing the current conception of science.

With this admission before us, we can return to our question: What is science? The average student will reply at once that science is knowledge. What kind of knowledge? That might prove awkward, but casual familiarity with scientific courses might suggest "organized knowledge." So far as that goes, it is probably a correct definition, but the nature of the organization will give us some pause. Most of us have been exposed to some form or other of analogy which pictures a boundless universe of ignorance with patient science hacking away, slowly but surely spreading its control further and further into a strange and awesome hinterland. Professor Dodge, in his *Human Variability* (1) presents this definition of science, "Science is the relatively permanent systematization of the unknown." He thus provides for false advances and necessary retreats in the war between science and ignorance.

Implicit in this definition are several assumptions generally subscribed to by all scientists. They should be clearly recognized by anyone attempting a study of any scientific subject. First, it is assumed that the events observed occur in a real world and not in an imaginary or "ideal" world. Second, it is assumed that this world and its objects and events are *knowable*—that is, they are susceptible of study and description and occur in a lawful order. This assumption clearly excludes the operation of unknowable or uncalculable forces or supernatural agencies. It is further assumed that any given event follows necessarily from its antecedent circumstances, and that nothing occurs by "chance." This is just another way of saying that science is deterministic, not in the sense the future events are foreordained with utter disregard of historical antecedents, but rather in the sense that whatever event does occur, occurs because it had to, inevitably, from the chain of preceding events or circumstances. Recognizing these assumptions as basic to science, we can now look for information concerning the nature of science. It might be rewarding to look at some scientists at work. We might be able to find out what they are by seeing what they do and how they work.

We know that a wide variety of tasks occupies a heterogeneous collection of individuals whom we identify as scientists. We see white-coated individuals peering into telescopes, microscopes, spectroscopes, etc. Others gaze intently at brain tissue, volcanoes, jet propulsion engines, "electronic" devices. A mass of charts, figures, slide rules, and "mechanical brains" surrounds the white coats. Can all of these people have something in common? Can they all be scientists, with each one working at something different from the others, using different tools, rules, gadgets, even different languages in terms of the symbols in which they express themselves? Is there a common element? There is the white coat, to be sure, but that appears trivial.

If we look closer at this array of diggers, viewers, measurers, calculators, etc., we begin to notice that their behavior does not appear to be impulsive or random. The telescope is not pointed just anywhere. If we track an archeological expedition, we do not find the archeologist saying: "It looks pretty soft here, let's dig awhile and see if we find something." On the contrary, he might pick out a most unlikely looking spot, far from the comforts of civilization, and proceed to his digging with apparent decision and definiteness. There is method to the apparent madness, and in every instance that we examine we will find that, although the content and equipment may vary, the method is basically the same; it is the scientific method.

We can now go back to our definition and amend it a bit: Science is organized knowledge, acquired by use of the scientific method. Our definition is not of much value unless we have a reasonable appreciation of what the scientific method involves. To acquire this appreciation, suppose we look at some imaginary and real figures in the history of our civilization and see what they did, and then decide for each whether he is a scientist or not.

Let us begin with a young and attractive witch of the Middle Ages, doomed to die an untimely death at the stake. Our witch has a small local reputation for helping people who suffer certain kinds of heart attacks. The sufferer purchases from the witch an unseemly brew which eases his difficulties and enables him to carry on. Legitimate barbers, the doctors of that bygone era, are furious about the witch, and through the powerful Barber Association try to have her condemned for practicing barbering without a license. The legitimate barbers get no heart-attack patients because they do them no good. The witch is doing all right herself. Her brew cures the patients. Is she a scientist?

A young barber out to make a name for himself bribes one of the witch's patients, secures a quantity of the brew, and attempts to analyze it. Because his chemical knowledge is inadequate, he fails and decides on other steps; he woos the witch and gets her to reveal her secret. The witch's brew, she says, consists of a soup based on the left hind foot of a female rabbit, the blood of a toad killed in the full of the moon, a hair from the tail of a dead horse, stagnant rain water caught in a wooden pail, and a handful of flowers from the witch's garden.

The young barber can hardly believe his ears. But he goes ahead, secures the ingredients, cooks up a brew, and tries it on a patient. The patient reacts as favorably as he would have for the witch. Our young doctor is incredulous; too impatient to wait for a full moon, he kills a toad at noon and prepares another dose. The brew is just as effective. He tries his hand again, but forgets the horsetail hairs; the brew is still good. Inspired, our hero tries again, leaving out the rabbit's foot in his haste. The brew still works. It does not rain for a while, and so he leaves out the rain water in his next attempt; it works. He finds to his surprise that he has omitted everything but the flowers, and the brew is still effective. He can't leave out the flowers and still have a brew, and in an idle moment of speculation, he concludes that the flowers contain the remedy. He examines the flowers; they are of a common garden variety—the foxglove. He now tries other flowers—no results. Foxglove works—nothing else does. Again he concludes: The distillation of the foxglove contains the remedy for heart attacks. (As a matter of fact, it does: The distillation is known as digitalis.) Is our young barber a scientist?

Let us leave the barber at his distillations and examine briefly the work of some individuals who are generally recognized as scientists. Perhaps by looking at what scientists *do,* we can find out what science *is.* We can begin on some street corner where a young lady stops an elderly gentleman and asks him for his co-operation in answering a few questions. She inquires into his religion, economic status, political affiliation, the furnishings in his home, and finally asks him for whom he plans to vote. She carefully records all of the answers, thanks the gentleman, and looks around for another person to interview. She chooses, this time, a smart-appearing businesswoman, and repeats the routine. All day long, for weeks at a stretch, she keeps recording answers. Every day she mails her record sheets to a public-opinion research bureau. Is she a scientist?

At the offices of the research bureau we might observe a young man tabulating on punch cards the results sent in by the young lady, running these cards through machines, recording totals, percentages, averages, etc. When he is not tabulating, he might be operating any of numerous calculating machines. At the start of his day, he is working on huge stacks of papers; at the end of the day, he might finish with a single sheet, perhaps with a single figure. Is he a scientist?

In another room of the bureau we might find an older man, puffing at a pipe and gazing out of the window. His desk is relatively clear. He may have a few slips of paper lying about, a scratch pad, and a pencil. He may have a number of magazines, newspapers, almanacs, and historical tomes about; but as we watch him, he is not reading, writing, calculating, or observing anything except the traffic. After a while he calls for his secretary and dictates a memorandum. We hear him announce: "There will be a landslide for Mr. Jones. He should win by an overwhelming majority, perhaps with 75 percent of the votes." Is he a scientist?

The next week, in another city, in another office, we might find someone musing over a newspaper report of the prediction quoted above and the election results published in his daily newspaper. He goes to his file and extracts a folder of clippings labeled "election predictions." After making some notes, he selects another folder labeled "attitudes toward politics." He continues consulting folders, books, articles, and journals. He jots down notes frequently. Finally he goes to his typewriter. We glance over his shoulder as he begins to type, and we read the title of what is apparently a chapter in a book: "A biosocial approach to political behavior." Is he a scientist?

What was your answer in each of the above instances? About the witch there should not be much doubt. Witches aren't scientists. Or are they? She was doing some good. She cured people. After her case sum had grown, she could be reasonably confident about her brew. Do modern doctors always know what are the specific causes of some of their cures? Take the case of injecting insulin or metrazol into depressed patients or, for that matter, of sending an electrical current through their brains. The patients are reported to be helped in some instances. Do the doctors using such techniques know why? Are they perhaps including some "toad blood" in their brew? How about that witch? Was she a scientist?

What was the young barber doing? The next chapter will suggest that he was following a very proper technique. He was experimenting. Scientists experiment. Was the barber a scientist? Are you sure? How about the young lady on the street corner? She was collecting data. Scientists collect data. What does that make her? But she was not experimenting. She did not do anything to anybody or anything—except to ask questions. What about the young man with the calculators? He was not even collecting data, much less experimenting. He was just organizing the data submitted by somebody else. What does that make him? What about the gentleman who made the predictions? Does prediction make a scientist, or does a scientist make predictions? Betters on horse races make predictions too, sometimes after a considerable amount of involved study of charts and records. Is there any difference between the predictions of a horse player, a weather prophet, an astrologer, and an Einstein? What about the chap who was writing the book? From the title we read, we can judge that he is going to do some theorizing. Does that make him a scientist?

None of the people we have just considered *looks* very scientific. After all, there were no white coats, no microscopes, no laboratory rats, in fact, nothing that looked like a laboratory. Can a street corner be a laboratory? The young man with the calculators seemed to have a serious air about him, and he did know how to handle his equipment. But where were the X-ray tubes, the flashing electrical arcs, the jet explosions? We could just as well have gone to research laboratories where we could have seen all these things, but if we had watched the people who were working there, would we have seen much more? We would have seen young and old ladies and men talking to or looking at other people, or at animals or dials.

The net result of the conversations or observations would be scratches in notebooks. The notebooks would then be subjected to the calculators, human or machine, and their contents digested until only a few sentences or figures, usually in a formula form, remained. Then someone would interpret the figures or formulas in terms of some event which could be arranged to occur or which would happen anyhow (an election, an experiment, or an eclipse). The correspondence between the formula and the event would be evaluated. Then someone would gather together numerous evaluated formulas and would see how they fitted together, how many were superfluous, or which were deducible from the rest. When a final collection of such evaluated formulas was obtained, somebody would probably start to write a book entitled: "A theory of . . ." Are you ready to say now whether or not we have been looking at scientists? Were any or all of the individuals described entitled to that description?

Maybe they are all scientists. Each of them—we can except the witch if you like—is performing an essential step in what has come to be called the scientific method. This method includes: (1) collecting data *systematically;* (2) analyzing and organizing these data into generalizations; (3) arranging these generalizations, which may be drawn from different collections of facts and generalizations, into theories; (4) drawing deductions from the theories in the form of predictions (such predictions are generally known as hypotheses or theorems); (5) "proving" the hypotheses by experimenting, or otherwise checking by controlled observation, trying to see if they are valid or invalid, and thereby supporting or discrediting the theories.

If we accept the above five steps as descriptive of the scientific method, we can then label anyone a scientist if he is active in any or all phases of the total method. When we stop to realize the scope of the problems of science, we can excuse an individual for not trying in his own lifetime to carry through all the steps; there are some scientists who have contributed to each phase of the scientific analysis of some problem, but they are relatively rare. The more likely case is that of the scientist who makes some systematic observations (Step 1); leaves them, and speculates about other observations reported by other investigators (Step 2); tries his hand at some theorizing (Step 3), but usually gives this up in a hurry; tries deductions (predictions) from some proposed theories (Step 4); occasionally experiments in connection with hypotheses suggested by other theorists (Step 5). In other words, a scientist may be occupied at different times with different steps of scientific procedure. There is no need that he be master of all of them or that he stick to one phase exclusively.

The steps in scientific procedure outlined above can be broken down into two general phases, the inductive phase (generalizing from the collected data) and the deductive phase (organizing the generalizations in theoretical form and developing the logical consequences of combined generalizations). The former of these procedures does not require much discussion in our special field of interest. The deductive phase is of greater prominence in psychology and will receive more consideration.

The average student of experimental psychology at one time in his life was probably fairly familiar with one famous deductive system, but if he is like most students, he has probably forgotten most of it and is now frowning in doubt. When you were in high school, you took a course called plane geometry. What was that course about? It had something to do with theorems, didn't it? Something about Q.E.D., proofs, a lot of angles. What did you do in that course? You recall something about axioms, definitions, postulates, and theorems.

What is an axiom? A self-evident truth—"a straight line is the shortest distance between two points." There won't be much of that in psychology. The only self-evident truth in psychology is that there are no self-evident truths. And even that isn't self-evident. It takes a little work and time to get to it.

Definitions? "The locus of all points in a plane at a given distance from a fixed point is a circle." That's reasonably clear. Not much argument there. Any clear definitions in psychology? Seems there were always several for any one term.

Postulates? Those are assumptions with some reasonable basis, aren't they? Euclid's famous fifth postulate was: "If a straight line incident on two straight lines makes the sum of the angles within and on the same side less than two right angles, the two straight lines being produced indefinitely meet one another on whichever side the two angles are less than the two right angles." Do psychologists make assumptions? You must have noticed some.

Theorems? How about the Pythagorean theorem: "The square on the hypotenuse of a right triangle is equivalent to the sum of the squares on the other two sides"? What is a theorem? That's what you were told to prove in this case of the triangle. It was a guess, but a good guess, a hypothesis. It followed logically from the assumptions, axioms, and definitions, if only you were able to think of which to use and when to bring them up. Presumably it was a truth, a piece of knowledge that lay dormant within the generalizations that Euclid labeled axioms and postulates. The prediction of an election was a theorem, a hypothesis. It was new information, brought into the light of day by logic. Such predictions and hypotheses are the essential aim of science. Scientists make generalizations (postulates), and by refining their terminology (definitions) they may be in position to develop *new* information (predictions) without working patiently for years to collect it bit by bit. Why wait for forty years for someone to stumble on a piece of information if you already have it in your scientific system and need but to work out all the logical implications of your system to acquire a great number of new "facts"?

The fourth step in scientific method is system or theory building. Not all areas of psychological observation are ready for systematization. In some cases, the necessary generalizations are lacking entirely or are wholly inadequate for systematic purposes; in some areas, for example, the field of learning, enough data have been gathered to give rise to at least four prominent systems. In some other areas, the frontiers of "the unknown" have not been pushed back far enough to warrant anything but patient data-collection. Psychology then, is actively involved in all five steps of scientific method. The experimentalist has more than enough to do. His work will occupy him, at one time or another, with all the steps, and at all times he can feel himself a scientist.

We have now looked at the various phases of scientific method in action. It is time to inquire into the background of science from a different viewpoint. What is the rationale behind science? Why does science exist? What are its aims or purposes?

The essential aim of science is prediction. *Prediction includes a broader meaning than merely foretelling an event.* It means understanding the necessary and essential relationships that exist between what the average man regards as cause and effect, but which the scientist more carefully describes as "antecedents and consequences." * In terms of psychology, it means understanding the basic relationships between stimuli and responses.

A little later we will have occasion to talk about stimuli and responses in their experimental aspects of "independent and dependent variables." For the present, we can limit ourselves to describing an independent variable as some object, event, or condition that we can introduce into an experimental situation and vary as we please. A dependent variable is an event, a response, or an aspect of behavior that we then observe with the purpose of noting changes, if any, that may occur as the independent variable is introduced or modified. If such changes do occur, we try to find out the nature of the relationship between the two variables. Such a relationship is usually termed a "function." When such a function is described precisely, usually in mathematical form, we then are in position to predict what will happen, and to what degree, for a given change in the independent variable. The scientist, in making his predictions, *knows* the relationships that exist between antecedent and consequence. He may be using some assumptions and, maybe, doing some guessing, but his guessing is not blind nor based on hope, faith, tradition, or rule-of-thumb.

Let us return to our young witch and her barber. The witch, in effect, made predictions: if the patient drank her brew, he would feel better. Her predictions, however, were poor things; they involved useless and unnecessary trimmings; they were not based on an appreciation of the relationships involved. When her barber swain arrived at the conclusion that the foxglove was the basic

---

* Scientists do not talk much about causes and effects, nor even about antecedents and consequences. Modern logicians like John Dewey, for example, emphasize that the true purpose of scientific or logical inquiry is to note relationships among variables, emphasizing strongly the fact that such relationships are *interrelationships*, each factor in a situation influencing the others and in turn being influenced, limited, or controlled by them. It is beyond the scope of this text to go into this problem extensively. The student is warned, however, to avoid the logical dangers involved in confusing his experimental manipulations with "causes" and his observations on interrelated phenomena as "effects."

ingredient in the brew, he was much closer to a scientific appreciation of what was going on. The fully scientific stage was reached,
however, only when the foxglove derivative, digitalis, was isolated
and its specific action on the physiology of the heart was detailed.
Many similar examples could be cited. The sailors on early "lime-
juicer" ships ate their scurvy-preventing fruit unaware of the vitamin that science was later to discover and relate specifically to
physiological factors. Such an understanding is what is meant by
scientific prediction.

Why is science interested in predictions? This question raises
the ancient question of the basic motivation or rationale of science. Controversies concerning the motives of scientists have
continued at least as long as there have been scientists. Some scientists, like some artists, claim they work for the love of their
work; others insist on more humanitarian goals; still others admit
to a more personal ambition for glory or financial success. This
question cannot detain us too long as we are unlikely to answer
it to general satisfaction. Hogben (2) in his *Science for the citizen*
tries to show that the scientist takes his problems from the practical needs of his culture and does not find them in a mystical
vacuum. The scientist is rarely too far ahead of his times. The
world has a way of making use of his discoveries, and there are
probably few scientists who would pursue for a lifetime a venture
that they thought would never prove useful to the human race.

References

1. Dodge, R. *Conditions and consequences of human variability.*
   New Haven: Yale University Press. 1932.
2. Hogben, L. *Science for the citizen.* New York: Knopf. 1938.

Experiment 2. An Experiment Dealing with
the Making of Scientific Assumptions

At Duke University, there is a building which houses the laboratories of parapsychology. In these laboratories for the past decade investigators have been examining the possibilities that certain individuals possess capacities which enable them to predict future events, influence future events, or have knowledge of events without resorting to the usual senses by which ordinary people acquire information, notably the eyes and ears. The "gifts" of these extraordinary people have been labeled by Joseph B. Rhine, a leader in this type of research, "extrasensory perception" or, more briefly, *ESP*. Not much is heard of this type of research at other universities, although considerable publicity has been given the Duke studies in national picture magazines, such as *Life* and *Look*.

In 1935 a nation-wide radio program undertook to assist Rhine in collecting data for his analysis. Amateur entertainers have tested numerous individuals at parties and socials for possible presence of telepathic or clairvoyant aptitudes, and the general subject of mind reading has long interested the general public. Dr. Rhine is a trained scientist, a botanist (Ph.D., University of Chicago) who began his researches in what he describes (3) as an attempt to put a scientific foundation under the folklore and old-wives'-tale type of evidence for such capacities which have been passed around for generations. He felt the need for serious scientific experimentation in this field, which has long been the more or less private property of fakers, quacks, entertainers, and others whose motivation might be much purer in nature.

Rhine is not the first person of serious training and background to consider this area of interest. Sir Oliver Lodge, an eminent physicist, is well known for his belief in spiritualism, as is Sir Arthur Conan Doyle, the writer of the beloved Sherlock Holmes stories and a physician by training. It was Rhine, however, who designed what he regarded as a technique for the establishment of proof of the existence of *ESP*.

Rhine developed a procedure in which subjects who have no sensory information concerning the nature of a series of events are required to try to report the nature of these events as they occur. In practice, Rhine used a set of 25 cards,* like a deck of playing cards, consisting of 5 newly created suits, with 5 cards to a suit. The suits were, instead of spades, hearts, etc., arbitrarily designed figures, a square, circle, star, cross, and wavy lines. The experimenter would view a thoroughly shuffled deck of these cards privately, generally indicating to a subject the time during which he was concentrating on a card, and the subject would write down the name of the card that he believed the experimenter was viewing.

Many arguments were raised and accusations hurled at Rhine that the experimenter was either consciously or unconsciously "tipping off" the subject, either through eye reflections, faint whispers, or otherwise, but Rhine conducted numerous experiments where experimenter and subjects were in separate buildings, often hundreds of miles apart, so that we can, for the moment at least, ignore these arguments, and accept the general statement that no cue was passed between the sender and receiver.

Now, the laws of probability indicate that if chance alone is involved in a series of 5 choices, one of the choices could be correct by chance alone. You can appreciate this fact by considering the choice of "heads" or "tails" when a coin is tossed. You have 1 chance out of 2 of guessing correctly. If a die is rolled, you have 1 chance out of 6 to guess the face which will show on top when the die stops rolling. So, with the cards, by chance, you should guess 1 out of 5. If you have 25 opportunities to guess, as you do in taking a "run" through Rhine's deck of 25, you should, by chance alone, get 5 right. Of course, by chance alone, you might also get more than 5 on any one run. Rhine claims that if you score consistently above chance over a long series of runs, there

* You can make up your own set by drawing the figures on cardboard.

must be some other factor present besides chance which is aiding your guesses. He calls this other factor *ESP*.

Suppose that we try a sample run through Rhine's cards to see how we come out. Record your score in Column 2 of Table 5. Your instructor will act as sender. You try to guess the cards at

Table 5. *Distribution of Correct Guesses ("Hits") and Incorrect Guesses in One "Run" through the Rhine Deck*

Card	Call (Guess)	Actual Deck	Control Deck	Card	Call (Guess)	Actual Deck	Control Deck
1				14			
2				15			
3				16			
4				17			
5				18			
6				19			
7				20			
8				21			
9				22			
10				23			
11				24			
12				25			
13				Total			

which he is looking as he looks at them. *Do not read further until instructed to do so.*

Well, how did you come out? Do you have *ESP?* Do any of your classmates? Group your data for examination in the spaces in Table 6. What is the class average? Is it anywhere near 5? How many people actually scored 5? In one of the author's classes the class average was 4.98. That seems to be close enough to 5, but only a few individuals scored 5. Were they the only ones who were guessing by chance? How about the ones above 5? Do you think they possess some special aptitude denied to the rest? What about those scoring under 5? Have they some negative aptitude that prevents their getting even a "chance" score? Maybe we'd better pay a little more attention to the meaning of this alleged "chance" score of 5.

A little reflection will bring you to the conclusion that a chance score of 5 represents an *average* chance score, from a great many measurements. If we flip 200 pennies, we expect, but rarely get, exactly 100 heads and 100 tails. We get rather 98, 99, 101, 102 heads, and so on. There is no special reason why we shouldn't get 200 heads, really; the point is that the 100 heads is the average result of a great many flippings of 200 pennies.

Now, we've already had occasion in our previous experiment to work up some averages or "means." We have noticed that roughly, there are about as many scores above the average as below it; we have also noticed that high scores raised an average, low scores pulled it down. We are now ready to draw a temporary conclusion: In any group of individuals, operating on a pure chance basis, just about as many individuals will score above the probabilities, *by chance,* as will score below probabilities, *by chance.*

Now what do you think of our high scorers? You probably want them to try again, to see if they keep it up. Suppose that they do, and also suppose that they keep it up, consistently scoring above chance. How long will you want them to keep it up to convince yourself that they have something? Fifty trials? 100? Would that convince you? (Would it make you feel that there's something to *ESP?*)

Let's change the subject a bit. You are playing bridge. The dealer hands you 13 spades. After you recover from your faint and bid a glorious 7-spade contract, the next dealer deals you another hand of 13 spades. What are you going to do? Now don't get excited. You think you have a rare hand, don't you? But stop a bit. Any bridge hand you have ever held is just as rare. The worst bust you ever had is just as rare as 13 spades. The particular combination of any 13 cards out of a deck of 52 is just as rare as any other particular combination. Every bridge hand is equally rare, and equally unlikely (or likely) to be repeated.

Now let's get back to Rhine. A high score of guesses might be impressive, and a succession of high scores, more so. But does a succession of high scores really prove anything, any more than a succession of rare hands in bridge? Remember, in order to get an average "chance" score of 5, there have to be scores above 5 to compensate for the scores under 5. Who gets them might well be considered immaterial. Just what is the meaning of a series of "above chance" scores made by some one person?

Suppose that we consider the following hypothetical example. A lot of people have been guessing at cards over the past years, well over 10,000. Suppose that we dismiss consideration of any who scored exactly 5 on any trial, and pick ourselves a population that scored either above or below 5. Let us not worry about the range of scores involved or the fact that there is some possibility of, by chance, ranging into higher-than-10 scores, although it is impossible to score less than zero on any trial, and just think in terms of above or below 5.

Now if we start out with 10,000 cases, and give each a run through the deck, half of them, or 5000, should score above 5, the rest below. Let's for the moment forget the low scorers and concentrate on the high. Give them another trial; half of these, or 2500 should score above 5 again, just by chance; give these 2500 another trial, and, by chance, 1250 should score above chance. Four times in a row, now 1250 people have scored above chance. Continuing the same procedure, there will be 625 above chance on a fifth trial, 312 on a sixth, 156 on a seventh, 78 on an eighth, 39 on a ninth, 20 on a tenth, 10 on an eleventh, 5 on a twelfth, 2 on a thirteenth, and we will wind up on the fourteenth trial with some stray character who has stayed above chance on every trial. What is more, assuming that he now turns about and starts getting scores below chance, he can continue for at least 13 more runs before he starts averaging 5, assuming that he does not fall below chance any farther than he had been above chance in his good trials. Our hero, then, can point with pride to a record of 27 trials during which he *averaged* above chance. Are you impressed? Remember, we started out with only 10,000 cases, and there are hundreds of millions of people.

When we take any particular human being out of the 2 billion alleged to exist, we do not know where he happens to fit in our selection. He may be the person who, *by chance,* will score above chance 100 times, 200 times, or oftener. Rhine does not set up extremely difficult standards for the acceptance of "evidence" of *ESP*. If you average 6.6 for 10 trials, you are considered "good"; an average of 6.9 for 10 trials is "very good." Such averages are not exceptionally difficult to obtain, as Rhine has demonstrated. The point is, of course, that no matter how high your average is, over no-matter-how-many trials, there is no evidence of anything working except the ordinary mechanics of chance.

But we want to be scientists; we don't want to engage in verbal bouts with mathematicians who point to the astronomical improbabilities of obtaining scores that Rhine has reported. We want to get some conception of a scientific approach to this problem. When we worked with drugs, we had to go to a lot of bother to demonstrate that it was the drug and not *suggestion* that might be operating in our experimental situation. In other words, we had to control our experiment. Control in that case, as in any other, meant that when we had our results, we knew, at least, that certain factors in the situation were not involved.

Has Rhine controlled his experiments? He indicates that he has paid the most scrupulous attention to preventing the passage of information between sender and receiver. Let us grant him this point (even though many psychologists are averse to being so liberal). Soundproof rooms, impenetrable screens, mechanical shufflers, independent scoring, etc.—all are forms of control; they eliminate the factors they are meant to eliminate. But a truly controlled experiment eliminates all the factors except the experimental variable. There is one crucial variable Rhine has not controlled, and that is the function of chance itself. It is not enough, in an experiment, to show that some event happens when a certain phenomenon is present (in this case, an alleged *ESP*). It is also necessary to show that it cannot happen when the agency is absent. Rhine should have demonstrated that it would be impossible to get high scores by chance alone over a reasonable period. Had he done so, there could be no really strong attack leveled at him; arguments would be limited to picayune details such as have been mentioned above.

In a simple little experiment, Leuba (2) decided to perform the necessary control experiment outlined above. He tried to see if he could get high scores in a situation in which *ESP* would be absent. His technique was extremely original and simple. All he did was to match two decks of Rhine cards, one against the other, giving the decks distinct human names as a means of identification. Each deck was shuffled and placed face down on a table; Leuba then took the top cards off each deck and scored them as hits if they matched and misses if they did not. He kept this up throughout the deck, and so had a record of hits and misses for a particular, though mythical, "subject." If the score was 5 or over, he retained the identities of the subjects and gave them another run. If the score was under 5, he just changed the identities and started all over. In this fashion, he ran "subjects" until they either earned scores of distinction according to Rhine's specifications or eliminated themselves by going under 5. After attempting some 87 "subjects," he found 3 that merited Rhine's approval as possessors of *ESP*. The remainder went into the same limbo which receives Rhine's discarded subjects.

Rhine was not satisfied that Leuba's results were obtained under sufficiently rigorous conditions, and the writer (1) undertook to meet Rhine's own specifications * on how such an experiment ought to be conducted. Using a mechanical shuffler and a predetermined number of runs for each mythical subject, the writer found 5 "subjects" out of 100 which Rhine's rules approve

* In a personal communication from J. B. Rhine.

as "good" or "very good." If it is possible to get the same phenomena that Rhine gets without the assumption of some as yet undescribed *"ESP,"* it seems that it is more appropriate to attribute the Rhine findings to chance than to the alleged "capacity."

Rhine, however, is not to be undone. To every argument he has an answer. To scoffers and critics he suggests that Galileo, Copernicus, and Einstein were abused and ridiculed. Columbus was laughed at. In fact, an extensive catalogue of scientists was eliminated at the stake or in the courtroom for trying to advance science. B. F. Skinner (4), in a scorching review of one of Rhine's books, points out that Rhine never exactly draws the conclusion from the syllogism implied in the subtle references to the laughter and scorn heaped upon Columbus and other great men, but from reading Rhine's books one can hardly fail to get the notion that, somehow, Rhine feels that attacks upon him are his finest tribute and best verification.

The student by now is probably eager to repeat at least one trial of a control nature on his little experiment. Suppose that you take another record of the cards. This time shuffle the cards and, without bothering to guess, simply record their identities in the third column in your table. Now compare this new set of identities with your original guesses. Remember you are comparing your guesses about *another* and different run, made some time before, with a card arrangement you did not suspect was even going to be presented to you for copying.*

How many hits did you make this time? What was the class average? Compare the two sets of results in Table 6. Did the class do better without guessing than with guessing? Don't be alarmed if your new scores are lower. It is very possible that they might be Your instructor is taking a chance that some of you will be disturbed if your new class average is lower. The student who has

---

* A more rigid control would be to compare the new run with the old one, and not with the "guesses." The present procedure is followed to get a large number of "runs" quickly; this is possible because each student's guesses are different from every other's. The other method would provide only one run, and this would demonstrate little or nothing.

Table 6. *Distribution of Number of "Hits" in a Group of Subjects (N__) in One Run through a Rhine Deck, Compared with a Control Run (No Guessings)*

Number of hits	Frequency	D	FD²	Number of hits	Frequency	D	FD²
	Experimental				Control		
15							
14							
13							
12							
11							
10							
9							
8							
7							
6							
5							
4							
3							
2							
1							
0							

followed the argument above will understand better, however. If you are still dubious, take a couple of decks of cards at home and repeat Leuba's study.

References

1. Bugelski, B. R., and Bugelski, S. A further attempt to test the role of chance in ESP experiments. *J. of Parapsychol.*, 1940, *4*, 142–148.

2. Leuba, C. H. An experiment to test the role of chance in ESP research. *J. of Parapsychol.*, 1938, *2*, 218–221.

3. Rhine, J. B. (ed.). *Extra-sensory perception after sixty years.* New York: Henry Holt. 1940.

4. Skinner, B. F. "Psi" and its manifestations. (A review of *The reach of the mind* by J. B. Rhine.) New York: *New York Times Book Review.* November 2, 1947.

4

The Content and Method of Modern Psychology

"In the beginning, mind was inextricably bound up with theological verbiage, but by the middle of the last century it had completely lost its soul at the hands of those who were trying to establish a scientific psychology. During the early years of the present century it began to lose consciousness under the blows of behaviorism. Finally at the present time, even its behavior is questionable." *

Psychology at one time was identified with the study of the mind. It is still so identified by the so-called "man in the street" and by the average college student. Most professional psychologists, however, disclaim any interest in "minds" or "mental" activities and prefer to emphasize an interest in *behavior* as the special content of psychology. But many aspects of "behavior" have a curious way of appearing "mental" to beginning students, and the definition of psychology as the study of behavior leaves many upset, irritated, and somehow unsatisfied. Nor are all psychologists ready or willing to give up their mental apron strings, and in their texts they speak of psychology as the study of behavior and *experience,* the latter term a substitute for the professionally frowned-upon "mind." This bringing in the "mind" by the back door results in confusing students to a point from which many fail

* The quotation has been taken from C. C. Pratt's *Logic of modern psychology* (4), p. 26. Much of the argument to follow is based on this challenging book.

to recover. Obviously, the experimental psychologist, who works directly with psychological problems, cannot be one of these confused individuals. He, at least, should know what he is doing and with what he is working.

In order to develop a working rationale as experimentalists, we must go back and find out how all the confusion and trouble began and try, if possible, to avoid the same mistakes. It would take us too far afield to follow through every one of the many aspects of, and solutions to, the traditional mind-body problem that philosophers and psychologists have propounded. Indeed, that approach is unnecessary in order to arrive at our goal of a basis for carrying on psychological observations in a scientific manner.

Introspection and subjectivity

The difficulty in which we find ourselves can be laid at the door of the Laboratory of Psychology, established by Wundt at Leipzig in 1879. Wundt, thoroughly convinced by his training and the scientific culture of the period that mental activity was an obvious characteristic of man, proceeded at once to the study of mental activity without bothering to describe or classify those acts which are mental and that are distinguishable from other acts which are not. Realizing that there could be no approach to the study of mental content by the customary procedures of the physical sciences, since the "mind" was commonly accepted as a nonpalpable entity that could not be weighed or measured by physical instruments, Wundt recognized the need for a new method of approach and proceeded to invent one. The method he developed came to be known as *introspection* and was for Wundt and his students the method suited par excellence to psychology. In fact, no other method was admissible. No other method could, indeed, be used by psychologists so long as psychology was identified as the study of the mind and its structure or function.

The method of introspection was a *technical procedure* for which one had to undergo special training. This training consisted essentially of learning to describe the content of the mind at a given moment without falling into the "stimulus error"— that is, including items of knowledge from past experience with the stimulus in the description of the "bare experience" or "existence" then in the mind. Such training for observing the mind in action was obviously difficult because of the absence of any tools or mechanism, sensory or otherwise, with which to make the required observations. To make any use at all of such a method, a framework had to be built in which the method could operate.

Wundt built the framework of his psychological "system" on the attributes of three assumed elements of the mind: sensations, images, and feelings. In spite of the restrictions of the method (which, if seriously used, would be quite sterile), Wundt and his students were able to accumulate a considerable store of facts (verbalized descriptions of events on which there is widespread agreement among individuals qualified to hold an opinion) * concerning sensory and perceptual reactions. Such information was obtained by asking subjects to report their reactions to stimuli in a laboratory situation, and, *except for the laboratory controls involved,* this process did not differ in any essential respect from the age-old customs of humans who, from the beginning stages of human speech, have greeted their neighbors with polite inquiries into the state of their health, their satisfaction with the weather, and their feelings concerning some proposition.

The results obtained by the Wundtian "structuralists" or "existentialists," as they were labeled, formed the extremely useful beginnings of a science concerned with sensory phenomena. Wundt, howver, assigned credit for these discoveries to the "introspective method," which, in practice, had nothing to do with such discoveries, since these were made by quite ordinary methods of observation and report such as are used by all humans, scientists or not. The reader should not infer from these remarks that Wundt and his students were not careful and rigorous observers.

* This definition of a fact is taken from Guthrie, E., and Edwards, A. *Psychology.* New York: Harper & Brothers, 1949, p. 24.

They were as scientific as they could possibly be in their work. It would indeed be difficult to find a more serious and critical scientist than Wundt or his most notable student, Titchener. Their difficulty lay in their definition of the subject matter of psychology and not in their method. As long as they worked in terms of mental processes, their method could be only sterile as far as theory was concerned, in spite of the tremendous amount of factual observation they accumulated.

Structuralism and the introspective method came under attack from a variety of sources and for various reasons. Gestalt psychologists attacked structuralism for its atomism and its emphasis on *analysis* into elements; the results of such analyses were identified by the Gestaltists with a perversion of the basic principles of mental organization. The functionalists attacked it as a "brass-instrument" psychology which refused to face the basic facts of life, its adaptive characteristics, and its functional integrity. The behaviorists attacked it for its sterility and its preoccupation with vague abstractions like "mind" and "consciousness" which Watson felt could not be studied scientifically. It was this last attack which led to our present difficulty. Watson was intent on making psychology "scientific." He identified science with the study of objects and events outside the observer and felt that until psychology got outside the self and became interested in "the other person" it could not become a science.

Watson incorrectly associated the study of the self, by some special technique such as introspection, with subjective observation. In his haste to get as far as possible from these empty and unscientific techniques, he urged that psychology get rid of *subjective* methods and become an *objective* science, like physics and chemistry. This emphasis on "objectivity" is the root of the difficulty. As Pratt points out, the word has at least nine different meanings, and its use is very likely to lead to confusion. By interpreting "subjective" to mean the opposite of the general meaning of "objective," Watson associated all the sins of introspection with the *only means of observation* that we have. According to Woodworth (7), he threw out the baby with the bath water.

In his attacks on introspection, Watson felt called upon to supply "objective" methods of studying human behavior. The technique of conditioning was coming into prominent use at the time, and Watson grasped at it as a panacea for the ills of psychology. Watson gave the impression in his writings that it would be better to condition a subject to respond with some movement to a color, for example, than to have him tell you he saw one. Today, after the smoke of Watson's battle against subjectivity has blown over, we tend to take a more realistic view. We realize more clearly what Watson found so hard to take, that in the last and final analysis someone has to look at the tracing on the smoked paper and the photograph and interpret what he sees in terms of his own sense organs, his own background, habits, and training, and his own weaknesses. There are few physical contrivances which react to stimuli, adjust thereto, and leave an "objective" report of the event. Even an automatic barometer which leaves a tracing of the atmospheric-pressure changes as they occur must eventually submit to human scrutiny, even if a way can be found for it to report itself and get itself classified and filed automatically.

The criticisms hurled by Watson at introspection were valid enough. To identify introspection with subjectivity, however, is a gross error. Subjectivity, if it refers to the use of an individual's sense organs and to interpretations of stimuli that impinge upon them, is the *only* method mankind has evolved for collecting information. The chemist, to whom the early behaviorists looked with respect, did not question the validity of his findings just because some of his tests depended upon his judgment of the color of a solution or an object. He just went ahead and reported "blue" or "pink" as his litmus paper changed color and never concerned himself with notions that science must throw out "subjectivity." The measurements that Watson so strongly desired had to be made by human measures, helped, we can hope, by adequate scales and balances, but depending upon the reaction of the observer's eyes.

By identifying objectivity with physical recording, the early behaviorists made a fetish of recording and "objectifying" instead of ascribing to such mechanical aids as records, photographs, etc., their basically helpful role of *preserving* some aspects of behavior for more leisurely study by the use of subjective sense-organ processes. This is not to deny the importance of recording, of eliminating whim and prejudice, of preserving data. Without such steps, litle progress can be made. On the other hand, to deny the scientific validity of personal observations because they are somehow "subjective" is to indict every measurement that was ever made. The word "objective" will be used hereafter, not as an antonym of "subjective," but as an indication that reasonable men, who have proper training and are prepared to observe some phenomenon, agree to its existence or occurrence, whether it be in the form of an X-ray photograph, a kymograph tracing, a photograph of an oscilloscope's wave reproductions, or simply a verbal report.

At various stages in the development of different sciences it may be necessary to deal with some types of events that cannot be directly measured or recorded until appropriate techniques are developed. In psychology, particularly, many types of events are far from the recording stage, yet they persistently demand our attention. Such events as emotional disturbances, "mental sets," choice behavior, attending, problem solving, etc., offer very little that can be recorded at present. However, this does not suggest that no study of these behavioral events should be attempted. With appropriate "social checks"—that is, repetitive observations by careful and trained observers—much information can be and has been obtained about such events. There is, after all, a continuum of accuracy between such activities as observing a dial pointer and observing reactions in a "fear" situation. "Objectivity" is a matter of degree. It will be realized, of course, that the "black-and-white" (better in color) record will allow future generations of reasonable men to agree about a recorded phenomenon, and so every effort should be made to get such records. Nevertheless, behavior having psychological interest will not be discarded and banished from science just because it cannot at the moment be recorded.

The Subject Matter of Psychology

We started out discussing the content of psychology and somehow wound up discussing its method. We dropped the "mind" rather hurriedly and allowed the word "behavior" to creep into our discussion. Will "behavior" comprise our subject matter? Is that what psychologists study? How does that distinguish them from physiologists, biologists, biochemists, and physicists? Don't they all study behavior? Behavior of living organisms, you say? Does that help? Total behavior? Adaptive behavior? A little consideration and you'll find that none of these is a crucial distinction. Time after time the psychologist in pursuing his studies runs into the territory of the physiologist, the physicist, the chemist.

Take, for example, the study of vision. The eye is like a camera, say the texts. It has a lens which bends light rays to a focus. Light rays are focused on a photochemical substance in the retina. Is this the language of psychology or that of physics and chemistry? When we think of neural correlates of learning we are getting physiological. The study of personality involves us with the endocrine glands; now we are delving into biochemistry. The alcoholic's behavior is due to a vitamin deficiency, says the psychology text; now we are part biochemist, part psychiatrist, part psychologist, and possibly part social worker.

Is intelligence a matter of brain-cell development? Is emotion due to thalamic imbalance? Are ulcers psychosomatic disorders? Are psychoses constitutional? Is color blindness a matter of heredity or vitamins? Do epileptic brain waves differ from normal? What are we talking about? Are intelligence, learning, emotion, personality, psychological problems? But the physicists, biologists and chemists are also working on those problems. To do a proper study in vision, the psychologist had better be a physiological chemist, an electrical engineer, an expert in optics, and a competent mathematician. Try audition as a psychological field. Better study acoustical engineering, with heavy doses of radio and physiology.

Does psychology *have* a content? That's a good question. Pratt answers with an unqualified *"No."* That's not so alarming as it sounds; no one, according to Pratt, has a subject matter with a content. Scientists just have different tools and have specialized in different techniques. They all study the same thing, the world and its contents and the interinfluences between the environment and its contents. Some scientists we call chemists, some anthropologists, some psychiatrists, some psychologists, etc., but all that we mean by such titles is a temporary subdivision of labor, possibly different points of view, and different temporary interpretations of the relative importance of the same materials or contents. For a competent and thorough analysis and understanding of the scientific world, all kinds of interests, aptitudes, skills, devices, methods, and techniques are important and necessary. Science is one. It is a unity, and to attempt to break it up into content divisions is to violate both reality and practice.

An example of Pratt's viewpoint will clarify the above. Psychologists traditionally have followed Pope's advice that the "proper study of mankind is man." But, in practice, they often find man too difficult to study and resort to animals in the fond hope that animals are simpler (certainly they are more practical to work on; they don't run off to keep appointments or forget to show up or eat when they should be starving, etc.).

In the course of study, some psychologists became interested in what came to be known as "instincts." Great controversies arose about the nature and number of instincts, lists running from 1 to 127, including everything from living to dying. (Freud retained the two extremes mentioned until his own death.) Some psychologists felt that animals had them, but men did not. Others wanted to include man with the animals; still others wanted to exclude instincts from both.

A series of remarkable studies purported to explain away the allegedly instinctive behavior of salmon nobly swimming the rapids for a thousand miles to return to the place of their birth, there romantically to mate, and more romantically to die. The migratory "instinct" of snowbirds was reduced to a relationship between illumination and gonadal changes, nesting behavior of pregnant rats to a loss of body temperature, rat killing of cats to learning, and so on. The instincts dropped one by one before the attacks of physiologists, physicists, chemists, and psychologists. But one beautiful "instinct" remained. The noble homing pigeon, hero of countless battles even in these electronic days, still flew home by instinct. Some psychologists feebly insisted that the home-flying was due to learning, that pigeons had to be trained to come home by gradually extending their travels, etc., but they were making little headway and really preferred not to talk about the matter. Instincts acquired a bad odor; scientifically they were out; no one was really alarmed if the swallows did not come back to Capistrano on time. That was just a pleasant myth. But the homing pigeons still came home.

A scientist who could not be happy with such unexplained behavior finally attacked the problem. He claims a great success for which we will not yet vouch, although he appears to have given a legitimate account of how and why pigeons fly home. Who was this scientist? A psychologist? Not at all; he was a physicist. Why is a physicist working with homing pigeons? Isn't that a psychological problem? One might well ask: What makes pigeons a physicist's dish? He is not supposed to be studying behavior. We might permit a biologist, or at worst a physiologist, to study pigeons, but a physicist? Maybe Pratt is right when he says that there is but one world to study and everybody is studying the same thing—behavior of the world's contents. Some use one tool, others another. Use whatever tool applies. If the tools of a physicist apply to homing-pigeon behavior, use those; maybe the tools of the psychologist do not.

The account of the physicist's study may prove illuminating. The physicist was familiar with the principles of magnetism and the distribution of magnetic-variation lines over the surface of the earth. Such lines follow roughly north–south patterns somewhat like lines of longitude. He speculated that such lines might provide an east–west orientation for a pigeon if it had some organ such as a compass that was magnetically sensitive.

East and west, however, are not enough to get you home. You might keep going north if you happened to be north of home; you need some way of locating a north and south coordinate to locate your position on the earth's surface in order to know when you have gone far enough north or south; in other words, you need a latitude-bearing as well as a longitude, just as does any navigator. Is there some physical force which might affect your behavior at different latitudes?

Being a physicist he knew, of course, about the Coriolis force which is measured as a change in the rotational speed of the earth with changes in latitude. The earth is narrower at the poles than at the equator, and the poles therefore rotate at a slower speed. Here we have a possible way of getting latitude, and with the magnetic lines for longitude, we have the basic procedures for locating a position on the earth's surface.

If this reasoning is correct, we should be able to confuse pigeons by taking them about the earth and releasing them in geographically strange areas which have the same Coriolis force and similar magnetic lines. In such an event, the pigeons should act as if they knew where they were going and fly to some specific location as though to their homes.

Now, our physicist lived at State College, Pennsylvania. Reference to suitable maps revealed that a location near Kearney, Nebraska, on the same latitude, had a magnetic line with the same directional orientation as did that at State College. If some pigeons were released in the Nebraska area, they should fly to some point on the State College latitude. He tried it, and they did. Our physicist concluded that pigeons fly home, not because of some mysterious instinct but because of the physical forces we have considered.

Do we have here a physicist solving a psychological problem? Or is it not more correct that we have here a scientist working at one of the problems of science with tools he happens to know well enough to use expertly? If you agree to the latter view, then it seems reasonable to agree that psychology is just another branch of scientific activity, with its own tools and viewpoints, its own techniques and methods. Our task is to learn how to use some of these tools, those of the psychological laboratory. The tools of the clinic and the tester we will not examine; those you can learn about in other texts and courses.

Many psychologists will not agree with Pratt's analysis. They will insist that psychology has its own "materials" or data. It is certainly true that the problems on which psychologists work do not overlap to any apparent degree the work of astronomers and geologists, for instance. The degree of overlap with biology and physics is more obvious, but the *type of problem* selected by the psychologist will still differ appreciably from that of the physicist or zoologist. Kinsey, for example, in his widely discussed study, *Sexual behavior in the human male,* is difficult to distinguish from a psychologist; after all, he mentions humans, behavior, and sex in his very title. Yet, Dr. Kinsey is a zoologist! An inspection of the Kinsey study, however, reveals it as a study of "classification," a well-recognized procedural preoccupation of zoologists.

A psychologist studying human sexual behavior would come out with a quite different report. His researches would probably deal with the *interactions of his subjects with their environments,* with the relationships between stimuli and responses. If psychology has a content at all, it is that of the relationship between stimuli and responses and, since it is quite obvious that the same objective stimulus is not always followed by the same response, the psychologist is forced to consider the nature of the organism exposed to the stimuli and how that organism, its history and its present conditions, affect and modify the resultant responses.

Science and Performance of Operations

There is one principle of procedure in scientific method which we have so far ignored but which we can now examine. The statement of scientific laws, which we have assumed to be the goal of science, involves a careful use of language and symbols. Scientific laws are usually stated as formulas; you are probably familiar with Boyle's law which states that when the temperature remains the same, the volume of a given mass of gas varies inversely as its pressure. In formula form it reads $PV = k$. The law of gravity also is stated symbolically as $F = \dfrac{mM}{r^2} C$. But when we ask for the translation of some of these symbols into words, we run into some difficulty. The physicist uses many expressions which seem to be quite meaningful in ordinary conversation, such as energy, force, acceleration, work, etc. Suppose that you try to define some of these terms, "energy" for example. What is it? Is it an "it"? Is work a thing? Is force a thing?

So long as physicists thought of energy and force as some kinds of real existences, which pulled or pushed other things around, they had no science and could not use these concepts. They found, eventually, that they had to remove energy and force from the objects they were endowing with such powers and define them in practical terms with which everyone would agree. They decided to call "force" by the mathematical expression: ma, or "mass" times "acceleration." In order to determine the amount of force involved in a given situation, it was necessary to measure the mass of some object and its acceleration. Such measurement gave meaning to the concept of force. Without the measurements, the concept had animistic, primitive, and unscientific connotations of some sort of power resident within a body. Energy is defined physically as $E = mc^2$ or mass times velocity of light squared. There again, measurements are resorted to in order to get some comprehensible meaning for a concept or "construct." Defining concepts in terms of the measurements involved amounts to describing the operations you perform in arriving at the concept.

This is nothing new to you, really; you've been doing it all your life. It just looks new because you haven't stopped to think about it. Take a concept like "heat." You know what it means. When you say "it's hot," and speak precisely, you really mean that, if you should take a temperature reading with a thermometer, the column of mercury would be above some standard reading. When you say something is "long" or "tall," you mean that if you should lay a meter stick alongside the object, the stick would indicate a given measurement, and that this would also be greater than some common standard. When you say that you've waited "a long time," you mean that the hands of a clock have traveled a definable distance in their daily circuits. In all of the above situations you have been describing things in terms of marks on instruments of one type or another. Without the instruments or some substitute therefor, you would not be communicating accurate information to your listeners.

When you enter discussions of human behavior, however, you tend to forget your measuring sticks, scales, instruments, and so on, and to talk about such things as "drive," "intelligence," "personality," as if they were entities of one kind or another. You make *things* out of them and act as if they were real, and your listener does not know what you are talking about because he also has made "things" out of them, only his "things" are not necessarily even close to what your "things" are.

Take such a concept as "intelligence." Your elementary texts define it for you in numerous ways. It is a capacity (that's a convenient and undefined word) to adapt or to adjust, or to use past experience, or to think, or to see spatial relations, or all these capacities put together. Few texts agree directly with each other, and the student is often annoyed, wondering why psychologists don't get together and decide just what intelligence *is*. But they can't do that (or they would have done so by now) simply because intelligence is not a thing or an essence or any other type of substantial reality.

One psychologist, despairing of any other approach, defined intelligence as "that which intelligence tests test." The student hearing this definition is inclined to laugh. It sounds silly; it's avoiding the issue or begging the question, he says. But is it so silly? What is length? After you worry over that for a while, you'll probably decide that length is that which length-testers test, or more simply, that which is measured by a ruler. Try your self out on "What is time?" After a few hours you'll be glad to agree that time is that which is measured by a clock, and let it go at that; but you'll not only be "letting it go at that," you'll also be scientifically correct.

Now how about intelligence? Psychologists would much rather talk about IQ's than about intelligence. Do you wonder why? Well, they know what an IQ is. It's $\frac{MA}{CA}$, that's what it is, and it isn't anything else; it has no other meaning and can have no other meaning in a scientific discussion. *MA's* (defined as the number of correct answers given to questions designed to be answered by normal children of different age groups) can be measured by tests; *CA's* can be measured; a division can be performed. An *IQ* is an operational concept; its meaning depends upon the operations performed to obtain it. We have already used several terms in our statistical manipulations which are good examples of operational definitions. The average or "mean," we found, amounts to its formula (the sum of the scores divided by the number of scores). The "standard deviation," we found, is: the square root of the mean of the squared deviations.

What is "learning"? Here we have no good formula as yet, although attempts are being made to work one out. John McGeoch (3) suggested a definition, in operational terms, which might not stand too close a scrutiny, but which at least is freer from mysteries than most definitions. He calls learning "the change in performance as a result of practice." We can measure performance, and we can measure practice (although we could get into difficulties there), and so his definition at least comes close to satisfying scientific demands.

Other concepts are not very easily defined; concepts like "drive," "motivation," "personality," etc., are extremely difficult to reduce to operational terms. We can approach a definition of "drive" in terms of specific drives, such as hunger, which we can relate to a certain number of hours without food, etc. "Personality" gives us considerable trouble. A favorite definition of personality defines it as the difference between one individual and all of the rest of mankind. That obviously leaves much to be desired, but it's on the right track because there is at least some hope of being able to measure the ways in which individuals differ. On the other hand, defining personality as the effect of some individual on others, or as the sum total of social and biological predispositions, is greatly removed from a working, laboratory description of a scientific nature.

There will be no use for any concepts in our work which have no *prospect* of reduction to operational terms. Occasionally, we may speak loosely and indulge in flights of fancy; on those occasions we will try to realize that, for the moment at least, we are no longer rigorously scientific. In the work to follow, it is expected that the student will practice reducing concepts and terminology generally to operational descriptions. He will stick close to his results and to his measuring sticks. Once he starts using terms which have no relation to any measurement he has performed, including counting and classifying, we can be fairly sure that he has left the field of science for the arts or metaphysics.

The student may have noticed in his elementary text that the author generally was careful to talk about behavior and not about alleged components of behavior. In discussing emotions, most authors do not talk as if there were such things as emotions; they prefer to talk about "emotional behavior" or "learning behavior" or "forgetting behavior" or "intelligent behavior."

This tendency to express psychological concepts in verbal or adjectival form is not just issue-dodging; it is a healthy development. There is some hope of reducing behavior to measurement; there is little hope of arriving at a thing we can call an emotion. As knowledge of psychological phenomena is increased, as our information broadens and develops, we are coming closer and closer to reducing our psychological concepts to measurement and formulas. When we are finally able to express certain kinds of behavior as functions (in a mathematical sense) of specific types of measurements, we will have arrived at science. Until that time, we can only keep trying.

Theories in Psychology

The place of theory or system-building in psychology is of primary importance for the student acquiring an appreciation of modern psychology. Because of the uneven development of various aspects of psychology, and because of the continuous introduction of new problems and "theories," the student should recognize just what is meant by a theory and know something of its use and function. Spence (5) points out that there are two kinds of theories which must be distinguished. One is of the Newtonian type, which organizes previously unrelated broad generalizations into a coherent system and serves principally to "explain" some aspect of the universe. We have not reached this stage of development in psychology. The other kind of theory is of a more speculative type, making considerable use of assumptions in an effort to provide a means of deducing theorems that can either serve as principles in their own right or assist in the accurate formulation of empirical laws which can later be fitted into a theory of the first type.

We can best illustrate theorizing in psychology by considering the general approach to the study of behavior by E. C. Tolman (6) and C. L. Hull (1). Tolman points out that we are far removed, in psychology, from the time when we can predict even such a simple event as the choice of direction a rat will make in a simple discrimination situation in a T maze. The reason for this difficulty is that there are so many variables which can determine the outcome and so many degrees of strength of each variable that it is quite impossible to appraise the potential influences on a given rat at a given time. Now, to study each degree of each variable is an impossible task; it could never be done even if all the world's psychologists devoted themselves exclusively to the problems involved. The solution, says Tolman, is theory.

How can a theory help in the absence of empirical facts and laws? Should not the facts and generalizations come first as they did in the theories of physics? But, says Spence, psychological phenomena are not so simple as are the relatively less complicated phenomena of physics. There are too many variables interacting in unknown ways with each other to allow ready generalization. At the present stage of development of psychology it is necessary to make guesses about the ways in which the numerous variables interact with each other in any given situation. Let us consider the example cited above in connection with Tolman's interest in theory.

Consider the rat faced with a right-left choice in a T maze. We can symbolize this situation with the familiar S—R formula. The animal's response, the behavior, or R, can be thought of as a function of the S. The S is a complicated series of influences involving both the external environment and internal conditions of the rat, but we can generalize that the response made will depend upon the resultant of the S factors. In other words, in this situation the R is a dependent variable. The behavior that occurs *depends* on the characteristics of S, which we can term the independent variable (since we can manipulate its various features experimentally).

We can picture the situation, following Tolman, in this fashion:

$$S \text{———————} f \text{———————} R$$

Independent variable   Dependent variable

which we translate: The behavior (dependent variable) is a function of the stimulus situation (independent variable). To predict behavior, then, it would appear that all we have to do is to describe the independent variables operating at a given time, and if we knew what effects these independent variables had on the organism, we should know what it would do.

This brings us to our difficulty: What is the effect of a given variable? Psychologists have arrived at sufficient sophistication to recognize that the effect of many variables cannot be stated simply. For example, what does hunger do to an animal? That depends on the degree of hunger and on the animal. Does it follow, for example, that the greater the hunger, the greater the activity? That appears to be so *up to a point.* After that, there may be less activity! Whenever hunger is a variable, then, it is necessary to know the precise degree of hunger and the relationship of this degree of hunger to behavior. At present we do not know the precise effect of a given degree of hunger, and we do not have time empirically to discover the exact effect of every degree of hunger that may function in a given behavior situation.

Are we then to give it all up as a bad job? That, says Tolman, is not the only alternative. We have the possibility of *guessing* what the relationship involved might be by taking advantage of the limited information we do have and interpolating and extrapolating on the basis of *assumptions* concerning the nature of the relationship. Such an assumption about the relationship existing between independent and dependent variables is what we meant above by the term "function." Tolman suggested the term "intervening variable" to describe such a "guessed-at" function. The intervening variables are, then, logical guesses which are used to tie together independent and dependent variables *operationally.* In effect, the intervening variables or functions are formulas based on tentative data and describable in terms of features of both stimulus and response or of independent and dependent variables.

An example from the field of electricity might help at this point. Physicists use the concept of "resistance" in describing certain relationships between the number of volts applied to a wire and the number of amperes of current delivered at the other end. The amount of current is supposedly related to the resistance of the wire. The resistance is an intervening variable assumed to function between volts and amperes. Various aspects of resistance can be *calculated* with respect to type of conductive material, its thickness, its length, etc. Resistance itself is never seen or otherwise experienced than as a mathematical derivative of the measurement of volts and amperes. It thus qualifies as an intervening variable, an assumption, a guess about a type of relationship, and it can be used in future situations or problems where it presumably operates as a variable.

In psychology the concept of intelligence as measured by IQ or $\frac{MA}{CA}$ has a similar status and role. By introducing an intervening variable, IQ, we can help out our predictions in situations where it is assumed to operate. In both the above examples we must note that, although we have referred to both resistance and intelligence by the term "it," no such *entities* are assumed to exist. These words are convenient shorthand symbols for types of functions or relationships between *measurable variables*. They are, or can be, strictly defined operationally and used for prediction without any assumptions concerning their "real" existence.

The above caution is suggested because some psychologists, such as Hull, on occasion make use of concepts or "hypothetical constructs" in the form of intervening variables that are also assumed to have a reasonable probability of actual existence in the form of some real entity. This might be an activity of the nervous system, for example, or some other physiological condition. Hull speaks, for example, of "functional anticipatory goal responses" as if they were real, even though they are as yet unobserved acts or movements of the organism. As MacCorquodale and Meehl (2) have pointed out, there is some danger of confusing the strictly operationally defined "intervening variable" of the Tolman type with a "hypothetical construct" having an assumed reality and a relatively independent existence. It is easy to fall into the error of endowing the "construct" with characteristics of its own which are not susceptible of measurement.

To return to our discussion of psychological theory, we can state with Tolman that "a theory . . . is a set of 'intervening variables.' These to-be-inserted intervening variables are 'constructs' which we, the theorists, evolve as a useful way of breaking down into more manageable form" the functional relationships between dependent and independent variables. A similar description of theory is offered by Hull in his statement that "a theory is a set of definitions and postulates proposed by the theorist (on the basis presumably of some already found facts) from which other empirically testable facts, or as he calls them, theorems, can be logically deduced." * If we substitute "intervening variables" for postulates in the above quotation, we can see the similarity between the approaches of Hull and Tolman.

The task of psychology, and of experimental psychology in particular, emerges from our discussion of scientific theory. It is the discovery and analysis of intervening variables or functional relationships between stimuli and responses. Such intervening variables when properly described will take the form of mathematical or logical formulas such as the well-known laws of physics $pv = k$,

$I = \dfrac{E}{R}$, $F = ma$, etc. Once the separate intervening variables are

suitably described, the subsequent task of discovering the intervening variables determining the relationships among simultaneously operating intervening variables themselves will begin. At that point psychology will arrive at the status of the first type of theory-building described by Spence.

It is hardly necessary to reiterate that psychology is far from such a goal at the present time. The student who has embarked on the study of psychology with the intention of learning how to control his fellows, or even himself, had best stop to take a fresh look at the situation. It is likely that the psychologist *of the future*

* Quoted by Tolman (6) from Hull, C. L. Mind, mechanism, and adaptive behavior. *Psychol. Rev.*, 1937, *44*, 1–32.

may know a lot about *people* but not much about specific persons, just as the meteorologist may know much about the weather but cannot tell us whether it will rain at a specific time and place. The variables determining human behavior are not likely to turn out to be less complex than those determining weather, yet meteorologists say that, in order to make accurate predictions, they would have to have ways of instantaneously evaluating the simultaneous influences of about two hundred constantly changing climate variables. With this final reminder of the nature of the psychologist's task, we can turn to a consideration of how he proposes to go about it.

Our next experiment will give the student a chance to cope with a typical psychological variable, that of "attention." This experiment will provide an opportunity to deal with an "intervening variable" operationally and should amply illustrate the considerations of the present chapter.

References

1. Hull, C. L. *Principles of behavior.* New York: Appleton-Century. 1943.
2. MacCorquodale, K., and Meehl, P. E. On a distinction between hypothetical constructs and intervening variables. *Psychol. Rev.,* 1948, *55,* 95–107.
3. McGeoch, J. *The psychology of human learning.* New York: Longmans, Green. 1943.
4. Pratt, C. C. *The logic of modern psychology.* New York: Macmillan. 1937.
5. Spence, K. W. The postulates and methods of "behaviorism." *Psychol. Rev.,* 1948, *55,* 67–78.
6. Tolman, E. C. The determiners of behavior at a choice point. *Psychol. Rev.,* 1938, *45,* 1–41.
7. Woodworth, R. S. *Contemporary schools of psychology,* rev. ed. New York: Ronald. 1949.

Experiment 3. The Measurement of the Visual Span of Attention

Introduction. From the viewpoint of this course we are interested in three aspects of experimentation which are suitably demonstrated by this experiment:

1. *The concept of operational definition.* In order to work scientifically it is a generally accepted maxim that all terms used should be operationally defined. An exact meaning must be communicated to the readers of your report; all the readers must be able to understand *in the same way* all the terms you employ in describing your work. The experiment you are about to do deals with what, traditionally, has been called the "span of attention." Some writers, however, chose to use the terms "perception" or "apperception" to describe the results of the type of manipulations in which you will engage. Presumably, the three terms are meant to describe either the same "thing" or are meant to convey shades or slight differences of meaning. It will be one of your obligations, in your report, to describe your findings in such terms that anyone with a knowledge of the language will understand *exactly* what you are talking about and where you obtained (or how you arrived at) your terminology.

2. *The concept of a criterion.* In many experiments you will use one or several criteria, or "cutting scores," in order to decide how long to continue an experiment or some aspect of its procedure. You might, for example, want to decide in a positive manner, for your purposes, how many trials to give in a learning situation before you accept some behavior as "learned," or, you might want to describe the hunger condition of animals in terms of so many hours without food.

Whenever your data are continuous in nature and you wish to break the continuity for some practical reason, you have a criterion problem. We might call it the "How-many-hairs-make-a-beard?" problem. It will occur in many of these forms: What level of intelligence of subjects should be used? What degree of various sensory or motor capacities, e.g., acuity of vision or hearing, should be expected? How much preliminary practice shall be allowed? How much rest should be given between trials? When has learning or conditioning occurred? Do you see the connection between operational definition and criteria? In the present experiment you are expected to answer the question: "How many dots can be seen in one glance?" Since the number will vary with different trials, your answer immediately takes the form: "That depends on the criterion you use." We will use 100 percent, 75 percent, and 50 percent frequency of correct response as criteria in our group analysis.

3. *Functional analysis.** The writing of scientific laws in many instances is reduced to describing the concomitant changes among variables as one of a pair of variables is systematically altered. In effect this amounts to plotting data in graphical form and showing the quantitative changes of the variables, which are described in steps on the ordinate and abcissa of the graph. A typical psychological example might be a curve showing the amount of activity of various kinds exhibited by animals at successive hours after removal of food. What functional analysis is demonstrated in the present experiment?

Apparatus. You will use a falling-door type of tachistoscope, set to expose a 5 by 8 white card for approximately 0.1 second. You will have a series of cards on which black dots appear. There will be one card for every number of dots from 3 to 15. There will be 4 additional cards for each of the following numbers of dots: 6, 7, 8, 9, 10. In your report, account for the presence of the additional cards, and give an adequate description of your apparatus, illustrating it by a working drawing. Figure 3 shows one of many possible types of tachistoscopes.

---

* The nature of a functional analysis is discussed in Chapter 5, pp. 95–97. It is desirable to work out such an analysis at this point for an illustration of the content of the next chapter.

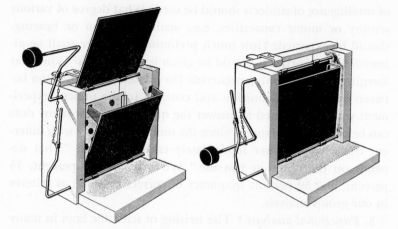

FIGURE 3. *A FALLING-DOOR TACHISTOSCOPE.* This device operates effectively and silently if a little care is taken in construction and adjustment. It consists essentially of two doors securely mounted on rods which turn in bearings. The lower door, while closed, keeps hidden the material to be viewed. As this door drops, the stimulus material is exposed momentarily, until the upper door drops and screens it. The weighted arm on the left drops with the upper door and strikes against the braided wire attached to the bottom door. This action closes the bottom door, screening the exposure material and preventing a second glance.

Mechanically, the system operates as follows:

1. The experimenter presses against a trigger which overbalances the upper door.
2. As this door begins to fall, the lower door also falls because it is held in position by the wire attached to the upper door, and the release of the tension allows it to drop.
3. As the upper door reaches the end of its fall, the weighted arm strikes the wire and resets the lower door.

Procedure. Arrange the tachistoscope in such a way that your subject has a complete view of the exposure area. Load your tachistoscope with the cards in random order. Signal the subject by saying: "Ready . . . now," and release the falling doors by a quick pressure on the trigger. Vary the interval between "ready" and "now" from 0.5 to 2 seconds. Record the number of dots re-

Table 7. *The Number of Dots Reported by One Subject after Viewing Tachistoscopically Exposed Cards Containing Various Numbers and Arrangements of Dots*

Trials	Number of dots on each card												
	3	4	5	6	7	8	9	10	11	12	13	14	15
1													
2													
3													
4													
5													
6													
7													
8													
9													
10													
TOTAL													
No. of correct reports													
Percent correct													
Overestimate No. of reports													
Underestimate No. of reports													
Group mean Percent correct reports													

ported for each card in the appropriate column of Table 7, regardless of its correctness. Shuffle the cards between each of the 10 trials.

Results. Report the percent correct for each number of dots for class tabulation. Present your subject's data along with the group data. Did your subject overestimate or underestimate? Consistently? Did he vary in his type of error at either end of the curve? How many dots could he see 50, 75, and 100 percent of the time? Cut your curve at these steps.

Discussion

1. Describe the sources of error, controlled and uncontrolled, that operated in this experiment.
2. Did the color of the background make any difference?
3. Was there any evidence of "learning" of the cards?
4. What are the basic problems involved in the use of a tachistoscope?
5. On the basis of your findings, define the "span of attention."

References

1. Woodworth, R. S. *Experimental psychology*. New York: Henry Holt. 1938, chap. 27.
2. Postman, L., and Egan, J. P. *Experimental psychology*. New York: Harper and Brothers. 1949, chap. 11.

5

The Nature of an Experiment

PSYCHOLOGY AND SCIENCE · BYSTEMS AS TOOL BOXES

AN EXPERIMENT, psychological or otherwise, is an attempt to discover the relationships that obtain between or among a number of factors called *variables*. A variable is any feature or aspect of an event, function, or process that, by its presence and nature, affects some other event or process which is being studied.

For example, in taking a photograph of some object, the photographer has to take into account such variables as the amount of light reflected by the object, the color of the object, its distance from his camera, its fixity or speed of movement, etc. He "controls" these variables by focusing his lens, adjusting the size of his shutter opening, and regulating the shutter speed. He may also use various types of filters and lenses for different colored objects, clouds, etc., and he will use films of special "speeds" and characteristics. Later he will choose different varieties of chemicals and photographic papers to develop and print his photograph. The resulting picture represents an observation by his camera; if he has attended correctly to all of the variables cited, his observation will have been a "controlled observation." As such, his picture is an experiment. Experiments are usually defined as controlled observations. Many people take pictures. Few people are photographers.

In the same spirit, many people observe human behavior, but few are psychologists. The psychologist in his controlled observations, his experiments, tries to do what the photographer does, to take account of the numerous variables that will affect his picture (analysis of an event). Unlike the photographer's, however, his variables are not "cut and dried" and relatively easily controlled by suitable equipment; in many cases, the variables are not even suspected, and, even when obvious, the apparatus or technique for controlling them may not be available. As a consequence, the results that come out of the psychological laboratory are not so clear cut and sharp as are those that come out of the darkroom. After the observation is made, it usually must be further described in elaborate reports which constitute an apology or rationale for the failures to represent clearly the event or object under observation. The report will be heavily loaded with figures and statistical treatments all designed to show what would have been the case if such and such factors had not entered or if they could have been controlled. The conclusion will be stated in possibilities, probabilities, tendencies, indications, and such modest terms as "it appears," "it would seem," and so on.

If this is discouraging to the beginning student, he might do well to reconsider his desire to enter a field that offers him little opportunity to stumble easily upon new elements, new continents, or great truths. Scientific psychology, like invention in the popular definition, is one tenth inspiration, nine tenths perspiration. The average psychological experiment takes relatively little time in doing. Much of the work comes in preparation, building and testing apparatus or materials, working out procedures, and finally in analyzing the results. One experiment of a simple sort performed by the author, took 20 hours to prepare, 1 hour to do, and 140 hours to compute data, analyze, and organize into a form from which conclusions could be drawn. In other types of experimentation, hours may be spent in monotonous repetition of presenting stimuli and recording observations. Such experiments lose most, if not all, of their glamor after the first subject. In some instances, the psychologist may watch a moving tape on which several markers are scratching out occasional signs representing the behavior of a rat in a darkened, soundproof box. The psychologist, in such instances, does not even have the opportunity of watching the rat; his function is reduced to watching a stylus or pen sporadically indicating the occurrence of a segment of the rat's behavior.

The Nature of Observation

To return to our definition of the experiment as a "controlled observation," we find that each of its terms requires additional explanation. To begin with the second term, "observation," we find several important questions to answer: Who does the observing? How? Why is the observation being made? Under what conditions? In an experiment, an observation is useful or meaningful only if an observer is trained to make the desired observation. It is a commonplace that different individuals see various objects or events differently. In an art gallery, the art expert sees things in a picture not immediately, if ever, apparent to the neophyte. At the concert, the musician hears tones and reacts to them in ways immeasurably different from those of a person with an "untrained ear." The "long hair" fails to hear the presumably delightful sound combinations in some boogie woogie rendition. We all find ourselves, on occasion, asking, "What does she see in him?" To observe, then, the observer must be trained; he must know what to look for, more or less what to expect, and how to see it.

The observer must, further, be ready to observe. We are familiar with the contradictory testimony of witnesses at accidents. Psychological experiments have repeatedly shown that unexpected events are not uniformly observed by assorted witnesses, although they have strong and profound convictions concerning their own reliability as observers and will swear to their evidence with "I saw it with my own eyes." To be ready to observe means, then, that the experimenter prepares himself for the observation. He arranges for the event to happen, and if he is not satisfied, he repeats the event for additional observation. If repetition is impossible, he secures a photograph, a recording, or other objective indication of certain features of the event, so that he can observe repeatedly at his leisure. He does not put his faith in "his own eyes" nor in those of other observers who may quite properly have 20–20 vision. When possible, he makes use of apparatus and instruments to make his observations for him.

In recent years the newspapers throughout the country reported numerous "observations" of "flying saucers" sailing about at various speeds and altitudes. No reputable scientist in the country even bothered to attempt to explain the phenomena being reported, even at the insistence of newspaper editors trying to satisfy an aroused public (aroused largely through the papers themselves). To the scientist there were no observations worthy of the name, and it would be pointless to consider the reports.

Consider the various factors that would have to be accounted for before a scientist could pause in his work to comment on an alleged "flying saucer": Are there any records, any photographs, any objective, planned observations? Is reproduction of the observation possible upon request? Are the observers trained to make such observations? Is there any consistency to the reports of members of groups of alleged observers? Unless such questions can be answered positively, the scientist pays no heed. He does not deny the occurrence of such a phenomenon; he is indifferent to it. Unless the phenomenon can be presented in objective reality, it is of no scientific importance for the time being. One might counter by reference to "shooting stars," whose reality is not doubted, but the astronomical scientist has sufficient objective evidence of what are popularly known as "shooting stars" to convince anyone. In sum, unless the observer is trained and ready, scientific observations are not to be expected.

The Meaning of "Control"

The term "controlled" offers more of a problem. In general it carries several connotations. In one sense, it means that irrelevant variables which might affect the observation have been eliminated; in a slightly different light, it means that the experimenter can be satisfied that what he has observed is real and meaningful, and that the relationships he has discovered in his observations bear at least an approximation to the truth.

The English philosopher John Stuart Mill * once attempted an analysis of the meaning of scientific observation and has left us a fairly comprehensive interpretation of the meaning of a "controlled observation." His suggestions were presented in the form of descriptions of five methods of scientific procedure. Only two such methods will concern us here (the interested student should consult any text on logic for the remaining three). The methods which concern us are known by the titles: the *method of agreement* and the *method of difference*.

Stated briefly, the method of agreement tells us that whenever some factor is always present as an antecedent to some phenomenon or event, and is present in numerous contexts, then that factor is a cause or part of the cause of the consequent phenomenon or event. The method of difference, on the other hand states that when some factor is regularly absent in the absence of a phenomenon, then that factor is a cause or part of the cause of the phenomenon. Stated negatively, if some event occurs in the absence of some factor, then that factor is not a cause of the event.

Let us examine each of these methods as they would apply to a psychological experiment. Suppose that we are concerned with the possibility of demonstrating a neurosis in some animal, say, a rat. We assume, perhaps anthropomorphically and also perhaps without foundation, that neuroses are caused by conflicts. Our problem appears simple, then: establish a conflict and see if you get a neurosis.

Means for establishing conflicts are allegedly available. You train a rat to make some response such as jumping a short distance through the air from a "jumping stand" toward some stimulus mounted on a collapsible door. As he hits the door with his feet, the door falls before him, he walks over it and eats some food on

---

* For a fuller account of Mill's methods, see Robinson (2).

a platform behind the door. When he has mastered the problem, you introduce an additional stimulus, resembling the first, mounted on an adjoining door. This door, however, fails to open when hit. Thus when the rat jumps against it, the result is a disturbing drop onto a net for the animal.

Let us use a circle as a rewarded stimulus and an ellipse as an unrewarded alternate. If the rat discriminates and avoids the original ellipse, we gradually alter the axes on the ellipse until it approaches a circle. The animal then allegedly begins to develop conflicts and does not readily respond to either stimulus. Since the rat is apparently refusing to make a choice, we use some method of forcing him to choose by making it difficult for him to remain on the stand. Suppose we decide to use an air hose which emits a sharp blast of air about the rat's hindquarters. The rat then jumps off the stand somewhat blindly, runs about the floor heedless of obstacles, appears quite frenzied, may hop vigorously, and may go into convulsions and a comalike state, during which he is quite plastic and catatonic. He acts like a "crazy" rat.

Suppose that we repeat this procedure with numerous rats and find that we get virtually the same pattern whenever we have established conflict, regardless of such things as age, sex, drive condition, previous laboratory experience, etc. We might represent the situation in the following form:

Factor present	Consequent event	Code	
A B C D E	Neurosis	A—age of rats	G—magnesium supply
		B—sex	H—nutritional level
F G H D E	Neurosis	C—species	I—insulin level
		D—conflict	J—metrazol level
I J K D E	Neurosis	E—air blast	K—oxygen
		F—vitamin B supply	consumption

Examination of the above table reveals that Factor D, conflict, is always present whenever there is a neurosis. Hence, according to Mill's *method of agreement*, conflict must be a cause or part of the cause of the event, i.e., the neurosis. But, the observing reader says, Factor E, the air blast, is also present on every occasion. That is necessary, says the experimenter, to force the animal to choose. At this point, if we agree, we must admit that conflict appears to be systematically associated with the neurotic behavior.

The experiment described above is not an idle invention. It represents many real experiments performed in the 1930's (1) which caught the imagination of the psychological world and aroused considerable controversy and additional experimentation. Alert experimenters, including the original investigator, were not content to accept the "necessity" explanation of the air blast. They did what, in retrospect, appears obvious. They dropped out Factor D, the conflict, retaining the E factor, the air blast. What was the result? The neurotic behavior remained. Here we have an application of Mill's second method, that of *difference*. If an event remains or occurs with the absence of a factor, then that factor is not a cause or part of the cause of the event. The experimenters went still further. They systematically dropped out all of the other factors A, B, C, D, K, until they discovered that when Factor E was present, so was the event; when that factor was absent, the event disappeared. Here we have a combination of Mill's two methods, the *joint method of agreement and difference*. The air blast was established as a basic contributor to the agitated behavior.

Still further experimentation revealed that some of the other factors listed were also involved to some extent: For example, not all rats respond neurotically to the air hose; some are resistant. Among those that respond, many of the listed factors seemed to play some part. In other words, more neurotic animals are found among animals who, for example, have insufficient vitamin B or magnesium in their diets. In 1947, it was reported * that a disease of the middle ear, common among rats, was very significantly cor-

* Patton, R. A. The incidence of middle-ear infection in albino rats susceptible to sound induced seizures. *Amer. Psychologist*, 1947, 2, p. 320. (Abstract.)

related with susceptibility to neurotic behavior following a high-pitched sound stimulus. The existence of this physiological determinant was obscured by a surface correlation between the event and the obvious factors observed by the experimenters.

The *method of agreement* is not an adequate experimental procedure. The *method of difference* is stronger but, by itself, inadequate. The two together are of the essence of experimentation, but even so they must be used with care. It took a long time to discover the disease factor by patiently breaking down the separate factors by the two methods. We are not sure, even now, that we know why the rat becomes convulsed. We are fairly certain that it is not because of conflict.*

The application of the methods of Mill as described above should have indicated the meaning of "control" to the reader. Theoretically, an observation is controlled when you *know* the actual relationship between variables and events. Actually such perfect knowledge may never be obtained. In popular language, when you know what factor caused what change in the event, or to what factors you can attribute the nature or characteristic of the event, you have a controlled observation.

Steps in Experimentation

The general nature of an experiment follows the pattern of a combination of the methods of agreement and difference. In effect, the purpose of the experimenter and his method are to observe some event, for example, the learning of a list of nonsense syllables by a subject, and to test each of the possible variables that might influence the learner's performance. By systematically changing one variable at a time (including it, changing its features, dropping it out) he eventually is able to indicate the relationship between the event and the separate variables.

It is, of course, possible to vary systematically either the event

* For a critical review of the experimental literature see: Finger, F. Convulsive behavior in the rat. *Psychol. Bull.*, 1947, *44*, 201–248.

or the variables, thus providing what appear to be two experimental methods, although they amount to the same general formula. For example, one might be interested in the effect of some drug, e.g., alcohol, on eye movements. In such a case, one would systematically vary the amount of alcohol given a subject, from no amount to some suitable limit, and record the changes in eye-movement behavior that corresponds to the several amounts. As many other factors as possible in the procedure would have to be controlled. On the other hand, instead of keeping an event (the eye movements) constant, one might be interested in the effect of a constant amount of the drug on a variety of events, knee jerks, reaction time, intelligence-test scores, learning scores, etc. In such an experiment, the significant variable would be held constant at a specific dosage while the observed event would be allowed to alter. In formal language, the factor that is specifically observed as a significant variable, that which is varied, is called a "variant"; the remaining factors which are held constant are the variables, the potential sources of error that must be controlled.

In science, generally, experimental research is aimed at finding relationships between variables, which are then expressed as "laws." Thus Boyle's law in physics describes the relationship which holds between the pressure and the volume of a gas. We translate the law practically as saying that, for a given amount of pressure, there will be a specific volume. Experimental data involving pressures and volumes would consist of a series of numerical descriptions of units of pressure and units of volume. Such numerical data could be plotted as a graph, in this case, a straight-line graph. By reference to the graph, one could read the expected pressure by simply noting the intersection point on the graph made by a perpendicular to the volume axis, and vice versa. One does not ask the physicist: What is the effect of pressure on volume? and expect a specific numerical answer. The correct form of the question would be: What is the effect of a specific increment of pressure on a given volume of gas?

The psychologist, too, plots his data in graphical form, showing the relative change in one factor as a consequence of, or accompaniment to, a change in another. Such a relationship is called a "functional relationship," and the aim of the psychologist is to make a "functional analysis" of a given set of data.

One might, for example, ask: What is the effect of smoking on college grades? A little thought will reveal that there are many variables involved in the answer to this problem. Suppose, for the moment, that our findings would justify to some extent a conclusion of a general nature that smokers receive lower grades in college than do nonsmokers. In considering the variables, we would have to take account of such factors as, for example, the sex of the students involved. Girls might be included. Perhaps the girls receive high grades and do not smoke as commonly as boys. This possibility might account for some of our results and should be controlled. How would you go about this? It might also turn out that wealthy students receive poor grades because of some lack of motivation for study. The wealthy student can afford cigarettes, the poor student cannot, and if poor students are perhaps motivated more strongly, we have another factor to consider. How would you control this factor? Then, perhaps smokers are more "nervous" than nonsmokers and their nervousness prevents their efficient study. How could this be controlled? Several other similar factors could be considered, but in any case, our basic data would have to be organized in terms of an answer such as we indicated above. The data will have to show how much effect on grades results from a given amount of smoking.

We can assume that an occasional cigarette probably has no effect on grades, whereas some abnormal amount of tobacco consumption has some effect. Our problem is to show the point-for-point relationship of the effect of each specific amount of tobacco consumption upon the event (grades). If our graphed data took the form of a straight-line graph running from the upper left to the lower right of our squared paper, we would then have a parallel to Boyle's law. We could then state a law concerning smoking:

The more you smoke, the lower the grade. Any other form of the curve would call for a different statement of our law. We might find, for example, that no effect on grades is apparent until we reach a scale position of 60 cigarettes per day, at which point grades show a strong decline. The formula for this curve could be computed and would be our law, just as scientific a law as $pv = k$. Psychological data will generally be presented in such curve or graph form (the formulas for the curves being the "laws" of psychology).

In short, then, the psychological experiment, like any other experiment, is a search for a functional relationship. "Learning" curves, "forgetting" curves, "fatigue" curves, are obvious examples already familiar to the student. The experiments to follow will often contain the instruction to the student: Plot your data. When doing this, remember that your graph shows a functional relationship, and if your experiment meets the standards of scientific rigidity, your graph is a "law."

Types of Experimentation

In our previous discussion of science, we found that scientific method encompasses a number of steps: collection of data, generalizing, organizing generalizations, deducing theorems, testing theorems by experimentation. These general steps indicate two stages in the method by which data are gathered, one at the beginning and the other at the end of the process, and suggest that two types of procedures can be called experimentation. One type, the collection of data, can be labeled "exploratory experimentation"; another, the testing of theorems, "confirmatory experimentation." These terms have some value insofar as they distinguish the relative stages of development of some area of study.

The exploratory experiments are just as valuable in the development of scientific theory as are the confirmatory, although they may in some instances appear trivial. At one stage in the development of "learning" theory, for example, many psychologists devoted their efforts to seeing whether various species of animals could be conditioned. As a consequence it was discovered by solemn experiments that rats, dogs, cats, guinea pigs, fish, pigeons, chickens, cockroaches, etc., could be conditioned. To do an experiment today to demonstrate that kangaroos could be conditioned would be of little interest, unless, of course, failure were reported. Still, it was important at one time to indicate that conditioning was not a specific feature of the behavior of some dogs in Leningrad.

In other instances, exploratory types of experiments may have little or no bearing on any theory of current interest. To discover, let us say, that left-handed people, on the whole, remove matches from the left-hand side of a match book might be of some interest to Sherlock Holmes but it would be of hardly passing concern to the behavior theorist. Even so, it is difficult to decide that any information, properly acquired, has no value. At some future date a relatively insignificant finding of today may be fitted into an important theoretical structure like a key piece in a jigsaw puzzle. European peasants had used mold for medicinal purposes long before the discovery of penicillin. The observations of Twitmeyer on conditioned knee jerks were ignored for almost twenty-five years. It is rare that a scientific report begins without alluding to some historical predecessor who had reported, perhaps casually, on some issue that has become prominent in current theoretical formulations. The exploratory experiment, if rigorously performed, will find its future theoretical resting place, if we assume the unity of science.

The confirmatory experiment usually acquires greater significance and greater current importance, because it is intimately related to some theoretical structure which either requires modification or is more strongly buttressed, depending upon the outcome. The confirmatory experiment is so designed that it tests the validity of a postulate or an assumption or the correctness of some defining term in a theory. Since a theory generally has one or several countertheories that oppose it, the attempt is usually made to design the experiment in such a way that it will support one theory and at the same time destroy another. Such an experimental design results in what is known as a "crucial experiment" and represents the high point in experimental science.

The confirmatory experiment purports to be a verification of a theorem deduced from a theory. Since a theorem is a logical conclusion from the simultaneous consideration of several postulates and definitions, it is obvious that, if the experiment is positive in outcome, it supports all of the postulates and definitions involved in the deduction. On the other hand, a failure to demonstrate the theorem may be due to the weakness or falseness of *any* or all of the postulates and definitions involved. Thus, the confirmatory type of experiment has a corrective function. The theorist is able to revise or eliminate postulates which are used in the deductions of theorems refuted by the experiment. It should be noted that positive results do not *establish* the truth of postulates involved in a deduction; they merely extend the life of these postulates and justify their continued use. Science is self-corrective, and the confirmatory experiment is the tool of self-correction.

In spite of their differences in the scheme of science, the two types of experiments described do not differ in their methods, needs, or the degree of scrutiny they must withstand. In each case, a functional relationship is the essential aim. The procedures follow a similar pattern. Events are observed under constant conditions, and variables are controlled as well as possible. Objective measures are taken. The only difference in the two types of experiments is in their immediacy of application or in their degree of absorption into the general field of science.

Apparatus and Experimentation

The beginning student in experimental psychology soon finds that psychological apparatus and equipment run a queer gamut from no equipment at all except pencils and paper to extremely complicated electronic devices, galvanometers, electroencephalographs, cathode-ray oscilloscopes, etc. In many instances he will find the local apparatus a collection of queerly constructed and complicated gadgets full of odd, and sometimes loose, wires, with queer names in an apparently foreign vocabulary. The heterogeneous collection of equipment often bewilders the student, and if, like most students, he finds allusion to electricity somewhat mystifying, he is apt to become negatively conditioned to psychological study. It is important at the outset to realize the purpose of apparatus in any scientific field and, in particular, in psychology.

It will be recalled that an experiment generally calls for an objective record of the observed event. Herein lies one purpose of apparatus. It is a convenient or, in some cases, the only possible way for getting this objective record. In psychology, the usual requirement is to obtain a record of the responses of the subject. If the responses are brain waves, then an electroencephalogram must be obtained. An electrocardiogram will be a record of heart beats. A pencil check might represent the occurrence of some simpler reaction. In any case, a response is recorded, and the apparatus must be designed for the specific purpose involved. If the response is simple, the record may be simple; on the other hand, some apparently simple responses may be extremely difficult to record. An eyelid blink, for example, may appear as simple a response as one could wish. However, an adequate record of an eyelid reflex in all of its characteristics involves a rather involved piece of "experimental machinery," as one student called it. In general, the experimenter should use no more apparatus, and certainly no more complicated apparatus, than his needs require.

The psychologist usually has to do more than record events (responses). He must also initiate these events in the form of stimuli, and it is generally necessary that a record of the nature, amount, and time of stimulation be made along with the response. This is just another phase of the general recording purposes of apparatus. The initiation of events, however, is a process that must be rigidly controlled, and it is often more easily done if the stimuli can be presented by mechanical means than by the experimenter. This, then, is the second purpose of apparatus: presentation and control of stimuli in their various characteristics. It is often especially important to have stimuli occur at specific time intervals. Generally, it is wiser to have this timing mechanically arranged rather than to leave it to an experimenter. In a "learning" experiment, it might be desirable to allow a certain length of time for learning one set of materials, and then an identical time for learning another. An experimenter who is not too careful might allow significant errors to creep into his timing through distractions, failure to keep a strict check of the passage of time, etc. In general, one can depend more on an automatic clock than on a psychologist.

If the student reminds himself continually that apparatus serves only the purpose of initiating stimuli and recording stimuli and responses, he need feel no difficulties in the matter of equipment. If he further warns himself that it must be no more complicated than is necessary for these purposes, he can at least begin to study the parts of the apparatus from an organized viewpoint.

At a symposium on trends in psychology, B. F. Skinner (3) described the nature of experimentation in psychology. The following selection from his address gives us a clear picture of an experiment with which to summarize our discussion:

In psychology, as in any science, the heart of the experimental method is the direct control of the thing studied. When we say, Let us try an experiment, we mean, Let us do something and see what happens. The order is important: we do something first and then see what happens. In more formal terms we manipulate certain independent variables and observe the effect upon a dependent variable. In psychology the dependent variable, to which we look for an effect, is behavior. We acquire control over it through the independent variables. The latter, the variables which we manipulate, are found in the environment. We manipulate them when we stimulate an organism, when we alter conditions of motivation or learning, and so on. The great majority of psychological experiments can be reduced to this form.*

* Quoted with the permission of Wayne Dennis, Editor, *Current trends in psychology*. Pittsburgh: University of Pittsburgh Press. 1947.

References

1. Maier, N. R. F. *Studies of abnormal behavior in the rat.* New York: Harper. 1939.
2. Robinson, D. S. *The principles of reasoning.* New York: Appleton-Century. 1936.
3. Skinner, B. F. Experimental psychology. In *Current trends in psychology,* Wayne Dennis, ed. Pittsburgh: University of Pittsburgh Press. 1947.

Experiment 4. Perception: Illusions.
The Horizontal–Vertical Illusion

Introduction. The difference between sensory and perceptual experience is strikingly brought out by the phenomena of illusions. With illusions we have dramatic demonstrations of the principle that "we see the world as we are, not as it is." Of late, Gestalt psychologists have brought the problems presented by illusions forcefully to our attention because of their basic objections to the one-to-one relationship between stimulus and response, which they insist is an assumption of the behavioristic S—R formula. Orthodox psychologists have long concerned themselves with illusions from the point of view of attempting to account for them in more or less mechanical (as contrasted with Gestalt) terms. An explanation of an illusion as due to eye movements, for example, might be, in general, more acceptable to the average American psychologist than the types of explanations offered by Gestaltists ("dynamic reorganization in the brain" for instance).

A well-known illusion which has long resisted adequate explanation is the horizontal-vertical illusion. When two lines of equal length are drawn so that one forms a perpendicular with the other, the vertical line commonly appears longer. In 1947 Finger and Spelt (1) attempted to demonstrate some of the factors involved in an understanding of this illusion. The experiment to be conducted here is, in effect, a repetition of their experiment with apparatus reduced in scale.

Apparatus. The apparatus is an illusion board, with movable screens so arranged that the horizontal-vertical illusion can be presented in four different forms. The separate forms are A ⌐, B ⌐, C ⊥, and D ⊢. One of the lines is of a fixed, standard length, the other is variable.

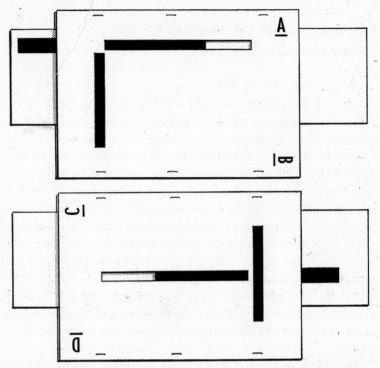

FIGURE 4. *THE HORIZONTAL-VERTICAL ILLUSION BOARD.*
Two pieces of cardboard are stapled together as shown. A 4-inch stripe
is drawn in ink on each side as indicated, and a longer slot (6–7 inches)
is cut in each cardboard. Another narrow piece of cardboard, with a
heavily inked stripe filled in on each side, is inserted between the two
original pieces. As this sliding piece is passed under the slots, it forms
the variable, or comparison, length. Holding the board in different
positions permits comparisons with the variable line in vertical or
horizontal positions. See letters in diagram for positions. For greater
durability, the board can be made of wooden frames with cardboard
surfaces.

Procedure. The E * arranges the board for the subject in one
of the four positions and brings the appropriate screen to the edge

* It is common practice to abbreviate "experimenter" as E and "subject" as
S. When the subject's responsibilities involve making judgments or observations, he is referred to as the "observer" or O.

of the standard line. The O then slowly slides the screen outward until he reports a judgment of apparent equality. E measures the variable line and records it in the appropriate block of Table 8. Ten such readings are taken with the board in each position. E and O exchange roles and repeat. Neither O nor E is to know the actual length of the standard line until the experiment is over. The O will assist the E in this matter by covering the standard while E is measuring. The O is not to know the measurements made by E and should look away while measurements are made. All measurements are made to the nearest mm.

Results. After recording your data in Table 8 below, report the average judgment of your subject in each board position to the instructor for group tabulation.

Table 8. *Judgments of the Length of a Variable Line in a Horizontal-Vertical Illusion*
(In positions A and C, the vertical line is the variable; in B and D, the horizontal is the variable.)

Position	Variable	Length of variable in mm										Mean	SD	Difference (H-V)
		1	2	3	4	5	6	7	8	9	10			
A ∟	|													
B ⌐	—													
C ⊥	|													
D ⊢	—													

Discussion

1. What variables in connection with the stimulus lines are controlled in this experiment?
2. Does the position of the horizontal line with respect to the vertical make any difference in the strength of the illusion?
3. Under which condition is the illusion strongest? Why is this so?
4. What is the effect of bisection as against a tangential relationship?

Table 9. *Average Apparent Difference in Length of Lines in a Horizontal-Vertical Illusion When the Horizontal Line Appears in Different Perpendicular Relationship to the Vertical*

(N =   )

Position of illusion	Position of H and V	Variable	Mean diff. in mm (H-V)	SD	SE		Critical ratio			
							A	B	C	D
A	∟	|				A	X			
B	⌐	—				B	X	X		
C	⊥	|				C	X	X	X	
D	⊢	—				D	X	X	X	X

5. What explanations have been offered in the past for this illusion? To what extent does your work confirm them?
6. What are the weaknesses of this experiment? Are there any uncontrolled sources of errors? Have enough positions been sampled? What others might be tried with some expectation of usable data?

References

1. Finger, F., and Spelt, D. F. The illustration of the horizontal-vertical illusion. *J. exp. Psychol.,* 1937, *37,* 243–250.
2. Underwood, B. J. *Experimental Psychology.* New York: Appleton-Century-Crofts, 1949, chap. 2.
3. Woodworth, R. *Experimental Psychology.* New York: Henry Holt. 1938, chap. 25.

6

The Choice of Subjects for Experimental Study

ALTHOUGH Alexander Pope urged that the "proper study of mankind is man," psychologists appear to have more difficulty in studying man than do the poets and often resort to other organisms in their quest for solutions to scientific problems. Before we can bring our account of experimental procedure to a close, we must consider the choice of subjects to be observed in the experimental situation.

It is hardly necessary to point out that human subjects are extremely variable in their reactions from day to day, even from minute to minute. There are individual differences in age, sex, anatomical and physiological characteristics (such as size, strength, sensitivity, and reactivity) as well as widespread behavioral differences resulting from personal history. If one is to discover truths about "man," he should not study woman or child or even *a* man. He should presumably study the "man" in the quotation marks. Such men, however, are not readily available.

It is nice to talk about the "layman" or the "man in the street." Certainly there are men in the street. But when we select a man in a street, he is likely to be 55 years old with poor hearing, a limp, a slight myopia, a nasty temper or a hangover, and possibly a cold or other complaint. Is he to be our "man"? Or should we select a college student, bright, alert, eager to cooperate, able to follow instructions, in the full bloom of youthful health, with all parts functioning in a satisfactory manner?

107

The student appreciates the fact that Pope's "man" and the psychologist's "man" are abstractions, or concepts derived from consideration of many men, of all nations, races, ages, temperaments, and other characteristics. There is, of course, no standard man to study. If we try to study the "average" man and do so by multiplying observations, using numerous "assorted" men, then we must realize that we are dealing with an abstraction, a mathematical fiction. Hence, when we obtain our results by experimental probing, the findings will apply to this mathematical fiction but need not necessarily apply to any single one of the men in the assortment.

This may appear somewhat alarming to the student. Of what value are data if they do not apply to man "in general"? Well, that is just the point, they do apply to man "in general." Find a "man in general" and the results will apply nicely. If you cannot find such a man, then the results apply only to the artificial, conceptual man you created by taking observations on many men.

The situation is not better in any other science. "Pressure times volume" is a constant "in general," or with "other things equal." It is a rare physicist who can give a perfect demonstration of this relationship because it is difficult to make other things equal. The acceleration of gravity equals $\frac{1}{2} at^2$ for objects falling in a vacuum, but birds, feathers, leaves, kites, and ladies' hats do not operate in a vacuum. In fact, a vacuum is a bit difficult to obtain. The scientist, however, is not discouraged when predictions cannot be made in a complex situation by invoking only one general law. If the prediction does not work out, it is because other general laws need to be discovered and invoked to take care of the other variables in the situation. The first problem is to find the general laws regardless of whether or not they can be immediately useful in prediction of complex events. Once all the laws are known and suitable account taken of the variables, the predictions will hold for the individual case, the "man in the street," and "man."

With the above general remarks before us, we can turn to the more specific problems involved in the choice of subjects to use in our experiments. Before we try to state what factors should influence or guide our selection, we should note that most of the experimentation reported by psychologists has been based on work done on two rather specialized groups, the college student and the white rat. What these have in common with each other or with "man" is a serious question and should not be avoided, especially since it appears that these two subject-groups will continue to be the favorite objects of study.

The obvious reason for using college students is that psychologists generally are located in colleges and find the students without much exertion. Whether students are suitable subjects depends on the problem involved. It is up to the psychologist using them to justify their use and properly to restrict his conclusions to a college population, if that is indicated. If the results are to apply to college populations, it is foolish to look elsewhere for subjects.

If the results are meant for "man," it must be established that college attendance *makes no difference.* Sometimes this is taken for granted, and no great argument need be prepared in defense of the procedure. If the psychologist is concerned with knee jerks or eyelid blinks, it is probably unnecessary to use a variety of subjects, or even a great many of them. If the only requirement involved is the capacity to close an eyelid, a college background should not disqualify a subject. If the problem is one in "learning," however, the question of subject legitimacy may well be raised. Basic conclusions about "memory," for example, might be radically different, if observations made on children are compared with those of college students, or those of college students with those of automobile mechanics.

It should also be pointed out that for some questions the way in which subjects are obtained is highly significant. Most student subjects are coerced into service either through financial want, desire to win approval, course requirements, or by other devices. If such coerced subjects are compared with volunteers, there may be a great difference in results.* Kinsey, in his studies of sexual behavior, is obliged to prove that his subjects, most of whom were volunteers, are not significantly different from the nonvolunteering population. Professor Gordon Allport has urged psychologists to take account of the differences between rats, children, chimpanzees, and adult humans. Failure to consider such differences may be disastrous to psychological research.

Let us turn now to a consideration of the general problem involved in trying to account for the popularity of the white rat as a psychological subject and indicate some of the limitations that should be observed in the use of this animal. It is intended that the remarks concerning rats be considered in connection with the use of other species, with due regard for similarities and differences known to be present.

It might be supposed that rats are used as experimental subjects because of their convenience—they can be easily housed, fed, bred, and manipulated. That this is no justification should be apparent at once. Such justification would apply if psychologists were interested in rats for rats' sake, and such psychologists are very rare, if, indeed, there are any. The only reason for studying the rat is the belief that results obtained will have some bearing on the problems engaging the attention of scientists; and for psychologists, in particular, these problems usually have their origin in the behavior of man. Unless the study of the rat in one way or another, directly or indirectly, bears on the behavior of man, there is little point to observing rats, except for possible naturalistic interests.

Now it is quite obvious that rats are not men, nor are men rats in spite of frequent identifications in impolite conversation. The differences in external appearance are obvious and need not be detailed. The question of importance is: Are the similarities of consequence?

It is well established that the rat's nervous system is similar in

* See the study of Brower, D. The role of incentive in psychological research. *J. gen. Psychol.*, 1948, *39*, 145–147. In this study Brower showed that students who were forced into a "steadiness" experiment differed significantly in their scores from volunteer subjects.

structure to that of man, and that the basic gross anatomical parts are qualitatively the same. It is necessary to point out, however, that the quantitative distribution of parts is by no means the same, that in the rat the proportion of so-called "sensory" areas is much greater than the remainder, usually called "association" areas. It would appear, then, that the behavior of a rat is much more under the influence of external stimuli, of sensory activity, than is that of man.

It is true, of course, that rats excel men in some kinds of activity, e.g., finding food by smell and response to high-pitched tones. On the other hand, their capacity for complicated maneuvers, delayed reactions, "symbolic" activity, etc., is extremely deficient in comparison with man's. In some activities that depend in large measure on sensory control, e.g., maze learning, rats can equal or surpass men. It seems, then, fairly legitimate to make relatively direct applications of findings from rats to men if the problems involved can be shown to be functions of certain mechanisms or processes that are the same in the two species. Where this cannot be shown, great caution is required.

It is customary in rat experimentation to use rats about 2 or 3 months old. The rat's life span is so short that older rats, even at 6 months, are slow, sluggish, indifferent as learners, and awkward as subjects. The results from rat experiments should be applied, then, to the developmental age in other species that compares with the maturity level of the rats used. In this connection it is important to note that, even with the rat, previous experience, amount of handling, and early environmental factors have a bearing on later behavior. Unless these factors are known and accounted for, the results are likely to be bewildering and inapplicable to other species not having had such prior treatment.

To illustrate, rats that are deprived of food when young, tend to hoard food when older; much less hoarding is observed in rats that have not been so deprived.* Similar results with other habits have been observed in other species. It is not legitimate to com-

* Hunt, J. McV. The effects of infant feeding-frustration upon adult hoarding in the albino rat. *J. abnorm. soc. Psychol.*, 1941, *36*, 338–360.

pare the first learning experience in one species with other than the first learning experiences in other species. In practice, psychologists generally use naïve, inexperienced rats in learning problems. It is highly questionable that any corresponding findings would be observed with sophisticated adult humans.

The two factors emphasized above, age or developmental level and experience, are perhaps the most significant variables to consider in comparing species or in trying to transfer principles. An equally important factor to consider is that the anatomical limitations of a rat force the psychologist to create a highly artificial situation for it, one that bears no resemblance to situations normally facing humans or, for that matter, rats. How such artificial situations in themselves affect behavior is not easily discovered. It is well known that human subjects in psychological experiments often react in undesirable and unexpected fashions to the equipment and apparatus surrounding them. This phenomenon has been called "backlash" and refers to the effect of apparatus or the experimental situation itself on the behavior. The student of rat behavior does not ordinarily take account of this backlash on the rat. He builds his apparatus to accommodate his needs and the rat's possibilities and lets it go at that. Different results in different situations are then argued about in terms of theories instead of in terms of the apparatus effect which may really be responsible.

In the above discussion we have talked about the rat as such. It should be emphasized that the remarks apply equally to the use of any other species. Beach * has pointed out the dangers of limiting research to the rat and ignoring other species. We are prone to assume that certain behavior patterns in the rat are learned, others unlearned. Unless we systematically check such assumptions with other species we may be making gross errors in our theorizing. There is also the danger that, unless we take immediate steps to investigate the applicability to man or other species of principles found by studying the rat, we will gradually come to

* Beach, F. The snark was a boojum. *Amer. Psychologist,* 1949, *5,* 115–124.

accept the principles as *general* laws simply through the continual reference to the animal experiment. Such a tendency is illustrated in the classical instance of Pavlov's dogs. These dogs are mentioned in every text, and over the years we have come to rely on them as proving something about behavior without stopping to analyze just what it is. The same types of experiments on humans are rarely discussed in general texts.

In view of the limitations indicated above, why do psychologists continue using the rat as an experimental subject? There are a number of important reasons for the practice, and these should be appreciated by the beginner:

1. Using any animal as a subject forces the scientist to be operational and objective to a degree that is not required with humans. This reason alone probably is enough to justify the practice. The use of introspective methods, as has been indicated, has not proved very fruitful for psychological theory. There is some danger of "anthropomorphizing"—that is, attributing alleged human faculties or capacities and processes to lower animals—but this can be detected and eliminated.

2. The scientific psychologist is under no delusions that results are immediately transferrable to other species. He is actually looking for *principles of behavior* that apply to the rat, and these he fully intends *to investigate further* on other levels, including that of man. There is no expectation of easy transfer. He is looking for principles for future *research,* not for application. The rat, paradoxically it might appear, is a source of ideas. It is, of course, hoped that, since the rat is an apparently simpler organism than man, principles of behavior might operate in it with less complexity and, therefore, be more available for observation. It is recognized, however, that great individual differences are observed even in rats, and often large groups must be used to establish reasonable conclusions.

3. It is highly probable that some kinds of behavior are based on similar functions in rats and in man, and it is easier to study these in rats than in man. If, for example, it is desirable to know

how mazes are learned, there is no point to building huge man-sized mazes when rat mazes will do. Extreme care, however, must be used in selecting problems where similar functions are expected to operate. There must be considerable preliminary checking to establish the fact of essential similarity. In all cases, it must be remembered that when rats are used, recourse is had to simple tissue conditions as motivational states; animals are forced to react because they are hungry or in pain. Humans rarely work for these reasons, and due allowance has to be made. What the effect is of hunger, as such, on the reactions of the rat is not known. Perhaps the rat is basically in a condition of frustration and is reacting on emotional bases instead of in terms of "hunger." These are problems for future research.

In general, if a problem can be studied more easily or more quickly in a rat, why bother with a man who will not keep appointments, or who will try to help or hinder the experimenter, depending upon his state of mind? If a problem involves several generations, who is going to wait for the children of today's subjects, and then for their children? If the problem is suitable for rat study, use rats.

It should be remembered that the psychologist uses rats for want of a better (in all respects) subject. He does not use rats to the exclusion of other subjects. They are not an end in themselves; they are only a help. So long as due precaution is used in interpreting findings, there can be no objection to the study of rats. In due time, it is hoped, they will contribute their share to the "proper study of mankind."

We can return now to some remarks of a more general nature regarding the selection and use of subjects. In most experiments it is desirable to give preliminary training, instruction, and "habituation" to subjects. It is necessary to devote, on occasion, considerable pretraining to subjects before taking actual observations. If highly trained subjects are required for some refined observations, there is no recourse but to train them. It is often desirable to breed laboratory animals for experimental use. Dogs picked up on the street may be friendly but otherwise quite useless. Casual volunteers for experiments in perceptual phenomena may also be of little value until thoroughly prepared. On the other hand, some experiments require complete naïveté from the subjects, and frequently deceit or other measures must be employed to control the variable of "knowledge of results" or personal interpretations on the part of the subjects.

On the basis of the above discussion we can now summarize our observations about the choice of subjects for experimentation. We recognize that the choice of subjects depends upon the problem under study, and that convenience and availability are not the criteria for selection. If possible, we chose those subjects in whom the phenomenon we wish to observe is most easily and clearly observable, with the fewest complications from irrelevant variables. If we choose "lower" animals, we are careful to defend their suitability and to describe their characteristics (age, sex, prior experience, hereditary factors, etc.) for duplication or approximation by other investigators. If we select college students, we detail the relevant characteristics that seem to bear on the problem and indicate how the subjects were obtained. Whatever the choice of subjects, we are careful, in drawing conclusions, to restrict generalizations to the population studied; and we make extrapolations to other populations (and other species) with great caution.

Although the problem more or less dictates the choice of subjects, it should still be recognized that there may be many ways of stating the problem and bringing it within the possibilities of investigation if the original way of stating the hypothesis turns out to require an unobtainable subject group. The same observation applies to the use of apparatus, and careful examination of a theorem may lead to its statement in such a manner that many ways of attack become open.

As a last suggestion, it should be noted that often one subject is as useful as many, if the problem involved is of the "is-it-possible" nature. Herman Ebbinghaus used himself as subject and contributed greatly to our knowledge of learning. Raymond Dodge studied his own knee jerk for several years and made notable contributions to our information about reflex action. It takes only one positive case to prove something can happen. Likewise, it requires only one negative instance to prove that something is not true always, no matter how often it has been shown to occur.

The actual number of subjects to be used depends upon many factors. There is no virtue in numbers, as such, but whenever statistical methods are to be employed, there should be enough subjects to justify the particular procedures followed. In recent years statistical techniques have been worked out for dealing with small samples and, for some measurements, as few as 10 subjects are permissible. Ordinarily one would not attempt refined statistical analysis with fewer than 30 subjects. In investigations where an unlimited population is available, it is considered proper to keep adding subjects until additional samples do not affect the measures of variability and central tendency.

With this chapter we can close our examination of the place of psychology among the sciences and the general nature of experimentation. In succeeding sections we will examine the characteristics of experimentation peculiar to psychological investigations. We have already seen that in psychological experiments our work amounts to presenting stimuli and observing responses. In the next two sections we shall consider the various kinds of stimuli that the psychologist may be obliged to use and what he does in the observing, recording, and classification of responses. The division of a discussion of experimental work into separate considerations of stimuli and responses is obviously artificial because of the intimate interrelationships involved. It will, of course, be impossible to ignore responses when studying stimuli and vice versa, and no such procedure is intended. But there are practical educational advantages in first looking at what the experimenter does to, or arranges for, his subject and then at what the subject does about the experimenter's manipulations. Thus, we may get a clearer idea of what is involved when psychologists experiment.

Part 2

The Stimulus in Experimentation

Introduction: What to Expect from Experiments in Psychology

IN THE PRECEDING CHAPTERS we have examined the nature of science and experimentation in general. In our examples we have wandered through various divisions of scientific labor, perhaps to the dismay of the student who is interested in getting down to psychological business. This introduction appears necessary, however, because of the failure of numerous students in various sciences to appreciate just what they are doing or why they are doing it.

Students in experimental sciences frequently find themselves bewildered in the laboratory. They do an experiment because it is required. They may find it difficult, and often resort to a common student practice of working out the experiment backwards. Knowing the expected results (from their texts), they manage to obtain them and satisfy the requirements. The laboratory work for many students becomes a chore and an obstacle instead of being an intellectual adventure. Experiments in chemistry and physics are often chosen to demonstrate "pure" principles rather than methods and procedures by which these and other principles could be studied or derived.

The purpose of the experiments included in this book is entirely and completely divorced from any desire to demonstrate psychological principles. If one is interested in facts, he can find

119

some in an appropriate text; if he wants a personal demonstration of a fact, he can probably achieve that ambition by much simpler means than will be presented in this text. It will, of course, be almost impossible to keep from demonstrating *some* facts in the course of our work. It is strongly hoped that the student will not feel that he has profited from his work when he finds that he has verified some alleged law. From the point of view of this course, the student in physics, let us say, who spends an afternoon or two in verifying the law of gravity is wasting his time; verifying Weber's law is equally unimportant. It is far more useful and scientifically rewarding for the student to understand *how* he verified this law, why he followed certain procedures, what other procedures were permissible or improper, and how the procedures can be used in other problems.

It will be the purpose of the experiments in this course to demonstrate psychological methods, procedures, and practices—good ones as well as bad ones. Some of the experiments are so designed that they are faulty in one or several respects. The results may often appear contradictory to expectation and to established findings. More often they will appear confusing or inconclusive. It is the point of view of the author that the student must gain an appreciation of the complexities involved in attempting to treat an intact human being or other organism as a laboratory specimen.

Clean-cut results are not the characteristic consequence of a laboratory session in psychology; any educational procedure that suggests otherwise is of dubious merit, if not dangerous. Courses in experimental psychology have often suffered loss of student interest and have been regarded as wasteful of time and effort because of the attempts by instructors to emulate foolproof experiments of the physical-science courses. In psychology, to make something work beautifully and all the time, one is forced to select some phenomenon which is so simple and inconsequential in terms of the more serious aspects of psychology that the intelligent student is bored and, in a sense, defrauded. It is a definite responsibility of a course of this nature to teach experimental methods as they are currently practiced and to prepare the student for serious thinking in psychological problems rather than to amuse or divert him.

The experiments which follow are chosen within the frame of reference described above. Their general purpose is to reveal the workings of common variables in psychological research. Each experiment is designed to teach the student how at least one variable influences the outcome of the experiment, and how that variable can be controlled or otherwise brought to account. If an experiment does not serve to point up a variable, it will be considered to have failed in its purpose. Nothing else is promised except what is implied in the problem of controlling the variables. This, of course, includes an appreciation of psychological procedures and methods which have been developed for the design of experiments and the control of the sources of error common to the investigation of psychological problems.

The student is expected to develop an appreciation of sources of error as the experiments are performed. There might be some virtue in simply providing a list of such sources of error and an indication of the control method. But the presentation of such a list out of context would appear lifeless and certainly of such a general nature that the student would, perhaps, faithfully learn the list, pay suitable lip service to it in responding to test questions, but never fully appreciate it. It appears to be better to learn the hard way. With this preamble before us, let us start learning something about variables and sources of error.

7

The Measurement of Stimuli: The Methods

of Psychophysics

The Use of Psychological Stimuli

A stimulus is usually defined as a change in the amount of energy impinging on an organism. The energy can be in the form of mechanical, electrical, thermal, or chemical activity. Much emphasis is placed in current physical theory on describing energy in terms of electromagnetic-wave motion. Psychologists in the future will probably have to concern themselves seriously with refined methods of measurement of wave energy in describing their stimuli. The work of Miles and Beck * in their discovery of a relationship between olfactory sensitivity and infrared heat loss from olfactory organ emanations is a case in point.

Important classes of stimuli, whose energy form is difficult to describe, are those originating in the internal organs, including the glands, and in the muscles, tendons, and joints. Although such "organic" and "proprioceptive" stimuli are variously described as arising from mechanical pressures and tensions, the measurement of such stimuli in physical terms has not yet become a practical reality. Proprioceptive stimuli play an important *theoretical* role in the systematic psychologies of Hull and Guthrie, but these writers make it clear that their use of such concepts as stimuli from "fractional anticipatory goal responses" and body movement is strictly on the basis of *assumptions,* and not on the basis of *measured* events. Aftereffects of stimuli in the form of "neural

* See pp. 209–210.

122

traces" are also made use of by Hull as basic *assumptions* for theoretical purposes. It is obvious from these considerations that the
nature of a theorist's and an experimentalist's work will depend
on his interpretation of "stimuli" as working constructs.

Thus far we have considered stimuli only from their physical
aspects as energy changes. It is well known from common experience that many energy changes occur which have no apparent effect on organisms. If we are to consider stimuli as somehow related
to behavior, it appears logical to set certain behavioral limits on
our concept of "stimuli." Because of this behavioral interest, stimuli are often defined as those energy changes which are followed
by responses. Such a definition is somewhat circular, although it
is operationally useful. It permits us to include absence, or the
abrupt termination and elimination, of energy as stimuli. The
stopping of a clock whose previous ticking did not evoke apparent
reactions commonly brings out a response; the stopping thus becomes a stimulus. Defining stimuli as energy changes which evoke
responses is in agreement with the stimulus-response formula,
which is a basic scientific assumption and the working hypothesis
of experimentalists.

One difficulty involved in defining stimuli in terms of response
is that the same physical stimulus does not always evoke a response because of conditions within the organism or in its external environment. The organism may become "adapted" to stimuli
and fail to respond; or the stimuli, for example, odors and sounds,
may be "masked" by other stimuli and evoke no response when
they would do so normally in the absence of the "masking" stimuli. Another apparent difficulty arises when we consider the nature of "subthreshold" stimuli. Such stimuli may not individually
evoke responses, but when they are rapidly repeated, a response
may occur. The explanation of such "summation" effects would
take us outside the scope of our present interests into a consideration of neural processes. For our present purposes, the problem of
subthreshold stimuli is important only on a behavioral and a
measurement level.

The Measurement of Psychological Stimuli

Thus far in our discussion we have spoken of stimuli as if they were distinct and specific features of the environment, acting separately and individually upon an organism which passively receives them and then reacts. Such a notion is, of course, naïve, artificial, and extremely dangerous for the experimentalist to entertain.

Although a full discussion of the problems involved lies beyond the scope of this book, we can at least point out the following obvious correction to the concept of the stimulus as a discrete energy change determining behavior in the absence of other qualifying and modifying circumstances: A stimulus never functions in a vacuum. There is an experimental or environmental situation in which the organism is already active in some fashion and to which it has become adapted, adjusted, or "set." Thus, in our reaction-time experiment, although we spoke of the sound as a stimulus, it was by no means the only stimulus present, and the energy change involved in the production of the sound impinged on a subject who was already reacting to a wide variety of stimuli (lights, sounds, pressures, etc.) as well as to what is called "the stimulus situation." The sound was, then, only part of a "stimulus complex" involving the apparatus, the experimenter, instructions, experimental area, etc. In another situation or circumstance the *same* "stimulus" would not evoke the reactions it did in the reaction-time experimental setup.

The "stimulus situation" cannot be ignored by the experimenter. It is easy enough to become confused or misled into believing that some *manipulated* aspect of the stimulus complex is the stimulus resulting in a given reaction. It is often likely that the subject is responding to cues or circumstances which the experimenter coolly ignores.

An example of such failure to consider the stimulation complex might prove profitable: In some of his experiments on "spatial" learning, Tolman found evidence for the conclusion that rats could more easily learn to go to a certain place, e.g., the west side of a T maze, than they could learn to make a certain kind of turn, e.g., a right turn. In his experiments, some rats would be started on the leg of an elevated T maze (see p. 202) and would find food at the end of one of the arms, say, the left. Then the entire maze would be turned about so that the animal would have to make a turn in an opposite direction to get to the same place. Tolman's rats had little difficulty in learning thus to reverse their turns, depending on the starting point. When started from the south, they turned left; when started from the north, they turned right. Other animals that had to turn *right* regardless of starting position had more trouble in learning. Tolman therefore concluded that place learning was superior to response learning.

In a repetition of Tolman's experiments, however, it was noted * that Tolman did not allow a great deal of time to elapse between trials, and it was suggested that because rats tend to *alternate* their turns on T mazes, if the time between trials is brief, just such a result should be found. On the other hand, if more time elapsed between trials, the animals would not tend to alternate, and "response" learning might be improved. The experimental findings justified this inference, and the experimenters concluded that Tolman's results were artifacts of the particular situation he employed. He had used an experimental situation in which he did not take account of the conditions present in his subject, or in other words, he ignored the "stimulus complex."

An equally important consideration with regard to the nature of stimuli is that not all subjects are equally affected by a particular stimulus because of individual differences in sensitivity or because of experimental circumstances. Such individual differences may be temporary or permanent conditions of the organism, and must certainly be taken into account. A head cold, to take an obvious example, should eliminate a subject from consideration for olfactory, and probably for most other, experiments, unless one is interested in the relationships involved with colds.

* Thompson, M. E., and Thompson, Jean P. Reactive inhibition as a factor in maze learning, III: The role of reactive inhibition in studies of place learning versus response learning. *J. exp. Psychol.*, 1949, *39*, 883–891.

Perhaps most important of all, especially for experiments in learning, motivation, emotion, abnormal behavior, and the like, is the prior experience of the subject with the stimuli or the stimulus situation. It is a common observation that people respond differently to what is physically the same stimulus. The same face arouses frowns in some and smiles in others. Snakes generally evoke a withdrawal reaction or at least a hesitance in approach, but we know this is not so for snake charmers. A psychotic may tremble at the sight of a kitten, and so on.

The relation between a stimulus and a person which depends on the previous history of the person is generally known as the "stimulus function." The significance of this "stimulus function" should not be overlooked in any consideration of stimuli. Although the usual emphasis in considerations of "stimulus function" is on "learning" experiences, we should not ignore the possibility of differences in stimulus function due to phylogenetic or physiological differences and which depend on structural variations. Interspecies comparisons, for example, may often be improperly drawn because the function of a stimulus for one species may be greatly different from the function it serves for another. Dogs and cats, for example, react differently to trees; horses differently from either, largely, we can assume, because of structural differences. In terms of stimuli more likely to be used in a laboratory, the lights, sounds, shocks, rewards, etc., that are commonly employed may have different functions for different organisms, and inferences from the behavior of the rat to that of a man may be incorrectly drawn if the stimulus function of a shock to a rat is misinterpreted and presumed to be the same as for a human.

The danger of anthropomorphizing is especially striking in experiments in which "lower" animals are required to respond to differences in stimuli, such as visually presented geometric forms. Without the most careful control observations, it is easy to fall into the error of assuming that when a rat is shown a square or a triangle it actually perceives a square or a triangle. In one experiment, for example, a careful experimenter (Karl Lashley) assumed that his rats were responding to broad horizontal and vertical lines. A control experiment by Ehrenfreund * indicates that Lashley's rats were responding only to the bottom sections of the cards and, for the rat, there was no difference between the stimuli.

In the light of the above discussion, the student might well stop worrying about what *a* stimulus is and concentrate on what *the* stimulus is in a given experimental situation. It should be plain that whenever an experimental report is presented, a most exacting and detailed description of the situation and the procedures followed should be included so that future experimenters who find divergent results can re-examine the original report and discover the "stimulus complex."

From our description of stimuli in terms of physical-energy change and response, we see that there are two ways of talking about stimuli. The measurement of energy change we can by-pass temporarily as a technical matter of the correct usage of suitable instruments like meter sticks and micrometers. The measurement of stimuli in terms of responses will be our present task. The primary concern is not one of simply noting whether a given stimulus produces a response, but rather one of discovering the range of stimuli that are effective and the range of responses that will occur.

In the 1860's the problem of measuring stimuli was considered the basic problem of what was then known as psychology. Philosophers in their eternal search for man's place in the universe were concerned with the relationships that existed between what went on inside and what went on outside the body. The "inside" was generally considered as consisting of the mind or consciousness; the "outside" was the physical world. Their statement of our present problem was: How much change must occur in the physical world in order that there be a change in "experience"? They attacked this problem by presenting carefully graded stimuli to a

* Ehrenfreund, D. An experimental test of the continuity theory of discrimination learning with pattern vision. *J. comp. physiol. Psychol.,* 1948, *41,* 408–422.

subject and noting his responses or reports of "lighter," "heavier," "louder," "darker," etc. The fact that they took these reports to reflect changes in "sensation" need not concern us today. They were actually recording responses, and their results were just as valid as their methods allowed, regardless of their metaphysics.

There were basically two kinds of problems that concerned these early investigators: (1) What are the lowest and highest amounts of stimulus to which a subject will react? and (2) What is the smallest amount of change in a stimulus value to which the subject will react with a consistent discrimination? The first problem is one of determining *thresholds:* the lowest value of a stimulus which will bring out a response consistently is generally called the stimulus threshold or "stimulus limen." The highest value is the "terminal limen." Because the early studies were reported in German, the German word for stimulus, *Reiz,* was employed. This word was abbreviated as R, limen as L, and the stimulus threshold came to be known as RL. The use of R to represent the stimulus is rather unfortunate, because American psychologists commonly use this letter to stand for a response. There appears to be no reason for perpetuating the older usage, and we may just as well use the combination SL to represent the stimulus limen.

The second problem, the determination of $DL's$ or *difference* thresholds was the major preoccupation of the early psychophysicists. Heinrich Weber discovered a relationship between stimulus values and responses that gave promise of a possible technique for the study of conscious processes. He observed that, as he increased the intensity or size of stimuli, it became necessary to add greater and greater increments to his standard stimulus for a subject to be able to give a consistent discriminatory response. This observation is not so startling today when we are fairly generally exposed to laws of "diminishing returns" and have at least some notions of relativity.

Your own experience has provided you with many practical observations on this point. Thus, turning on one light in your living

room at night makes a great difference in illumination. Turning
on one additional light, however, does not *double* the visibility.
If more lights are turned on, each additional light contributes less
and less to the total visibility. The same general principle holds
in reverse; thus, if one bulb burns out in a brilliantly lighted
room, we may notice the event, but our visual efficiency will not
drop to zero as it would if it were the only light present. Even a
sharp-eyed child will not notice the absence of *one* chocolate from
a bagfull, but to detect one missing from a total of two is an easy
performance.

Weber found that as he increased his standard stimulus, a *proportional* increase would have to be applied to his comparison
stimulus if the subject was to discriminate the difference. This
proportional increase can be described as a percentage or a fraction. Weber found that different fractions were involved in the
different types of "sensory" reactions which he studied. In order
consistently to tell one light intensity from another, the fractional
change had to be somewhere around 1 percent or $\frac{1}{100}$; for weight,
the fraction was $\frac{1}{30}$ or 3 percent; for sound intensity, the fraction
ran from $\frac{1}{4}$ to $\frac{1}{5}$. When you are asked to "turn down the radio,"
you may as well plan on a fairly heroic twist of the dial. The intensity must be reduced about 25 percent if the objector is even to
notice the decrease, must less approve. A slight reduction will not
meet the requirements of the difference threshold.

Weber considered the fractions listed above as "constants" and
expressed his general conclusion in the form: $\frac{\triangle R}{R} = C$ which we
can translate as $\frac{\triangle S}{S} = C$, where S is the "size of the standard stimulus, $\triangle S$ is the amount of change (plus or minus) necessary to
evoke a report of a difference, and C is a constant, a fraction depending on the sense involved." This formula is the famous
Weber's law. The reader will note that it is purely operational
construction. It says nothing about what is alleged to be going on
in the "minds" or nervous systems of the subjects. It deals only

with measured stimuli and describes the general observation that
stimuli must be changed by certain definite fractional increments
for the subject to respond consistently to the difference. Thus, for
the discrimination of a difference in brightness, a Weber fraction
of $\frac{1}{100}$ would be inserted in the formula in place of C, if we
found that a standard stimulus (S) of 100 units had to be changed
by 1 unit $(\triangle S)$ in order for a subject to report a noticeable difference.

It remained for Gustav Theodore Fechner to add the mentalistic embellishments in his restatement of Weber's law. Fechner's
own observations led him to believe that a more accurate generalization would obtain if the stimulus size were described, not in
absolute measurements, but in terms of logarithms. Fechner was
also interested primarily in what he thought of as the "amount"
of sensation. His law took account of this "psychological continuum" in his use of the "sensation" strength, or S, in his equation
or law: $S = k \ log \ R$.*

The early interest in relationships between stimuli and conscious processes is no longer of special concern to psychologists.
The methods used by the early psychophysicists, however, are still
very much alive and of great value for a wide variety of psychological uses. In the study of behavior it is often necessary to work
with materials that cannot be measured or otherwise evaluated by
physical instruments. How would you proceed as a judge in a
beauty contest? On what basis would you choose Miss America?
How would you study the reactions of civilians to military bom-
bardment? How do you select the candidate for whom you will
vote? How does your English instructor evaluate your themes, or
your psychology instructor decide that you are a $C+$ instead of a
$B-$ student? How does a manufacturer or merchandiser decide
which designs or brands will attract his market? These are all
psychological problems, and to the people engaged in finding the
answers, they are important problems.

Yet in the fields of esthetics, morals, politics, social attitudes,

* In modern terms, it would be better to write $R = k \ log \ S$. Why?

consumer relations, education, to mention only a few, there are no yardsticks or Toledo scales. But measurements must be and are made in daily practice. The methods used, in one form or another, go back to Weber and Fechner. We call them psychophysical methods because of their past associations, but they are only experimental procedures for dealing with certain kinds of variables and controlling sources of error in observation. There are basically only three "official" or commonly recognized psychophysical methods, although each method has a variety of names and "special cases." The array of names and different statistical procedures often proves bewildering to the student. This bewilderment is both useless and unnecessary for a practical appreciation of the methods. The statistical procedures are *not* part of the psychophysical methods as such. The mathematically sophisticated student can delight himself in the elaborations devised by one investigator or another. The average student can study the methods as basically simple and logical methods of presenting stimuli to subjects.

Lest the above remarks prove discouraging to the reader, he should realize that he has probably used each of the methods at one time or another in his daily life, although he probably did not bother to keep a record of his subject's or his own responses and probably did not attempt to achieve really refined and objectified data. The housewife dividing a pie into equal sections or the schoolboy dividing an apple or candy bar into two equal-appearing sections (hoping to avoid the "just-noticeable difference") are approximating the *method of average error*. The bather in his tub or shower adjusting the hot and cold taps by slow stages is using a modest variation of the *method of limits* in his efforts at reaching a blissful mixture. The purchaser of a necktie trying to pick one from the display is involved with the *method of constant stimuli*. In the laboratory you have already performed one experiment in which you used the *method of average error* as a formal part of the procedure. When you allowed your subject to try to equate a horizontal and vertical line and averaged his errors to find his percentage of illusion, you were at the same time calculating his "average error." There is nothing especially formidable about the psychophysical methods. We shall now examine each more formally and determine the distinguishing features of each.

The Methods of Psychophysics

The following account of the main psychophysical methods will serve only to differentiate one method from another. It is expected that the student will learn the methods adequately only through performing experiments which make use of them. The methods have already been described much more fully and adequately than can be done here, and the student will consult the standard references for more elaborate descriptions of procedure and methods of analysis. See especially Garrett (1) or Thurstone (2) and Woodworth (3). The student is advised to read about only one method at a time, do the corresponding experiment, and then go on to the next. He should, however, glance over the discussion of general sources of error (pp. 136–138) before experimenting.

1. **The method of average error.** This method is also described as the method of equation, method of equivalents, method of adjustment, and method of reproduction. The chief distinguishing feature of this method is that the *subject* tries to equalize the stimuli. In general, the subject tries to adjust some variable stimulus to look, feel, or sound like some known standard stimulus. The extent and direction of his error is determined for each trial. Assuming an adequate number of trials, usually at least 30, the average error is then calculated, first, regardless of sign (direction of error can be in the relationship of *more* or *less* than the standard), and then with due consideration for algebraic sign. Thus, in the horizontal-vertical illusion experiment, the subject attempted to match a variable line with a standard four-inch line. Suppose he exactly matched the stand-

ard four times, overestimated by $\frac{1}{16}$ of an inch on three trials, and underestimated by $\frac{1}{16}$ of an inch on three trials. He would then have a total error-score of $\frac{6}{16}$, if we disregard the direction (over- or underestimate), and an *average error* of .6/16 for the 10 trials. If we pay attention to the *direction* of error, his overestimates would cancel his underestimates, and his average error would be zero. If a subject overestimated *or* underestimated on a majority of trials, the average error would then be prefaced by a sign (plus or minus) to show his tendency.

The average obtained when signs are ignored indicates the sensitivity of the subject or his ability to approximate the standard. It is assumed that the average error marks the limit of the just-noticeable difference for that subject. Stimuli lying within the plus or minus limits of the average error are presumed to affect the subject in the same manner as does the standard.

The average error computed with signs included indicates any tendency on the part of the subject to overestimate or underestimate the standard. Such a tendency is called a *constant error*. This type of error, and several others, will be considered later. Since the subject performs manipulations in this procedure, there is often a danger that his adjustments of the variables are affected by his muscular control; he may overreach himself and submit a "match" or comparison which is faulty because he is unable to control the instrument being used. This is especially possible when righthanded subjects are required to adjust items from the left side. Any such muscular-coordination deficiencies should be taken into account in the interpretation of the results. The student has already used this method in Experiment 4, and will use it again in Experiment 6.

2. *The method of limits*. This method is also known as the method of just-noticeable differences (J.N.D.), the method of equal-appearing intervals, the method of serial exploration, and the method of minimal change. The several names suggest the nature of the method itself. This method is best adapted for determining *SL's* or *TL's,* although it also serves adequately for *DL's.* In its usual form, when used for the determination of a threshold, or *SL,* the experimenter starts with a stimulus value well above threshold and proceeds to diminish this value by small, but measured, equal amounts. With each presentation of the stimulus, the subject reports whether or not he hears, sees, smells, tastes, or feels the stimulus. As the stimulus value diminishes, the experimenter arrives at a value which no longer brings out such a response. The experimenter then assumes that the threshold lies halfway between the last stimulus (no response) and the one just previous to it. The series just described is known as a *descending series.*

The experimenter now starts with a stimulus value well below the just-determined threshold and proceeds to increase the value until the subject responds positively. Again the threshold for this *ascending series* is determined as the halfway point between the last stimulus for which there was no response and its successor. The ascending and descending series are repeated in suitable frequency for the purpose involved, and average threshold values of each series are computed. The two separate thresholds may now be averaged for a grand threshold value.

For the *DL* determination a similar arrangement is followed with the necessary exception that a standard stimulus is presented and the variable is altered until the subject reports that the variable is less (in the descending series) or more (in the ascending series) than the standard. For some purposes an "equal" response is permitted, and the range of values in which the subject responds with "equal" is considered to represent the *DL* limits. A variety of sources of error enters into the use of the method of limits; these will be described shortly. The student will use the method of limits in Experiment 6.

3. The method of constant stimuli. This method has a variety of corollary methods or submethods associated with it, all of which can be generally classified as "frequency" methods. The several frequency methods are each designed to handle specific kinds of problems and require special study. Two such frequency methods (the *order of merit* and the *method of paired comparisons*) will be studied in Experiment 8 and in Experiment 12. In general, the method of constant stimuli involves the presentation of a standard stimulus in company with one of several graded stimuli which have been previously selected by a tentative use of the method of limits or the method of average error.

The comparison stimuli may be limited to two or three values close to the standard value. The subject is asked to report on each comparison stimulus in terms of its relation to the standard. In a weight-judging experiment, for example, he would report the comparison stimulus to be "heavier" or "lighter" than the standard. Equal judgments might also be permitted. Each comparison stimulus would be presented repeatedly to meet statistical requirements (30 to 50 trials for each stimulus are suitable for rough purposes), and the *frequency* of correct judgments would be tabulated for each comparison stimulus. The subject is expected to have a large percentage of correct reports with the extreme stimuli at either end of the range employed, and a progressively smaller correct percentage as the stimulus values approach the standard. The stimulus which is judged correct 50 percent of the time is considered the threshold stimulus, and the difference between this and the standard is regarded as the *DL*. Generally, the data are plotted in graphical form, and two curves of opposite contour are the result.

As the comparison stimulus values decrease from greater to lesser toward and beyond the standard, the percentage of responses of "greater" also decreases. As the stimulus values increase, the percentage of reports of "smaller" decreases. Such a pair of curves will cross somewhere in the middle of the graph. The point at which each curve crosses the 50-percent level on the ordinate is the "point of subjective equality" (PSE), or the point at which the subject is unable to discriminate a difference with better than chance success. The comparison and standard stimuli are, as far as the subject is concerned, the same. To make better than chance judgments, the comparison stimulus must be increased or decreased. The points at which the comparison stimuli are judged correctly 25 percent and 75 percent of the time are often taken to represent plus or minus 1 DL, because these values lie halfway between chance and certainty. The plotted curves of data collected by the constant stimuli method are known as "psychometric functions."

Sources of Error in Psychophysical Experiments

Several special types of error may affect the results obtained by use of the methods described above. These errors, although especially noticeable in experiments involving "judgment," intrude into other types of studies, and it behooves the experimenter to design his procedures to avoid such influences. The sources of error involved are the following:

1. Constant errors. If stimuli are always presented in one order, e.g., from greater to smaller, or from right to left, the obtained results differ from those collected if the order is reversed. Such "spatial" errors can be controlled to some extent by systematically varying the direction of the starting point in a given series. In studies involving a standard stimulus which is removed before a comparison stimulus is present (as in judging weights or tones), it is generally found that a "time" error is present. The stimulus which is presented second appears to have a value advantage from the fact that it follows the preceding one. The obvious control is to present the standard first in only one half of the trials. In the "spatial" error, control of arrangements is not always successful because of biases of subjects which make it easier or necessary for them to react from left to right, say, than the reverse.

THE MEASUREMENT OF STIMULI

2. *Variable errors.* The subject will not always arrive at the same threshold determination. If he did, there would be no need of repeating readings. For numerous reasons *beyond control,* the subject will vacillate within a limited area. Sometimes he will continue reporting "heavier" or "larger" far beyond the point where he stopped on a previous trial. The only control here is to multiply observations and describe the results statistically in terms of deviations.

3. *Habituation and anticipation.* Subjects often act as if they had become accustomed to responding in the way in which they started, e.g., "larger," and continue to do so for no apparent reason other than "habit." On the other hand, they know that eventually a change will occur, and they may "anticipate" this change before they might normally (statistically) be expected to do so. These two erroneous practices tend to counterbalance each other, but it is desirable to institute controls for their more complete elimination.

To ensure adequate responses, it is necessary to keep the subjects interested and alert; rest pauses help cut the sometimes unavoidable monotony. By far the most effective control is to vary the number of steps and the order in which changes are made in the stimulus. If the subject has sometimes 10 and sometimes only 3 presentations before he is at threshold level, he is unable either to get "adjusted" or to anticipate. Where possible the standard stimulus itself may be presented after the comparison in half the trials (see above for "time" error). This procedure forces the subject to change the type of response. If he has been saying "louder" for a comparison stimulus, he must now say "softer" if the standard comes first.

4. *Miscellaneous errors.* The possibility is always present of drawing a subject for study who is highly skilled in a given type of discrimination or of drawing one who, on the other hand, may require special preliminary training before he is able to comply

with the instructions. Some subjects, for example, do not quite understand what is meant by "brightness" or "saturation," and such concepts must be explained to them. In the use of "differential" tuning forks, some subjects have difficulty in discriminating pitch differences because the forks do not start out with their fundamental pitch but only gradually "settle" into it. In the process of settling from the general noise resulting from the contact of the hammer, the forks give out a series of pitches which trouble the discriminating listener.

Because psychophysical experiments are often time consuming, subjects tend to become bored. To escape boredom, they may attempt new ways of going about their tasks; they thereby change their "sets" and criteria. They may become supercritical or indifferent, and consequently their thresholds will change radically. The experimenter must watch for such unusual changes and take suitable measures in the form of rest periods, re-examination of the instructions, introduction of control series—e.g., the experimenter pretends to change the setting but does not do so—and so on.

References

1. Garrett, H. E. *Great experiments in psychology.* New York: Appleton-Century. 1930, chap. 15.
2. Thurstone, L. L. Psychophysical methods. In *Methods of psychology,* T. G. Andrews, ed. New York: John Wiley and Sons. 1948.
3. Woodworth, R. S. *Experimental psychology.* New York: Henry Holt. 1938, chaps. 17, 18.

Experiment 5. Psychophysics I: Determination of the Weber Fraction by the Method of Average Error *

Introduction. The psychophysical method of average error is already familiar to the student from Experiment 4. In that experiment, however, the method was used as a technique for the determination of the extent of an illusion. The method itself was so obviously and logically a part of the procedure that some of its features may have been overlooked. The present experiment is designed to emphasize some of these possibly overlooked "control" features of a psychophysical procedure in a relatively "pure" situation.

In addition to this examination of "controls," the experiment serves to introduce a series of experiments in which "judgments" will be the responses to be studied. Because judgments form such a large part of the experimental data in a variety of psychologically interesting areas, it is necessary for the student to observe the circumstances and conditions which operate on even the relatively simple judgments he is asked to make. An incidental aspect of the experiment is the determination of Weber's law in the discrimination of lengths.

Apparatus. Each student serves as his own subject or observer (O). The necessary material consists of a finely pointed pencil, a millimeter scale, and a sheet of paper with a series of printed lines. In the experiment to be performed there will be 40 lines, 10 each of 50, 75, 100, and 125 millimeters length. The lines are printed in random order and in irregular positions on the paper. Two blank sheets of paper will be used to provide a screen so that only one line is observed at one time.

Procedure. 1. In general, the observer will try to locate the middle of each line as accurately as possible and will mark this point

* This experiment is slightly modified from one described in *Class demonstration in psychology* by G. Milton Smith and Robert S. Woodworth, New York: Henry Holt. 1940.

lightly with his pencil. He will then measure the lines (after all have been marked) and locate the actual mid-point. In Table 10 he will record as errors the differences between his judgments and the actual mid-points. Each error should be identified by a sign (plus or minus) indicating that the error consisted of going too far to the right of the mid-point (plus) or too far to the left (minus). All errors should be reported in millimeters.

2. It is expected that the O will move his pencil along the line until he reaches the alleged mid-point, with some probability of going beyond and returning. The O should start his pencil-tracking of the first line from the right, second from the left, and so on. The O should attempt to judge on appearance alone and not try to estimate various lengths on the basis of personal experience.

3. Obtain the mean error score, with and without signs, and find the percentage of error for each length by dividing the average errors for each line by 50, 75, 100, and 125, the number of millimeters in the several lines.

Results

1. What is your Weber fraction? What is the group Weber fraction? (Average the four percentages of error.)
2. Because you were, in effect, comparing one half of a line with another half, or, in other words, estimating lengths of 25, 37.5, 50, and 62.5 mm., should you not use 25, 37.5, 50, and 62.5 as the divisors in calculating percentage of error? What is the Weber fraction with this change in divisors?
3. Express the meaning of the Weber fraction you derive in ordinary language. In other words, what can you say about the probable degree of error subjects will make in judging lengths visually?

Discussion

1. Why did you calculate the percentage of error for each length? What was the result? How much error would you make in estimating the mid-point of a yardstick? A football field? A mile-

Table 10. *Average Errors of Estimation of the Midpoint of Lines of Several Lengths for One Observer and a Group (N =   ) of Observers*

Trials	Lengths							
	50 mm		75 mm		100 mm		125 mm	
	O	Group M *	O	Group M	O	Group M	O	Group M
1								
2								
3								
4								
5								
6								
7								
8								
9								
10								
Total 1 †								
Total 2								
Mean 1								
Mean 2								
% Error								

* For group "mean" insert the average scores of each individual in the group for all 10 trials. Sufficient space is provided to take care of 30 subjects if you divide the column into 3 sections. Use only "mean 1" for the group data.

† Total 1 and Mean 1 are obtained without regard to sign. Total 2 and Mean 2 are calculated with signs included and will necessarily be smaller.

long road, assuming you had some vantage point for viewing?

2. Why did you omit signs in the group results?

3. What were your own scores with and without signs? What does the sign indicate? Why were you asked to approach alternate lines from different ends?

4. What would be the effect of introducing some artificial cue, such as a spot on your screen, as a guide for your estimates?

5. Did you have any trouble in controlling your pencil so that

your mark fell to one side of the place you desired to mark? What would such an error be called?

6. What are the prominent differences between the method you used and that used in the operation of a Galton bar?

References

1. Postman, L., and Egan, J. P. *Experimental psychology*. New York: Harper and Brothers, 1949, chap. 2.

2. Woodworth, R. S. *Experimental psychology*. New York: Henry Holt, 1938, chaps. 17, 18.

Experiment 6. Psychophysics II: The Method of Limits. Determination of the DL for Brilliance

Introduction. The experimental features of the psychophysical methods are well demonstrated by the method of limits. This method is one of the simplest procedures for the determination of both terminal and difference thresholds or limens. The present experiment will deal only with the determination of a difference threshold, but the modifications necessary for determination of absolute or terminal thresholds can be readily inferred by the student who follows through the logic involved in the calculation of a difference threshold. The experiment to be done will involve determining the *DL* for brilliance.

Apparatus and Procedure. *Brilliance* is defined by Brennan, Burnham, and Newhall (1) as "that attribute of any color or visual sense-quality in respect to which it may be classed as equivalent to some member of a series of grays ranging from black to white. Distinguish from brightness, which has reference solely to stimulus magnitude." In effect, we can secure different degrees of brilliance by changing the proportions of black and white in a stimulus. An easy way of altering the composition of a stimulus in terms of black and white is to rotate interlocked disks of black and white paper on a "color mixer" (a variable-speed motor which can be made to rotate the disks rapidly enough to eliminate flicker and provide a fused stimulus). To determine a *DL* for brilliance, then, we can use a color mixer with a pair of disks (black and white) which can be altered to provide various shades of gray. Such shades can then be compared with a standard gray stimulus (*SS*) and adjusted until they appear to be equal. The difference in degrees of white between the standard and the comparison stimulus will be a difference threshold or limen. The standard stimulus might consist of a gray disk on another color mixer adjacent to the comparison, or it might consist of a smaller gray disk mounted over the comparison or variable disks.

FIGURE 5. *A BRIGHTNESS DISCRIMINATION BOX.* A wooden box is divided into two compartments. At the front, ground-glass windows are inserted in suitable frames. In each section a 60-watt bulb is wired in series with a rheostat. The lights should be placed near the sides and rear of the compartments to obtain an even illumination. Holes are drilled in the top to provide ventilation. Either light can be used as a standard by selecting some rheostat setting below the maximum illumination. The experimenter then changes the comparison light intensity by adding resistance to the other circuit at the subject's instructions, until the subject is satisfied about his judgments of "brighter," "darker," or "equal." When the box is in use, the experimenter provides screens above and at the sides to prevent external lighting from affecting the stimulus windows. A convenient scale is mounted behind the rheostat knobs, and readings are taken in the scale units. These readings can then be translated into electrical or photometric units if appropriate instruments are available. Turning the box upside down reverses the position of the standard and comparison stimuli.

A simpler method of obtaining the difference threshold is to make use of two ordinary 60-watt electric light bulbs wired in series with suitable variable resistances so that each bulb can be dimmed by adjusting the resistor knob. The bulbs should be mounted behind a milk-glass screen which is placed in a frame designed to provide windows about 1½ inches square. The inside of the box should be painted black and ventilated by boring holes in the top. Either light can serve as a standard. The standard light should be dimmed to about half its power as measured by a photometer or by a suitable voltage indicator, which can be provided easily by mounting the resistor knobs on 180° scales (a protractor will serve). The experimenter then asks the observer to judge the comparison stimulus in terms of the standard—that is, the subject is required to report "lighter" or "darker" or "equal" as the comparison stimulus is manipulated by the experimenter. The specific steps in the procedure (see below) will be explained for the type of apparatus just described, but they are readily modifiable for either of the above-mentioned methods.

Specific procedural steps. (1.) *Ascending series:* Start with the right window obviously darker than the left. Ask your subject to report on the right window, the variable. Add 1 unit of light. Repeat. Continue in steps of 1 unit until O says "equal." Record this point in Table 1 as the average between this setting and the one just previous. Thus, if the last point at which he said "darker" is 150 units of light, and the first point at which he says "equal" is 149 units of light, it is assumed that somewhere between 150 and 149 is a point at which his judgment changes. You would, therefore, report 149.5 as your finding for this point, which is known as the lower threshold for the ascending series (Rla). Continue increasing the amount of light until the subject changes from "equal" to "lighter." Again record the average of these two points for the same reason. This new point is called the upper threshold for the ascending series, or Rua.

2. *Descending series:* Start with the right window obviously lighter, and reduce its brightness by 1-unit steps until the subject reports "equal." Average the two points (as above) for your first upper threshold of the descending series (Rud). Continue through "equality" until the subject reports "darker." Again

average the two readings for your lower threshold in the descending series (*Rld*). You have now obtained four threshold values.

3. Repeat the above procedure 10 times, recording the separate values of your threshold in Table 11.

Table 11. *Distribution of Values of a Comparison Stimulus When Judged as Equal to, Darker, or Lighter than a Standard Stimulus*

Trials	Ascending series		Descending series	
	Rla	*Rua*	*Rud*	*Rld*
1.				
2.				
3.				
4.				
5.				
6.				
7.				
8.				
9.				
10.				

4. Special precautions: Do not start with the same values of intensity in each trial. Vary this amount from trial to trial, sometimes starting with more, sometimes with less intensity. This will make your trial series vary in length. Do not make your series so long as to tire your subject nor so short that he does not have a chance to acquire a reference value. Comment on the reason for varying your series length with each trial.

Results

1. Average the lower values of each threshold as follows: Add the two upper thresholds together, and subtract the two lower thresholds from this amount; dividing by 4 will give you the

average difference limen. The following formula expresses the above instructions:

$$DL = \frac{Rud + Rua - Rld - Rla}{4}$$

2. Locate the "point of subjective equality" by *adding* together *all* four thresholds and averaging by dividing by 4. This point is that "variable stimulus magnitude which seems, on the average, to be equal to the standard" (2).
3. Compute your "constant error" by subtracting your standard stimulus value from the point of subjective equality.

Discussion

1. Why did you make your observations in both ascending and descending series?
2. Why did you vary the lengths of the series?
3. What are habituation and expectation, or "anticipation," errors? Do you have any evidence that such errors were made by your subject?
4. Why bother about locating points of equality in your series? Why not just go right through the equality points and record only the points where the judgment changes from darker to lighter, or vice versa?
5. What major source of error was not controlled in this experiment?

References

1. Brennan, J. B., Burnham, R. W., and Newhall, S. M. Color terms and definitions. *Psychol. Bull.,* 1948, *45,* 207–230.
2. Postman, L., and Egan, J. P. *Experimental psychology.* New York: Harper and Brothers, 1949, chap. 2.
3. Thurstone, L. L. Psychophysical methods. In *Methods of psychology,* T. G. Andrews, ed. New York: John Wiley and Sons. 1948.
4. Woodworth, R. S. *Experimental psychology.* New York: Henry Holt. 1938, chaps. 17, 18.

Experiment 7. Psychophysics III: Constant Stimuli. An Evaluation of the Methods of Paired Comparison and Order of Merit

Introduction. The method of constant stimuli involves the use of a number of stimuli near the threshold value (*SL*) or near a standard stimulus when *DL's* are being determined. The subject is asked to judge in the latter case whether one stimulus is stronger, lighter, better, etc., than another. The percentages of reports of all types are then plotted to determine *DL's* at certain criterion points. The present experiment is a variation of this method applied to, in this case, an esthetic judgment. The same procedure can be applied to a wide variety of other situations, e.g., evaluating baseball teams, movie actors, peanut butter, college professors, etc. The method to be used is known as that of *paired comparisons*. In effect, it is a formal procedure wherein each item in a series is compared once with every other item. As an aid in evaluating the lengthy paired-comparisons method, the *order-of-merit* method will also be used.

Apparatus and Procedure. (1.) *Apparatus.* Any assortment of objects with some common factor or involving some dimension (better, stronger, prettier, etc.) could be used. Advertisements of the same product could be rated for buyer appeal, attention-getting value, etc. A little consideration of the problems involved in comparing advertisements will quickly indicate that several factors may be present which confuse the stimulus situation, so that knowledge about specific determinants cannot be obtained. It is desirable to have as simple a situation as possible for this demonstration-of-technique experiment, and for this reason the items selected for judgment should vary in only one characteristic. The characteristic that we will use is that of "preferred proportions of a rectangle" as determined by responses to changes in the ratio of length to width.

What are the most pleasing proportions of a rectangle? This

is an ancient problem which has never been solved to everyone's satisfaction. It has been suggested that when the sides of a rectangle are in the ratio of 6:10, the rectangle will then be most pleasing. This ratio is known as the "golden mean." It should be noted that in the usual experiment in which this "pleasantness ratio" is tested, no account is taken of the area, which is allowed to vary (see Thorndike's results, Woodworth, 3, p. 387). In our experiment we will keep the area constant and vary only the length of the sides of a number of rectangles.

As apparatus, then, we require a number of rectangles of similar area whose sides vary in known ratios. For purposes of this experiment, we can use black paper rectangles mounted on white backgrounds which are cut to present uniform borders ($\frac{1}{2}$ inch) all around the black rectangles. The subjects can be shown the rectangles according to the procedure detailed below and should indicate their preferences. The rectangles we will use are all 100 square centimeters in area. Their lengths and widths vary as follows:

Rectangle	Width	Length	Ratio of Width to Length
A	10.0 cm.	10.0 cm.	1.00
B	9.5	10.5	.90
C	9.0	11.1	.81
D	8.5	11.8	.72
E	8.0	12.5	.64
F	7.8	12.9	.60*
G	7.5	13.3	.56
H	7.0	14.2	.49
I	6.5	15.4	.42
J	6.0	16.7	.36

* (Approximately the "golden mean.")

2. *Procedure.* Two kinds of comparisons will be made. In each type of comparison procedure, the subjects will rate the several rectangles for pleasantness of appearance. They should be in-

structed to consider only the shape or form of the rectangles and not to attempt to use any categories of objects as guides.

a. *Order of Merit.* The stimulus cards should be placed before the subjects in a random order in a position of good visibility. In a classroom they can be set up on the chalk tray at the blackboard. Each subject indicates his first choice, second choice, etc., in Table 12. As much time as desired is allowed. Each subject should make a preliminary survey and then go about his selections.

b. *Method of Paired Comparisons.* The instructor presents two rectangles at a time for group comparison. Pairs are selected at random, and subjects indicate their preference for one member of each by checking in the column of the preferred rectangle in Table 13. The check marks should be placed in the *column* of the preferred stimulus and in the *row* of the less-preferred stimulus. Thus if a subject favors C over G, he places a mark in Column C, Row G. This procedure is repeated with successive pairs until every rectangle has been compared once with every other rectangle. The experimenter will alternate an equal number of times the sides (right and left) of exposure of each stimulus. What procedural error will this alternation avoid?

Results

1. Which rectangle was most preferred by the order-of-merit and the paired-comparison methods? Which was least preferred? Can you explain these preferences?

2. What were the "rank order coefficients of correlation" (ρ) between the two methods (*a*) for the group of subjects and (*b*) for you as an individual judge? How well do you agree with the group in both methods of judging?

3. Do you find any evidence for a "golden mean"? Plot your results, using the width-length ratios as abscissas and the mean or median rank orders for ordinates. Does the shape of the curve indicate any trend?

Discussion

1. Why is the method of paired comparisons considered a psychophysical method by Thurstone (1)? How does it qualify as a method of "constant stimuli"?

Table 12. *Order of Merit Ranks Assigned to 10 Rectangles of Varied Proportions but of Equal Area by One Subject and by a Group (N =   ) of Subjects*

Rank	Rectangles									
	A	B	C	D	E	F	G	H	I	J
Own										
Mean										

Table 13. *Paired-Comparisons Ranks Indicating Preference for 10 Rectangles of Varied Proportions by One Subject and by a Group (N =   )*

NOTE: The table is to be read in terms of columns versus rows; thus a preference for Item E over Item J would be indicated by a tally mark in Column E, Row J.

Rectangle	A	B	C	D	E	F	G	H	I	J
A										
B										
C										
D										
E										
F										
G										
H										
I										
J										
Own total										
Own rank										
Group total										
Group rank										

2. Which method gave the best results? What is meant by "best" in this case? If you were an advertising manager selecting suggested advertisements from a group submitted by your artists, which method would you use?
3. What sources of error did the experimenter control? Which were left uncontrolled?
4. What factors in everyday life can you relate to your experimental findings?

Table 14. *Rank-Order Correlations between Order-of-Merit Rank Order and Paired-Comparisons Rank Orders in Judging Pleasantness of Proportions of Rectangles*
$$(N = \quad)$$
NOTE: For procedure for calculating rank-order coefficients of correlation, see the following chapter in this text.

Rectangle	1 Own rank (Merit)	2 Group rank (Merit)	3 Own rank (P. Com.)	4 Group rank (P. Com.)	1 & 2 D D²	1 & 3 D D²	2 & 4 D D²	3 & 4 D D²
A								
B								
C								
D								
E								
F								
G								
H								
I								
J								

$$\rho = 1 - \frac{6\Sigma D^2}{N\,(N^2 - 1)}$$

References

1. Thurstone, L. L. Psychophysics. In *Methods of psychology,* T. G. Andrews, ed. New York: Wiley. 1948.

2. Underwood, B. J. *Experimental psychology*. New York: Appleton-Century-Crofts. 1949, chap. 3.
3. Woodworth, R. S. *Experimental psychology*. New York: Henry Holt. 1938, chaps. 16, 17, and 18.

8

A Little More Statistics

A STUDENT once reported to the writer, "the more I study, the lower the marks I get." He thereupon talked himself into the logical conclusion, and ceased studying. As it happened, his grades dropped to new lows, and he felt obliged to renew the grind. Had his marks improved, we would have been presented with a new fairy tale whose attraction would be irresistible for many students. Most of you have wondered about the methods followed by instructors in arriving at your grades and those of your classmates. How much does "intelligence" enter into the problem? Do beauty and brains go together? Beauty and grades often seem to. How would you go about finding out about the factors that determine grades or "go with" them?

Most of your life you have been handling such "go with" problems. In warm weather you wear light clothing; in the winter you bundle up. The clothes you wear "go with" the weather. The good looking girls "go with" the boys who have more money; success "goes with" hard work (so "they" say). Such examples occur to you by the dozen; it also occurs to you that they do not always work out. Occasionally a congressman pads his payroll, and a stock exchange president perpetrates a fraud or two, and you begin to wonder about "honesty is the best policy" or "the cream always comes to the top."

It would be very convenient for scientific purposes if one could predict the degree of success of some person if his honesty or work habits were known. You recall that the practical aim of science is prediction, and much of its practical work involves the construction of instruments which, to some extent, at least, predict coming events. A barometer, for example, predicts to some extent the weather to come. The basis for such predictions is found in the past history of both barometers and the weather. A certain barometric pressure "goes with" certain kinds of weather. Any measuring instrument "goes with" something. What does an intelligence test "go with"?

The work of the psychologist, like that of any scientist, is to find out what "goes with" what, so that in the future he can predict a condition or state of affairs by knowing something about *one* of the pair of items that go with each other. Thus the clinical psychologist studies the reaction of various personality types to a special kind of test, say the Rorschach ink-blot test, so that in the future some aspects of personality, otherwise unknown, might be detected. The modern scientific question is not "what causes what," but "what goes with (or before) something else," or more generally "to what degree does a change in one variable accompany a change in another variable?" This question can be labeled, for convenience, the question of "concomitant variation."

If every time we changed one variable a certain amount, a specific change occurred in another variable, we would be in a position to predict freely back and forth from one variable to the other. If we had a graph of the relationship between the variables, we could read off the value of one variable on the abscissa if we knew the value on the ordinate. But such graphs are not easy to plot. There are few instances of pairs of variables that change together in precise amounts. Some physical events come close to such an ideal. We know, for instance, that if we increase the pressure on a gas, the volume decreases, and vice versa. But when we turn to behavior problems, our variables are not so neatly allied. The most intelligent student does not always get the highest grades; people who are aggressive or honest in one situation may be shy or dishonest in others. Even in more physical aspects of personality such as height and weight, for example, we do not always find the tallest to be heaviest, and so on.

Our problem is one of discovering to what extent one variable changes as another changes. Even if the changes are not perfectly synchronized, it is of considerable value to know the degree to which they are synchronized.

If we find that a given change in one variable accompanies a change in another at least part of the time, we are in a position to begin predicting, at least on a percentage basis. Perhaps other variables are present which will account for the remaining percentage. We can look for those later if we know they exist, and the failure to get 100 per cent predictability is a guarantee of their existence.

But how can you go about discovering such relationships between variables? It is not so difficult as it might seem if you approach the problem logically. Since we are dealing with two variables at a time, it seems logical to begin by measuring each of the variables. It is obvious, however, that one pair of measurements might be quite meaningless and unrelated, and so we go about accumulating more pairs. Suppose we take the question of grades and intelligence as a sample problem. We can assume that the grades represent a measurement of a sort and that the same is true of intelligence-tests scores. Assume we have such information about 10 people. For convenience, let us line up the grades obtained from highest to lowest and indicate the I.Q. of the person obtaining each grade in an adjacent column. The data are tabulated on page 157.

How does this information strike you? Do grades "go with" intelligence? Not exactly? Well, we can hardly expect exact results when neither measurement is absolutely pure; besides there may be other factors. Is there any tendency for grades to accompany I.Q.? There certainly seems to be a trend. In general, the high grades go with high I.Q.'s and the low grades with low I.Q.'s. In some cases there are reversals—a lower I.Q. goes with a higher grade; but these reversals do not seem too outrageous or upsetting.

Person	Grade	I.Q.
1	98	125
2	95	130
3	90	118
4	89	115
5	88	110
6	83	116
7	75	95
8	74	97
9	71	88
10	57	80

Is that all we can say? Can we give a more precise statement of the degree of relationship present?

If the highest grade accompanied the highest I.Q., the next highest grade the next highest I.Q., and so on down the list, we would be obliged (if we had a lot of cases) to say that there was some basis of predictability in the list. Knowing a position in the I.Q. list, we could state the position in the grade list which accompanied it. The difficulty with our sample, however, is that no such clean-cut arrangement is apparent. There are too many instances where a lower I.Q. precedes a higher one. If we had some way of indicating the extent of such variations from a perfect correspondence, we might be in a position to evaluate the relationship between the two lists.

It is possible, of course, to see to what extent the position in one list differs from the position in another list. Let us determine this difference for our 10 cases and see what it amounts to. For convenience we can line up both groups of scores again, and since we are interested in the extent to which a position in one list varies from a position in the other, it is necessary to assign a position-score or rank to each measurement. We can put the grades into one column of ranks (Rank I) and rank the I.Q.'s in another column (Rank II) and then obtain the difference (D) in a third column as follows (forget the D^2 column for the moment):

Person	Grade	I.Q.	Rank I	Rank II	D	D²
1	98	125	1	2	−1	1
2	95	130	2	1	1	1
3	90	118	3	3	0	0
4	89	115	4	5	−1	1
5	88	110	5	6	−1	1
6	83	116	6	4	2	4
7	75	95	7	8	−1	1
8	74	97	8	7	1	1
9	71	88	9	9	1	1
10	57	80	10	10	0	0

Total 11

To get the differences, we subtract Rank II from Rank I. When we do this, we find that we get involved with plus and minus signs. We know that such a difficulty is easily eliminated by the process of squaring. That accounts for the D^2 column. By adding up the D^2 figures, we have an indication of how much difference there is between our two sets of measurements. This will become a very useful figure if we first stop to interpret it. Consider what D and D^2 would amount to if both "Ranks" columns were identical. In that case, D and D^2 would be zero throughout, and the sum of D^2 would also be zero. That would mean that there would be a perfect correspondence or relationship between I and II, and we could freely predict the position of any person in Column II by knowing his Column I standing, and vice versa. We could use his grades as a measurement of intelligence, or vice versa. We could halve our work as far as measuring these aspects of personality are concerned. Now consider what would happen if the sum of D^2 amounted to a large figure. That would mean that the D's must be great, and that in turn would indicate little prospect of prediction.

For convenience we would call a perfect relationship, such as described above, "unity" or "oneness" and assign it an arbitrary value of 1 to represent such perfection. Then any deviation from

such perfection would represent a D score above zero and, therefore, a D^2 score above zero, and the relationship would be somewhat less than 1, depending upon the number and extent of the
differences. We could represent such a case as $1 - (x)$. Note that
if the ranks in either column were reversed, so that the highest
I.Q., for example, accompanied the lowest grade, and so on, the
Σ of the D^2 would amount to a very high total. In such a case,
the amount of x might be so great as to give us a negative answer
to our subtraction of $1 - x$, and our answer would carry a negative sign.

Because we could predict just as easily, however, in such a case
of perfect reversal, the relationship could still be indicated as 1
with a minus sign before it, thus: (-1). In order to accommodate
the possibility of such an occurrence in any real set of measurements, certain constants and factors have to be applied to the x
component in our equation, which we can now state as:

$$\text{degree of relationship} = 1 - x$$

The factors to be added are introduced to prevent the x component from ever exceeding the value of $+2$. Thus, there can never
be a relationship exceeding 1 or -1. In effect, if the D^2 score is
small, the result will be between 1 and 0; if the D^2 score is very
large, the score will be between -1 and zero. The factors added
to the D^2 score are a constant multiplier, 6, and a divisor,
$N (N^2 - 1)$ where N equals the number of pairs in the ranking.*
The complete formula now reads:

$$\text{Degree of relationship} = 1 - \frac{6\Sigma D^2}{N (N^2 - 1)}$$

Suppose we apply this formula to our ΣD^2 of 11. We have

$$1 - \frac{6 (11)}{10 (100 - 1)} = 1 - \frac{66}{990}$$
$$= 1 - .006$$
$$= +.93$$

* To go into the derivation of the complete formula would take us far beyond the mathematical preparation assumed for this course.

Before we try to interpret this result, assume the case when the ranks of Column II are a perfect reversal of Column I. You will find that ΣD^2 will then equal 330. Substituting this figure in our formula, we have

$$1 - \frac{6\,(330)}{990} = 1 - \frac{1980}{990}$$
$$= 1 - 2$$
$$= -1$$

The figure, $+.93$, is very close to 1, or unity, or perfection. We can take it to mean that a strong trend exists for high scores in one measurement to accompany high scores in another measurement. Trends expressed in such figures as we have just obtained are called "correlation coefficients." There are many ways of obtaining coefficients of correlation. The method described here is one of the easiest to use with small numbers of cases. It is called the *rank difference method,* and the correlation thus obtained is usually called *Rho* (symbolized by ρ).

Because correlation coefficients will be part of your equipment as a psychologist, it will be your obligation to learn when and how to use them, what type of procedure to apply to different data samples, and what the correlation figures that you obtain mean. For your present purposes, we can content ourselves with pointing out certain commonly accepted meanings. We can unhesitantly appreciate correlations of $+1$ and -1 as indicating perfect relationships between two sets of variables. Zero correlations are also easily interpreted as indicating no characteristic trend or relationship whatsoever. Because students are inclined to interpret correlations as indicating a type of percentage relationship, it should be pointed out that a straight percentage interpretation is not justified.

Correlation values up to .45 are considered "low" to "very low." From .46 to .75 they rate from "low" to "moderate," and from .76 to .90 they are considered "high." Correlations above .90 are rarely obtained in psychological work (except in limited types of studies) and are considered "very high" by statisticians.

You will have many occasions to use correlation techniques in psychological investigation. Although other scientists use them frequently, the coefficient of correlation is almost a symbol of the psychologist. You had best become not only familiar but intimate with it.

References

(See Chapter 2)

9

Experimentation in Vision

THE BEGINNER in the experimental psychology of vision must equip himself with certain tools of the trade. He must familiarize himself with the basic terminology, the units of measurement, and the important variables. The scientific knowledge in the field of vision is voluminous, and simply becoming acquainted with the literature of the field as a whole would require a lifetime. The subject has received the attention of physiologists, physicists, and chemists as well as of psychologists, and the student will do well to acquire a background in the work of these scientists if he is to comprehend, much less contribute to, the understanding of vision.

The classical work in vision was done by H. von Helmholtz, whose three-volume work on physiological optics is still a standard reference, though published in 1865. The analysis of vision as a photochemical process has been presented by Hecht (4). A currently useful reference is Bartley's *Vision* (1). Woodworth (5) finds it important enough to devote five chapters to the subject. Despite the amount of work done by psychologists alone, many puzzling problems remain for future solution, and the existence of several theories of color vision, for example, indicates that the investigation of vision will long continue.

The experimental study of vision has spread out over so many types of problems that we cannot hope even to begin a serious consideration of experimentation in the field as a whole. What-
162

ever the question, however, we can note that experimenters often take cognizance of two factors of important laboratory concern: (1) In terms of the observer, a laboratory distinction is often drawn between monocular and binocular vision; and (2) In terms of stimuli, a distinction is usually made between chromatic (colored) and achromatic (black and white) stimulus objects. Because each of these distinctions is of considerable laboratory interest, we shall attempt to deal with them in the experiments in this section.

Certain basic factors regarding the nature of the visual response and its mechanism must be appreciated before one begins experimentation. The student will do well to consult texts on the anatomy and physiology of the eye, as well as a chapter on light in a standard textbook of physics. Material on lenses and mirrors is especially useful for the psychologist. In nearly all elementary texts, the eye will be compared with a camera, and the analogous relationships will be brought out. Familiarity with photographic materials and processes is most desirable. The simple fact that the ordinary human observer has two cameras mounted about two inches apart (interocular distance), with sets of muscles performing as automatic universal joints, is not brought out so frequently, but cannot be ignored by the experimentalist. What we think of as a visual reaction usually begins with the introduction of light rays into the eye through the pupil. We might best begin our own study with an examination of these stimuli to vision.

The Stimuli for Vision

The eye normally reacts to objects which reflect or generate light. Unless an object does reflect or give off light to some degree, it cannot be seen. It is impossible for anyone, cats and bats included, to see in the dark, if "dark" means the absence of light in any degree. The physical nature of light is not yet fully understood, although it is now generally thought of as a form of energy which exists in minute amounts called "quanta." Whatever the essential nature of this "radiant" energy, it is also thought to exist in the form of an electromagnetic wave motion.

These electromagnetic waves or vibrations are so rapid in motion that to discuss them in terms of frequency would involve awkward units of measurement. Consequently, the waves of light are customarily described in terms of wave length. Even so, the measuring units are exceedingly minute. Wave lengths of light are measured in millionths of millimeters, or "millimicrons," usually abbreviated mμ. (The angstrom unit, one-tenth as large, is also used.)

Only those wave lengths of "radiant energy" that lie in the so-called visible spectrum (380 mμ to 780 mμ) affect us as visual stimuli. Waves longer than 780 mμ are known as infrared (beyond the red), while those below 380 are the ultraviolet. Ordinarily, neither infrared nor ultraviolet rays serve as visual stimuli, although they may have their own stimulus values in other respects. The wave length of light being reflected into the eye becomes of consequence in a consideration of color (see below). As psychologists we may have little occasion to concern ourselves with a description of light in terms of wave length, and we may satisfy our needs by describing a stimulus in psychological terms. Eventually, however, an accurate physical description will probably become necessary, and the spectrometer will become the common tool of physicist and psychologist.

Nor can we ignore the study of wave energy and of the electromagnetic spectrum in other areas. The current interest in the relationships between the sense of smell and infrared wave lengths is an indication of the degree of technological specialization a psychologist may find he must attain.

In elementary experimentation the student will be more immediately concerned with relatively less complicated measures of stimuli. His problem will be more one of describing the size, strength (intensity), complexity, and quality of his stimulus. To these features we now turn.

1. *The size of the visual stimulus.* For some purposes it is adequate to give a simple inches-and-feet description of the boundaries of the object under observation. Whenever such sizes are
reported, it is necessary to report the distance of the object
from the observer, because the size of the visual image on the
retina varies with the distance. When one is interested in reporting on some general visual principle that is not concerned
with the distance of the object, or when the actual object cannot easily be measured, it is desirable to measure the angle
formed by the object in relation to the eye, and to report the
size of the object as so many degrees or minutes of arc. A measurement of this kind is also reported as so many degrees of
"visual angle."

The Snellen Eye Chart commonly used to measure visual
acuity has letters of different sizes arranged in rows. A subject
who has 20/20 vision can read the letters of a particular row
from a distance of 20 feet. The height of the letters in this row
correspond, at 20 feet away, to 1 minute of arc. The use of
degrees for measuring size is of obvious significance in many
perceptual problems involving judgment of size. In the famous
moon-size illusion, for example, it can be shown that the "visual angle" determined by the diameter of the moon is the
same regardless of the moon's position, although the moon
admittedly looks larger on the horizon than at its zenith.*

Sketchers often make use of visual angles for measuring the
relative sizes of items they are attempting to reproduce graphi-
cally. They hold a pencil before their "sighting" eye and note
how much of the pencil must be exposed to cut off, or blank
out completely from the visual field, the object under view. A
larger object requires more such exposure than a small one.

* The moon-size illusion is not strictly and completely an illusion because
of increased refraction of light near horizon, but the same phenomenon can
be shown with small disks in a domed room where differences of refraction are
not important.

The artist then adjusts the dimensions in his sketch to correspond with the lengths of pencil exposed. If the pencil is always held at the same distance from the eyes, say at arm's length, the artist has a readily available scale by which to measure proportional lengths at a distance.

To make a crude scale for measuring the size of objects at a known distance, take a thin piece of stiff paper or plain wood, about 8 inches long, hold it at arm's length, and mark off on it the distances from the top down that you must expose in order to cut out of view sections of a yardstick standing vertically at a distance of 20 feet. If you make a mark on your scale for every 3 inches of yardstick, you should be able to estimate the length of some unknown object at the same distance within an inch and a half. Make another scale by moving the yardstick forward a foot at a time. You can then tell how far away a 3-foot object is, if it is within 20 feet. Can you figure out with such a scale when the object is 40 feet away?

Size and visual angle: the artificial pupil. Because we measure the visual angle from a fixed position, it is necessary to control the location of the pupil. This can be done easily by mounting some object with a circular opening of fixed size, say 1 mm., just before the subject's real pupil. The subject makes his observation through this opening. All angles are then calculated from the position and size of the artificial pupil.

2. Strength of the visual stimulus. The intensity (brightness) of a visual stimulus depends upon the amount of physical energy (amplitude of light waves) present, and upon the composition of the wave lengths of light entering the eye. The intensity also depends upon the state of readiness of the eye for reacting to such light. This state itself depends upon such factors as pupillary diameter, retinal adaptation, location on the retina affected by the light, and the field or "surrounds" forming the background of the stimulus object or light source.

a. *Measuring physical intensity.* We can speak in terms of amount of light if we are describing the source of the light itself or of the light being reflected from the source into the eye. The amount of light physically present can be measured with physical instruments such as are familiar to the average camera user (light meters, illuminometers, photometers) and the measurements can be reported in foot-candles, millilamberts, or other convenient units. The amount of light affecting the observer depends upon the distance of the subject from the illuminated object (it varies as an inverse square with the distance), and so the distance of the observer must always be stated. This principle has been incorporated into the manufacture of some photographic light meters in which the readings are made at the camera lens instead of near the object being photographed.

b. *Measuring complexity or composition of wave-lengths.* Unless the experimenter starts out with light sources whose compositions are known or arranged through the use of filters of known characteristics, it is necessary to employ some form of spectrometer or spectrophotometer to determine the light frequencies present. The measurements involved in such determinations are beyond the normal possibilities of an elementary laboratory course in psychology and will not be considered here. The student will have an opportunity to make some observations in this area from a subjective rather than physical viewpoint in an experiment on color mixture (see Experiment 10).

At this point we are concerned only to make clear the fact that wave length itself is an important component of intensity. Failure to consider this factor may invalidate the results of some experiments in which subjects may be reacting to brightness differences between stimuli when the experimenter believes that only wave-length differences are involved. Thus, in an experiment in which an attempt is being made to discover if dogs or infants are able to see colors

(react to wave-length differences), it is of the first importance
to equalize the intensities of the stimuli employed. The fact
that a dog can learn to stop and go with traffic signals is no
evidence that he sees red and green. He may be reacting to
a brightness difference.

The experimenter must always be careful to note the
sources of illumination in visual experiments. Various electric light sources have wave-length characteristics of their
own. When such lights are used for viewing stimuli, they
modify the light reflected by the object so that the object
is not the same, psychologically speaking, as it would be under other lighting. Daylight itself is not free from complications; the presence or absence of clouds, the time of day,
even the composition of window glass, affect the composition of wave lengths that will be reflected by a stimulus object. The description of the stimulus object in terms of the
light characteristics it reflects is by no means a simple task,
and should not be attempted without a proper consideration of the physics of light.

When the physiological and psychological aspects of vision are brought into consideration, the description of a
stimulus object becomes much more complicated. We then
encounter such factors as afterimages (negative and positive), summation and induction effects, learning factors,
emotional factors, as well as a variety of factors stressed by
Gestalt psychologists, such as constancy, visual aftereffects,
figure-ground relationships, etc. To describe a visual stimulus actually being used in an experiment with a human
subject is a task of major proportions. In a simple experiment involving flicker fusion, one experimenter set up controls for 21 factors before beginning to obtain data. Other
sources of error were left to be controlled by increasing the
number of subjects and readings in the hope that they
would counterbalance themselves.

c. Readiness. (1.) *Surrounds.* The visibility of a stimulus object (often called a "target") depends upon the background illumination, both in terms of intensity and quality (color, hue). The background is often spoken of as surroundings or more commonly "surrounds." Obviously a "target" on a "surrounds" of equal quality and intensity will be difficult to see. Black on white is seen more easily than white on black. Red on green is difficult to detect at some distance. A careful description of the surrounds is necessary in any report of visual stimuli.

(2.) *Adaptation.* The eye adapts to the basic level of illumination present. We all have experienced the apparent failure of vision upon entering a dark theatre, but have found that often in a short time we can pick out objects which were at first invisible. This type of adjustment is called "dark adaptation." In 40 minutes (in the dark) we are almost completely adapted, that is, we will be at peak efficiency for responding to light stimuli. Dark adaptation is usually accomplished by keeping the subject in a dark room for a time corresponding to the desired degree of adaptation. Certain types of red goggles can be used for adapting under less trying circumstances. As we leave a dark area for a brightly illuminated one, the reverse type of adaptation occurs, and we overcome the dazzling effect which at first prevents satisfactory visual orientation. These adaptive adjustments depend upon structures in the retina which need not concern us here, but the phenomena themselves indicate the necessity for carefully describing the adjustment level of the eye in reporting the results of experimentation.

3. The quality of visual stimuli. In this section we shall talk about the psychological or response aspects of visual stimuli. We shall think of the functional relationships between wave length, amplitude, and complexity of light waves and the reactions of observers. It is easy to become confused in consideration of such functional relationships and attribute to stimulus objects those characteristics which belong to the observer. Thus we often speak of colored objects as if they possess the color. The color, however, is a reaction to such objects made by an observer capable of certain kinds of responses because he possesses certain physiological structures. For the color-blind person, the red apple is not red, at least not in the same way as for the non-color-blind. Rats do not see color, chimpanzees do.

It is perfectly possible to experiment in the visual area without discussing any of the physical characteristics of light. Most psychological experimentation is of this nature, largely because it is more convenient to use psychological terms where actual physical measurements are awkward or impossible, as yet, and would be difficult to use for communication. The average individual is not used to terms employed in physical measurement and is more familiar with terms referring to his own reactions to stimuli of different wave lengths, intensities, and complexities. For such individuals, such reactions are lumped together under the general term "color." An object is reported to have color, a lot of color, to be colorless, etc. The more sophisticated persons, influenced perhaps by Technicolor movies, will discriminate among objects as having color or as being "black and white." In either case, they are referring to their own discriminated responses and are naming their own reactions.

Experimental psychologists, however, are not content with the omnibus term "color," and prefer to discuss the reaction aspects in more specialized terms. The visual response is ordinarily analyzed into three different features, which parallel to some extent, but do not exactly coincide with, the physical features described before (wave length, amplitude, and complexity). The three corresponding psychological functions and terms describing them are: hue, brilliance, and saturation. We shall describe these three aspects of visual response separately, but we must first distinguish between chromatic and achromatic responses.

a. *Achromatic stimuli.* The normal human subject is said to be able to discriminate 570 different steps or stages of gray, ranging in a continuum from black to white. Physically, *black* is the absence of light of any kind, but in terms of discriminated response, black is a definite and positive reaction. It is almost impossible to obtain an object which will be described as "pure black" because all *seen* objects reflect or generate some light or they would not be seen. Black velvet is as nearly perfect a black as we can perceive because it consists of, in effect, a series of holes tied together. Blackboards are not black in the physical sense, as can be observed by placing a piece of black velvet on a blackboard, which then looks gray by contrast. A convenient way of describing achromatic responses is in terms of scales of gray, such as that of Hering, or in terms of the proportions of black and white that must be combined on a color mixer to elicit a judgment of "equal" from the subjects involved.

b. *Chromatic stimuli.* Chromatic, or "color," responses are difficult to describe exactly because a complete description involves a consideration of all three psychological functions (hue, brilliance, and saturation). There are about 300,000 discriminable combinations of these variables, and this makes any attempt to list all of the chromatic responses virtually impossible. Any particular chromatic response, however, can be identified as having a scale position in each of the continua mentioned. In the practical world of paint manufacturers, one company advertises 1000 different colors, or about 0.3 of 1 percent of all those possible.

c. *Hue.* "Hue" is a more correct term for "color" as the latter term is generally used, and refers to some position on the visible-spectrum scale. There are as many hues as there are discriminable spectrum steps. Boring (2) states that 156 different hues can be distinguished around a "color circle." Most texts illustrate hues as if they were arranged on a circle formed by joining the red and violet ends of the spectrum. If we remember that this is merely a convenient way of representing certain principles of color functions, we can accept the circle, keeping in mind always that the actual spectrum array consists of wave lengths from 380–780 mμ.

Names of hues often cause difficulty because of a wide variety of terms introduced by painters, stylists, and paint manufacturers. It is safer experimentally to describe a hue in wave length, than by any special color name. The following table presents some common usages:

Color (hue) names and corresponding wave-lengths *

Hue	Wave-length
Red	from end of the visible spectrum to about 660 mμ
Orange	from about 660 mμ to 590 mμ
Yellow	580 mμ
Yellow-green	from about 560 mμ to 525 mμ
Green	510 mμ
Blue-green	from about 510 mμ to 480 mμ
Blue	476 mμ
Reddish blues	from about 476 mμ to 435 mμ
Violet	from end of the visible spectrum to about 435 mμ

* These values are reported in: Boring, E. G., Langfeld, H. S., and Weld, H. P. *The foundations of psychology.* New York: John Wiley and Sons, 1948.

d. *Brilliance.* This feature of color refers to that response aspect which depends upon the amount or intensity of light reflected by an object and upon the visual angle. It is measured in terms of a position on a scale ranging from *dark* to *light,* usually arranged in connection with a series of grays such as described for measuring achromatic stimuli (see above). The term "brilliance" should be distinguished from "brightness." The former refers to a response function, the latter to a physical characteristic of a stimulus.

Brilliance is often referred to by artists as "value" or "tint" (light) and "shade" (dark). The terms "tint" and "shade" are commonly misused in ordinary conversation and should be used with caution.

e. *Brilliance and hue.* Any hue, then, can be considered as having a certain degree of brilliance, depending upon the scale position of gray that it matches. A convenient (though impractical) way of thinking of brilliance might be as follows: Suppose that you start mixing black and white paint or inks in a series of test tubes. Into the first tube pour 1 cc. of white, 9 of black; into the second pour 2 cc. of white, 8 of black, etc. When you reach the fifth tube, you will have half of each, and a hypothetical neutral gray. (Actually paints and inks do not function in this fashion, and the half-and-half mixture will be very black; the 1 cc. of white will have no appreciable effect on the 9 cc. of black either.) A hue that matches this neutral gray by subjective estimate can be described as neutral in brilliance. A hue matching a combination with more white is more brilliant, one matching a mixture with more black is less brilliant, or darker. In practical painting, or in color mixing by use of colored papers, the brilliance can be heightened by adding white, and decreased by adding black. This procedure, however, results in a change in saturation, which we shall consider next.

f. *Saturation.* Saturation of color is sometimes called "chroma" and refers to the richness of hue present, or its relative purity or freedom from mixture with other hues or gray. To understand saturation, think of your tube of neutral gray, and take a bottle of ink of some hue, say red. Assuming the latter to be pure spectral red, add 1 cc. of your neutral gray to 9 cc. of red. You have now cut the saturation 0.1. Add 2 cc. of gray to 8 of red, and you cut saturation by 0.2. As you add more gray, you get less and less red, until you wind up with neutral gray. In this procedure we do not alter the brilliance if it is assumed that a completely saturated (pure hue) has the brilliance of neutral gray.

Now do the same for any other mixture of black and white and your red. If you add a lighter gray to your red by similar stages, you will wind up with a lighter gray, systematically cutting saturation. It is easier to think of adding hue to the gray if you are working above or below neutral gray, because as you use lighter or darker grays you find that you cannot distinguish as many degrees of saturation as you add gray. If you add even a small amount of a very light gray, you cut the saturation much more than at the neutral level; the same holds for the dark end. Adding a small amount of black immediately decreases the saturation so much that not many stages of change in saturation can be detected. The "color" rapidly becomes black.

To go further into the problems involved in visual experimentation would take us beyond the scope of this work and would involve us in a consideration of content and theory which is adequately covered in the standard references listed below. The student would do well to pursue a glossary of visual terminology prepared by Brennan, Burnham, and Newhall (3) before attempting serious reading in the literature on vision.

A Partial List of Variables in Visual Experimentation

In the eye (monocular and/or binocular):
1. Adaptation level.
2. Visual acuity.
3. Visual defects
    a. Myopia, astigmatism, etc.

     b. Color weakness, degree and kind.

     c. Efficiency of convergence and accommodation.

  4. Pupil size.

  5. Retinal area under study (color zones, blind spot, fovea—cone or rod vision).

  6. Possible autokinetic phenomena, afterimages, induction effects.

In the stimulus and surrounds:

  1. Nature, size, steadiness, distance, and position of fixation point.

  2. Maintenance of fixation point (head, chin, eyelid rests).

  3. Hue, brightness, and saturation of target or "test object" and of surrounds.

  4. Time of exposure (duration of stimulus).

  5. Possible non-visual factors facilitating or inhibiting the reaction to the visual stimulus.

References

1. Bartley, S. H. *Vision: a study of its basis.* New York: D. Van Nostrand. 1941.
2. Boring, E. G. *Psychology for the armed services.* Washington: The Infantry Journal. 1945.
3. Brennan, J., Burnham, R., and Newhall, S. Color terms and definitions. *Psychol. Bull.,* 1948, *45,* 207–230.
4. Hecht, S. Vision: II, The nature of the photoreceptor process. In *Handbook of General Experimental Psychology,* C. Murchison, ed. Worcester, Massachusetts: Clark University Press. 1934.
5. Woodworth, R. S. *Experimental psychology.* New York: Henry Holt. 1938.

Experiment 8. Vision I: The Blind Spot; Monocular Vision

Introduction. At the place in each eye where the optic nerve leaves the retina there are no receptor cells for vision and consequently no vision. These areas of no vision are known as "blind spots." In the eye they are as large as the area of the optic nerve (about 1½ mm.²). We fail to see any object the light from which falls on these areas.

The extent of visual area to which we are blind depends upon the distance of the object from the eye. Thus, at a suitable distance, we might not see an elephant, a truck, or a building, if the light from such objects was falling on the blind-spot area. We do not usually miss such objects because we normally look at objects with both eyes, and since the blind spots are not at corresponding points on our retinas, what is missed by one eye is picked up by the other. By keeping our eyes in motion we also manage to direct the light from our blind-spot area onto the *fovea centralis* or other nonblind areas.

So well do we handle our visual apparatus that, as a matter of fact, very few people ever discover that they have blind areas in each eye. Our own present interest lies not in the problem of blind spots so much as in learning about the nature of visual projection and in becoming acquainted with the concept of visual angle as a measure of the size of objects. The blind spot offers a convenient means of fulfilling these experimental needs.

Apparatus and Procedure The apparatus consists of a headrest (see Figure 6), an eyeshield, an object to serve as a fixation point (say a tack), a target stimulus (this can be a black dot ¼ inch in diameter on the end of a paper wand), and a sheet of paper.

1. Arrange the subject in the headrest. On the wall at a distance of 50 cm., in front of and on a level with the subject's left eye, place the fixation point.

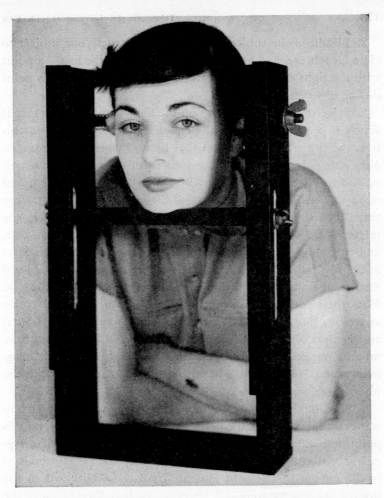

FIGURE 6. *A SIMPLE CHIN AND HEAD REST.* The position of the head must often be made constant for certain kinds of observations. The head rest pictured illustrates one type of arrangement. The thumb-screws at the sides are adjusted to keep the head steady. The head sides of the screws are padded. The chin piece is adjustable for different lengths of heads. In use, a C-clamp would hold the head rest securely to the table. Since the upper jaw is a fixed part of the head, and consequently moves with it, some stabilizers are constructed so as to utilize this principle. To stabilize the head, then, subjects rest their upper teeth on a "biting board" (tongue depressors serve well) fixed in a desired position.

177

2. Blindfold the subject's left eye, or instruct your subject to close his left eye, and have him look straight at the fixation point with the right eye. He should never move his eye from this point during observations.

3. Place your target stimulus on the fixation point and move it slowly in a straight line to the right. At some point along this line, the subject should report that he no longer sees the target. Note this point and now place your sheet of paper on the wall so that its center covers this point. Repeat your observation and mark the point of disappearance of the target on the sheet. Continue in a straight line, and the subject will report seeing the target again. Mark this point. Join the two points with a line, and run a light pencil line vertically through the middle. Start at the mid-point of this line and slowly move the wand upward first, then downward, until the subject reports seeing the dot. Mark these points and join them vertically. You will now have an approximation of the center of your blind spot with horizontal and vertical bisectors. Bisect each angle formed by these horizontal and vertical lines, and you will have eight radii of an imaginary circle. Number these in order from 1 to 8, starting with the top of the center vertical.

4. Start at the center of your circle and move the target outward on radius 1. Note the point of appearance. Start beyond this point and come in toward the center. Mark the point of disappearance. Repeat for each of the radii. Keep the points obtained in the outward movement separate from those obtained in the inward movement. Repeat 5 times for each radius. Measure the distance of each point and enter these figures in Table 15.

5. Move the subject to a distance of 100 cm. and repeat the above procedure.

Results

1. Plot on graph paper the outlines of the blind spot ("means" of 5 readings at each radius) obtained at each *distance* (for this, use only the "going-out" readings). Plot the two spots in

Table 15. *The Projected Sizes of the Blind Spot at 50 cm. and at 100 cm. as Measured along 8 Radii from an Approximated Center*

(Readings were taken from the center out, and from beyond the boundary toward the center.)

Readings	Radii															
	1		2		3		4		5		6		7		8	
	in	out	in	out	in	out	in	out	in	out	in	out	in	out	in	out
At 50 cm. 1																
2																
3																
4																
5																
Mean																
At 100 cm. 1																
2																
3																
4																
5																
Mean																

terms of their distance to the right of the fixation point and in terms of their location above or below that point.

2. Plot the outlines of the blind spots obtained at 1 m. in terms of the "means" of each 5 readings for the "in" and for the "out" procedures. Note: Should you discard single readings that are at marked variance with the others? Why?

Discussion

1. Account for your results. Which blind spots are larger? Does position, direction, and size change with the distance of the fixation point or with the direction (in or out) of the target?

2. What would be the diameter of the blind visual area at two meters? 1000 meters?

3. What difficulties did you experience in obtaining your results? Can you account for any irregularities in the shape of the spot as it was "projected"?

4. How "big" was the blind spot you plotted?

5. What sources of error did you control? What sources were left uncontrolled?

References

1. Dennis, Wayne. *Readings in the history of psychology*. New York: Appleton-Century-Crofts. 1948 (chapter by Mariotte).

Experiment 9. Vision II: Depth Perception; Binocular Vision

Introduction. The problems of vision expand enormously as soon as we transfer attention from monocular to binocular vision. We immediately meet the fact of binocular parallax (the fact that the image on the retina of each eye is slightly different from that on the other). Because the right eye sees a little more of the right side of an object, and the left eye a little more of the left side, we are faced with the question of how two separate views result in the impression of a single object with depth and position in space. Although this question is an old one, there are still no good answers to it, and today it continues to command considerable attention. The results of the study of binocular parallax and its consequences (retinal disparity) have had wide application in the recent war in a variety of problems where depth perception was involved (range finding, mapping, flight training).

Apparatus and Procedure. Only simple equipment is necessary to provide examples of retinal disparity for study. The subject sits with his head in a chin rest and fixates a truncated wire pyramid (small end toward the subject) set on a level with his eyes at a distance of 100 cm. He closes one eye at a time and views the pyramid with the other. On a previously prepared form he draws the apparent position of the small end of the wire pyramid. The view with the right eye is indicated in the right square; that with the left eye in the left square. The lines connecting the corners are then drawn in, and the two figures inked. The card is then viewed in both a Brewster stereoscope and a Wheatstone stereoscope (the latter made by the student) and the observations recorded. Additional observations are made by reversing the images presented to the two eyes in both stereoscopes. The experimenter will also describe his observations in viewing 5 standard stereoscope slides as well as 5 slides personally manufactured for use in his Wheatstone type of stereoscope.

Instructions for preparing the stereoscope slide. (1.) On a
$7\frac{1}{2} \times 3\frac{1}{2}''$ card draw a line half way from the top of card
across its length. Place a dot $1\frac{1}{2}''$ from the right end of the line
and $1\frac{1}{2}''$ from the other end. Place dots $1\frac{3}{4}''$ nearer the center
from each of the first dots. Erect perpendiculars from each of

FIGURE 7. *A TRUNCATED PYRAMID.* The pyramid shown is easily constructed by shaping pieces
of wire into a small and a larger square. The
corners of the two squares are then joined with
four short lengths of wire. Each joint is secured
with a drop of solder. The pyramid is then
mounted on a rigid support. The model shown is
mounted on a rod which fits into a tube where a
set-screw can hold the rod at the desired height,
although this is not an essential feature. The as-
sembly of such a truncated pyramid provides a
satisfactory introduction to the art of soldering
for the uninitiated.

the four dots so that they extend $\frac{7}{8}''$ above and $\frac{7}{8}''$ below
the line. Connect the two right-hand perpendiculars at top and
bottom and do the same with the two left-hand perpendiculars,
thus forming two squares $1\frac{3}{4}''$ in size, whose adjacent sides
are $1''$ apart.

2. Make 5 additional cards of a similar nature with the following
   items, one on the right and one on the left side: (a) vertical
   and horizontal line; (b) small circle and larger circle; (c) blue

FIGURE 8. *A WHEATSTONE STEREOSCOPE.* Many arrangements are possible to secure the desired results. All that is essential is to mount two small mirrors (ladies' handbags are excellent sources) at 90° to each other. The mounting can be achieved simply, with adhesive tape or, more permanently, by grooving slots in a wooden base. Some method of holding the stereoscope cards must be devised, and for this the only essential is that it be possible to bring the cards into line with the mirror faces. If a wooden block is used to mount the mirrors, then side arms can be pivoted on this block to provide for swinging the inspection material into focus. A sliding card holder can be mounted on each side arm if this refinement is desired.

square and red square; (d) diagonal lines slanting in opposite directions; (e) two numbers and two letters. For use in your Wheatstone stereoscope, cut the cards in two.

Instructions for making the Wheatstone stereoscope. The diagram in Woodworth (2), pp. 655–656, is sufficiently clear to enable the student to arrange his apparatus (see Figure 8). Basically, only two small hand mirrors are required. These should be mounted on some support at 90° to each other. Two projecting arms with carriers for holding the slides are then attached. The arms should be free to swing. The carriers' distance should be adjustable.

Results. Submit drawings of your stereoscopic views and descriptions of their appearance in the stereoscopes. What happens when you reverse the views of each eye?

Discussion

1. What variables and sources of error did you observe, control, or fail to control in this experiment?
2. What other indications are used in the perception of depth besides binocular vision?
3. How is the perception of distance related to depth perception?
4. Would you approve of driver's or pilot's licenses for people with only monocular vision?

References

1. Postman, L., and Egan, J. P. *Experimental psychology*. New York: Appleton-Century-Crofts. 1949, chap. 9.
2. Woodworth, R. S. *Experimental psychology*. New York: Henry Holt. 1938, chap. 26.

Experiment 10. Vision III: Color Mixture *

Introduction. The early researches of Thomas Young and James Maxwell established the fact that any part of the spectrum can be matched by projecting on a white surface suitable proportions of any three widely separated monochromatic lights. According to Evans (1) this fact is the foundation for our basic knowledge of the color sensitivity of the eye. From this fundamental fact as a starting point, certain additional important generalizations concerning color vision have developed. These generalizations are variously known as color laws or color rules, and in one form or other they cover the following observations listed by Evans:

1. The mixture of any two wave lengths of light will give rise to a color falling between the two in the spectrum, except at the extreme ends, where they form a series of purples related to the extreme short-wave-length colors (around 400 in the region known as violet). The exact wave length matched varies with the relative intensity of the two, being continuous from one to the other as the percentage varies from 0 to 100.
2. There is a whole series of pairs of monochromatic lights which, when mixed, will give white light. These pairs are called the complementary wave lengths.
3. There are no complementary wave lengths for the central region of the spectrum (the greens).
4. Any known color may be matched by light of a single wave length mixed with white light, with the exception of the colors which we call "purple" or "magenta."
5. Those colors which cannot be matched by monochromatic plus white light may all be made into white light by the addition of some line from the green spectral region (i.e., they are all complementary to some spectral region).

---

* This experiment is slightly modified from one described in a mimeographed manual used at Brown University, entitled "Experimental Demonstrations in Psychology."

In the experiment to follow, some implications of these laws have been restated into hypotheses for you to verify.

Apparatus and Procedure. The statements listed above refer to mixtures of lights and apply primarily only to such methods of mixture. In your own experiment you will be able only to approximate the required conditions, as you will use colored paper discs rotated rapidly by a color mixer to represent the colored lights. The procedure you will follow is known as color mixing by addition, in contrast to color mixing you may have done with pigments; the latter type of mixing is known as subtraction of colors. In working out the suggested hypotheses you will use large and small discs of colored papers, interlocking these on the color mixer in the manner already familiar to you from Experiment 6. The specific procedures and hypotheses to be tested follow:

Hypothesis 1: An achromatic mixture (white or gray) may be obtained from complementary colors in the proper proportions. E selects a large yellow disk and a large blue one and interlocks them for rotation on the wheel. Interlock a small white disk with a small black one and place them over the blue and yellow disks on the wheel. E adjusts the wheel so that it is illuminated by the electric light overhead and is *not* illuminated by light from the window. E rotates the wheel rapidly enough so that S, seated as far as is convenient from the wheel, reports a fusion of the colors. E changes proportions of yellow and blue, under the direction of S, until finally an achromatic mixture of the two is reported. Then the proportions of the small white and black disks are adjusted until the mixture matches the yellow-blue one as closely as possible. At this point E changes places with S in order to verify the match for his own eyes. If the match is satisfactory to both partners, the amounts of yellow and blue, and those of black and white, are entered into the equations for hypothesis 1 in the space provided below for

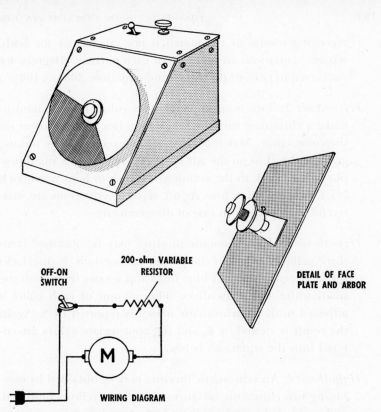

OFF-ON
SWITCH

200-ohm VARIABLE
RESISTOR

DETAIL OF FACE
PLATE AND ARBOR

M

WIRING DIAGRAM

FIGURE 9. *AN INEXPENSIVE COLOR MIXER.* The essential features
of a color mixer are: a motor with a speed control (rheostat) and an
arbor for holding disks of colored paper in place while they rotate.
The disks have a slit from center to circumference so that they can be
interlocked. As shown here, a small motor (F. A. Smith Mfg. Co.,
Rochester, N. Y. Pilot 59-A) is mounted at a slight angle on a wooden
box frame which provides the necessary stability. The shaft of the
motor protrudes through the box face plate. An arbor is attached to
the motor shaft with a set-screw. The 200 ohm variable resistor controls
the speed of rotation from a very low r.p.m. up to a speed high enough
to overcome flicker. The simple wiring diagram shows the necessary
connections. The whole apparatus can be built for under $5.00.

When using the mixer, the operator must be sure to interlock the
disks so that the exposed edge travels in the direction of rotation. If desired, a neutral background screen can be mounted between the face
plate and the arbor.

187

recording results. If the match is not satisfactory for both, separate equations are written for each partner. (Degrees are converted to percent for the second equation: $360° = 100\%$.)

Hypothesis 2: Two noncomplementary colors may be used to make a chromatic mixture whose hue lies between them on the color circle. Match a large yellow-green disk by mixing green and yellow on the wheel. If necessary, add a small proportion of black to the yellow-green disk to help you match brightness as well as hue. Again, separate equations are written for each partner in case of disagreement.

Hypothesis 3: An achromatic mixture may be obtained from three primary colors in the proper proportions. E interlocks the large red, green and blue disks and rotates them with the small white and black disks. The amount of each color is adjusted until an achromatic match is reported by S. Again the result is viewed by E, and the appropriate values are entered into the equations below.

Hypothesis 4: An achromatic mixture may be obtained by combining two chromatic mixtures. The large yellow, blue, red, and green disks used in procedures 1 and 3 above are now adjusted on the wheel so that each is in the same *proportion* (but half the total *amount*) as in the original achromatic mixture (i.e., 180° of the new mixture is made up of yellow and blue in the same proportion as in procedure 1, while the remaining 180° consists of red, green, and blue in the same proportions as in procedure 3). The same blue disk provides the necessary amounts of blue for both parts. Now the small black and white disks are used to match the new mixture. Complete equations, as before.

Hypothesis 5: An unknown color may be matched by an unsaturated mixture of three primary colors in the proper proportions. E places a small disk of a relatively unsaturated "unknown" color (with black added) over the large disks of red, green, blue and white. S obtains a match, and the amounts are measured as before. Again E makes a separate match and equation if necessary.

Results

Hypothesis 1. Achromatic mixture of complementaries.
..... ° B + ... ° Y = ... ° white + ... ° black
..... % B + ... % Y = ... % white + ... % black

Hypothesis 2. Chromatic mixture of noncomplementaries.
Yellow-green color = ... ° G + ... ° Y + ... ° black

Hypothesis 3. Achromatic mixture of primaries.
..... ° R + ... ° G + ° B = ... ° white + ...
° black
..... % R + ... % G + % B = ... % white + ...
% black

Hypothesis 4. Achromatic mixture of achromatic mixtures.
..... ° R + ... ° G + ... ° Y + ... ° B = ...
° black + ... ° white
..... % R + ... % G + ... % Y + ... % B =
..... % black + ... % white

Hypothesis 5. Equation for a given color, X.
X = ... ° R + ... ° G + ... ° B + ... ° white
X = ... % R + ... % G + ... % B + ...
% white

Discussion

Complete the following sentences:
1. Complementary colors are ....
....
....

2. Primary colors are ....
....
....

3. Matching an unknown color by a mixture of three primaries
   has the following significance for three-color processes of print-
   ing and photography: ....
....
....
....

4. Brightness is ....
....

5. Saturation is ....
....

6. You add black to a monochromatic stimulus when seeking a
   match with a mixture because ....
....

References

1. Evans, Ralph M. *An introduction to color*. New York: Wiley.
   1948.
2. Postman, L., and Egan, J. P. *Experimental psychology*. New
   York: Appleton-Century-Crofts. 1949, chap. 7.
3. Woodworth, R. S. *Experimental psychology*. New York: Henry
   Holt. 1938.

10

Experimentation in Audition

THE STUDY of auditory phenomena is an extremely complicated pursuit and involves a high degree of technical specialization, especially in the use of electronic devices. Like the subject of vision, audition presents problems that can be approached from the viewpoints of physicists, physiologists, and psychologists. Possibly no other problem shows more clearly the interdependency of the allegedly different sciences. Some psychologists (at least, they are members of university psychology departments) spend many of their working hours stimulating the eighth nerve of a carp and recording the neural action currents that result. One such psychologist was asked, "What's a psychologist doing that kind of work for?" His reply was, "I don't care what they call me. There's a problem, and somebody's got to work on it. If someone wants to call me a 'physiologist,' let him."

To do justice to the complications involved in the study of audition in a general course in experimental psychology is impossible. We can at best hope to indicate the breadth of the problems and some of the methods involved in approaching them. A convenient way of considering the several aspects of audition is to examine the three traditional approaches of physics, physiology, and psychology, even though we do not accept such a breakdown as in any sense genuine. As a matter of fact, we shall find ourselves unable to keep the discussion on any one of these levels without getting involved with the others.

The Physics of Sound

What is the nature of the physical stimulus that results in a "hearing" response? The average psychology text presents the answer in terms of a questionable analogy. We are taught that sound is a form of wave energy or wave motion. This definition is generally accompanied by a drawing of a cyclical, two-dimensional wave with a crest and trough.* Any such notion of sound is misleading and only bewilders students as they get involved in the future development of the subject.

Actually, instead of being pictured as such a transverse wave, sound may better be considered as made up of alternate compressions and rarefactions of the molecules of some suitable medium. Such condensations and rarefactions should be thought of as taking place only on a longitudinal plane, and not on a transverse one. The longitudinal alternations of the medium are further to be considered as occurring in concentric shells, which expand into the surrounding medium as they leave the source. The concentric shells advance through the medium with diminishing intensity (energy), which varies inversely with the square of the distance. The speed of the advance varies with the medium and the temperature. (Speed of sound in air at 0° C. = 1087 ft. per sec. In a classroom at 22° C. sound travels about 1130 ft. per sec. The speed of sound increases 2 ft. per sec. with every degree centigrade rise in temperature.)

The alternations of condensation and rarefaction in the air, which are our chief interest, are produced by the periodic movement or vibration of any body free to oscillate or vibrate when set into motion by the transfer to that body of energy from some source. The rapidity of the alternations is generally a characteristic of the vibrating object, and is spoken of as its "natural period" or natural "frequency." The frequency of vibration is one

* Actually such a curve represents a plot of pressure in terms of time and distance, and is of value for various kinds of measurements; it is of little value, however, for showing a student what a sound wave "looks like."

way of characterizing a sound. If the frequency is small, we speak of a low "pitch." If it is great, we speak of the sound as "high." We will return to "pitch" in the next section. We mention it now to indicate the impossibility of separating the discussion of the "physics" and the "psychology" of sound. Even the physics texts do not always attempt to do so.

In connection with vision we found that light is measurable in wave lengths. Sound can also be measured in terms of the longitudinal distance to which any single compression and rarefaction of the medium extends. Thus each vibration of a tuning fork vibrating 256 times per second compresses the air in a room at 72° F. for a distance of about 4 feet. The length of any wave from the crest of one to the crest of the next can be calculated by dividing the speed of sound by the frequency of the vibration. It is assumed that after the object has been vibrating for one second, the compressions and rarefactions have traveled 1130 feet by the process of systematically agitating successive sections of the intervening air. If the object is still sounding at the end of 1 second, it is assumed that the space is filled with 256 lengths of such disturbances, each about 4 feet long. Because the speed varies with the medium and the temperature, it is safer to describe sound in terms of the frequency of vibration, which presumably does not vary.

It is practically impossible to produce pure sounds, because sound, as a form of energy, sets objects in the environment into vibration. Such objects include not only our ear drums but also walls, tables, and other furniture, which in turn reinforce the original sound. Such "forced" vibrations result in a complication of the vibrations reaching the ear and make basic research in sound to a large extent a problem of eliminating the environment. In addition to the "forced" vibrations, and more importantly, there are *reflections* of the original sound from many surfaces, sometimes from many different angles and with different efficiencies, resulting in a complex sound pattern from a relatively simple source. The Bell Telephone Company has spent a small fortune in designing a laboratory which, in effect, amounts to a room without a floor, walls, or ceiling, at least as far as "reflection" of sound is concerned. They did this by an ingenious arrangement of sound-absorbing materials, which project into the room at various angles and to different distances, so that sound is absorbed and not reflected. In such a room a speaker hears his own voice as "pure" sound for the first time, and even this purity is violated by the resonance complications initiated in the ear mechanisms, which themselves alter the characteristics of sound waves. The alternative to using such a room as described above is to work high in the sky without visible or, at least, sound-reflecting means of support. Sound reflection and reverberation (irregular and repeated reflection) are the chief sources of error in many varieties of auditory study, and a minimum prerequisite for even noncritical work is a good sound-absorbing room which is also "shielded" from external sound sources. (A "sound-proof" room is a figure of speech, and not a reality, with the possible exception of such a room as described above.)

The reflections from the environment are not the only sources of confusion of the sound vibrations. The vibrating objects themselves vibrate, not only as a whole, but also in parts. The vibration of the whole is identified as the *fundamental* frequency, and the sectional vibrations are called "harmonics." These sectional vibrations result in a complex number and variety of periodic compressions and rarefactions of different intensities, and provide what is called the "timbre" or "quality" of the sound. They are responsible for the individual differences or characteristics of sounding bodies and enable us to recognize a particular voice, musical instrument, dog, or auto horn.

The intensity of a sound is the third feature for us to consider. This is not to be identified with "loudness," which is an individual matter, and which varies with the pitch as well as with the efficiency of our ears. Intensity in physical terms is a matter of energy or pressure. Pressure is usually measured in dynes per cm². To measure sound in dynes, however is not meaningful, since the basic question of interest is one involving a human listener, and his reactions do not keep pace with pressure increases as direct functions. In other words, doubling the pressure, for example, does not double the loudness.

A convenient way of representing the intensity of a sound is in terms of decibels. Decibels are mathematical ratios relating the intensity of one sound to another. One decibel represents a ratio 1:1.13, or a 13 percent increase in intensity of one sound over another. The commonly accepted arbitrary "zero" for sound pressure is 0.0002 dyne/cm². * One decibel is 13 percent more than this. Two decibels are 13 percent more than the result of the previous addition of 13 percent to the zero level, and so on. In more socially useful terms, we have to reach a level of 40 to 60 decibels to be able to hear conversation easily; 40 decibels are enough for whispers. The top limit is about 120 decibels. After that the intensity is so great as to be painful.

Some texts present descriptions of decibels as if they were equivalent to J. N. D.'s or the Weber fraction. While this type of presentation may help the student appreciate the ratio feature of the decibel, it is not accurate, as one decibel is not a "just noticeable difference." The Weber fraction for sound intensity varies greatly, depending upon pitch and loudness, but it is about $\frac{1}{5}$, or 20 percent, while the decibel is a fraction representing differences in intensity of only 13 percent. The decibel, thus, is little more than $\frac{1}{2}$ of a just noticeable difference.

The Physiology of Hearing

The experimental approach to the physiological aspects of hearing can receive only sketchy attention here, because the study of hearing in relation to the anatomy and physiology of the ear is quite beyond the possibilities of an elementary laboratory course.

In general, the physiological approach relates the physical as-

---

* This is an arbitrary base, and any other, say that of normal conversational speech, might be taken as a base. The choice of base depends on the problem.

pects of sound stimuli to the structure of the ear, especially to the cochlea and its structures, and to the auditory nerve. The most useful procedures thus far developed consist of: (1) attaching recording devices (including powerful amplifiers) to the cochlea or auditory nerve, and recording the action currents that result when the ear is stimulated; (2) destroying sections of the cochlea, either by surgically obliterating or removing them, or by exposing experimental animals to prolonged tones. The animals are then studied by noting their reactions to tones to which they were previously conditioned, or by examination of damage done to the cochlea at autopsy. Such observations as that of the "cochlear microphonic" effect have been described as a consequence of the first method. The second procedure has led to the discovery of tonal islands and gaps, presumably related to damaged fibers on the basilar membrane.

Recent studies of electrical activity in parts of the body other than the ear indicate that muscular action currents can be recorded when a subject is exposed to a tone. Davis,* for example, has recorded such currents from the arm when the subject was instructed simply to listen and make no movements. What the significance of such findings is has not yet been established, but it is clear that investigators of auditory phenomena are turning to the response aspects of hearing, and are no longer limiting themselves to the ear.

The student planning research in the physiology of hearing will have to acquire an appreciation of electronic equipment, especially amplification and recording systems, some surgical skill, thorough grounding in the neural anatomy of his experimental subjects, and in addition a practical familiarity with conditioning procedures commonly used for testing purposes. Only the last of these factors will receive treatment in this course. The others, as is obvious, require additional courses and special preparation.

* Davis, R. C. Motor effects of auditory stimuli. *J. exp. Psychol.*, 1948, *38*, 257–275.

The Psychology of Sound

The experimental approach of psychologists to hearing has resulted in the isolation of a number of problems which overlap the areas of physics, mathematics, aesthetics, and communication, as well as physiology. In this section we shall point out some of the special problems and procedures that have interested psychologists.

Auditory acuity. How weak a sound can you hear? How strong must a sound be before it begins to hurt? How low a sound can you hear? How high a sound can you hear? These are questions of acuity and of thresholds. Much auditory experimentation depends on accurate determination of such absolute or "terminal" and difference thresholds, and a great deal of practical communication and personal pleasure depend on the acuity of your ears. How much of an orchestral concert can you actually hear? For many older members in a concert audience, some of the musicians may often be wasting their time, as there is an extensive loss of hearing for high tones with advancing age. The modern, scarcely noticeable, "hearing aid" has replaced the ear trumpet, but the large sales volume, if not the number of visible trumpets, gives evidence of this common human failing. A young person with normal ears can hear tones from around 16 or 20 c.p.s. to 16,000 or 20,000 c.p.s. He will hear these tones with different efficiencies, however, depending on the loudness. The low and high tones require greater intensity to be heard effectively.

Equipment for the usual methods of threshold measurement of pitch includes audiometers of various types for normal hearing ranges, beat-frequency oscillators for pitch values throughout the hearing range, lamellas for lower frequencies, and specially constructed air columns (Galton whistles) for the higher pitches. A variety of relatively simple measurements of auditory acuity in terms of intensity can be made by finding the greatest distance at

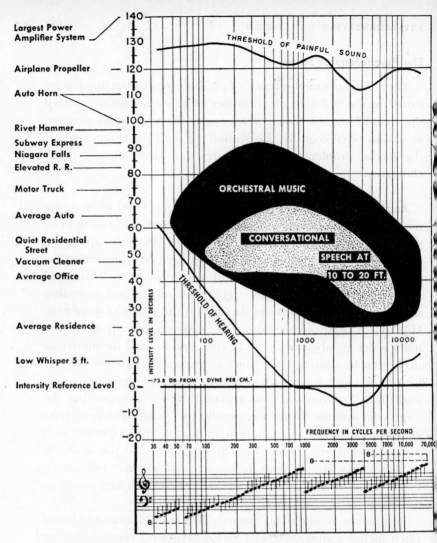

1. Can be only partially helped by most powerful vacuum tube aid. Some cases total loss. 2. Severe cases of hearing loss requiring most powerful vacuum tube hearing aids. 3. Cannot carry on normal sound life without aid. 4. Should be fitted with aid. Loss severe enough to affect speech in time. 5. Handicap experienced. Occasional use of aid. 6. Hearing loss begins to be noticed.

FIGURE 10. *RANGE OF HUMAN HEARING*. Note the horizontal units (frequency in cycles per second) are not equally spaced. Note changes in threshold values with changes in frequency. (Courtesy of *Radio Today*.)

which a ticking watch or clicking coins can be heard, or by using small weights (e.g., buckshot) which are dropped from various heights onto a sounding plate.

Timbre. The complexities introduced into the pattern of pressure impulses by overtones or harmonics provide what is described as the "quality" of the sound. Sound quality is of considerable special interest to musicians and listeners to music, and it also represents a special technical problem for telephone and radio manufacturers who strive to reproduce the quality of musical instruments and of the human voice. The highest overtones of musical instruments are not faithfully reproduced by the average radio or telephone. Even the overtones of the voice, especially those involved in the diphthongs (like *oi, ou, ai*), the sibillants (like *f, s, sh, th, v*), and the sound *ee*, are difficult to transmit by telephone. The overtones in radio communication became a major problem in communication between pilots and radio towers during the recent war. Special languages had to be developed which included words of high "communicability value." The same problems were important in the training of pilots and tank crews, where intercommunication was difficult due to the "masking" noise of the engines. Some military psychologists were detailed to research on microphones and speech transmission; others became teachers of speech and microphone technique. The problems are by no means solved, and such concerns as the Bell Telephone Company are engaged in extensive research programs whose central problem is "timbre."

Timbre is of interest to physiologists because of the complications in neural patterns and in the movements of the structures of the ear, especially of the basilar membrane, that must be postulated to account for the discrimination of sounds. The problem is even more complicated by the finding that the cochlea itself adds overtones to supposedly "pure" sounds without harmonics of their own. From the physical viewpoint (and this requires some physiological explanation) the problems of sound become enormously complicated by the introduction of one additional tone when a tone of different pitch is sounding. If the frequency of the new tone is close to that of the other (having less than 30 vibrations difference), the two tones alternately reinforce and counteract each other, so that "beats" result. At greater frequency separations, the two tones produce a third tone which has the frequency of the difference between the two originals (this is a "difference tone"). In addition to the difference tone, the two tones may produce a fourth tone which has the frequency of the sum of the two originals, or a summation tone." The student will readily appreciate the difficulties that emerge in trying to define his stimulus when he is using even what he considers a pure tone.

The relative pleasantness or unpleasantness, or the "consonance" of tones, is another timbre problem which has received considerable attention. "Noise" is usually described as a complicated pattern of aperiodic vibrations. The mathematical analysis of consonant and dissonant musical combinations or chords is of special interest to some investigators. This type of investigation has been approached from the viewpoints of mathematical analysis and of culture, some investigators claiming that the culture determines what will be called "pleasant" or "consonant."

Localization of sounds. It is not commonly appreciated by the layman that sounds, by themselves, are poorly localized in both spatial direction and distance. We make so much use of our eyes and of information from other sources concerning the quality of sounds and the location of their producers that we rarely appreciate the fact that sounds from above or from below, or from in front or from behind us, are almost impossible to localize without other cues. To investigate the problems of localization some device must be employed which can present to a subject an auditory stimulus from various angles in relation to the planes of the head. A "sound cage" is such a device.

To make it possible for us to determine on what basis a subject localizes sounds coming from both right and left, it is necessary to be able to control three aspects of sounds: their intensity, phase, and time of arrival at each ear. A device which provides for the control of these variables can be arranged from telescoping tubes which can be connected to the same or to separate sources. In this way, sounds of different intensities can be sent to the two ears so as to arrive at the same time and in the same phase, i.e., with the same aspect of the wave, e.g., the crest, entering each ear at the same time. Similarly, the other variables can be varied or held constant. A controversy still continues as to which of the three factors is basic in localization. The determination of distances of sounds has not been investigated extensively. The loudness and clearness of tones are considered the basic variables in this connection.

Practical applications. The interests of psychologists in sound have led to investigations of musical talent in terms of acuity tests for pitch, timbre, intensity, rhythm, and other aspects of tones. Studies of "absolute pitch" have resulted in a controversy about the heredity and training variables in regard to this musical accomplishment, some psychologists claiming that even "tone-deaf" individuals can be trained to have "absolute pitch." * Other psychologists have entered the area of musical appreciation and have developed tests in which selections from the masters are played (in random order), both in the original form, and then with some variation of harmony, melody, or rhythm. The listener reports which he prefers, and his score is based on the number of times he is able to recognize the original and the nature of the variation. Progress in this aesthetic area has been limited.

A practical problem of great importance is the relation of noise to efficiency. The degree to which noises "mask" sounds which are meant to be heard has already been alluded to in the discussion of the problems of communication. The study of efficiency is in itself a vastly complicated problem, and the introduction of a noise

* Neu, D. M. A critical review of the literature on "absolute pitch." *Psychol. Bull.*, 1947, *44*, 249–266.

variable creates an experimental situation involving so many variables as to preclude any but the most tempered conclusions. A similar situation prevails in studies purporting to show the influence of music on the mood of mental patients, on department-store sales, or on industrial productivity. An appreciation of the variables involved in such research may be obtained by an examination of the Western Electric studies of industrial efficiency.

The variety of problems referred to above should show the student the ramification of the problems involved in the psychology of sound. Our own special interest is in a consideration of the variables or sources of error that should be noted and controlled in investigations of such problems. The following summary list includes only some of the basic variables in auditory experiments (others are specific to the problem under investigation).

The Variables in Auditory Experimentation

In the subject (Acuity of the two ears.):
1. Defects of hearing, tonal gaps, hearing range.
2. Special training or ability, e.g., "absolute pitch."
3. Attention (set) of the subject, e.g., tensor tympani efficiency.
4. Individual differences in thresholds and *D.L.'s* for pitch, intensity, timbre, time, rhythm, and consonance.

In the stimulus, the sound and its source:
1. Number of overtones or harmonics in addition to the fundamental.
2. Presence of beats, difference, summation, and masking tones.
3. Limitations of microphones, ear phones, speakers, and transmission systems, especially for high and low tones.
4. Development of the tonal stimulus (its "attack" and "settle").
5. Differences in time, phase, or intensity of tones in localization studies.
6. Measurement standards (reference level for decibels).

7. Intensity values at different frequencies (the "hearing envelope").
8. Possible complications of a conditioned-response nature (synesthesia).

In the environment (these must still be considered part of the stimulus complex):

1. The acoustical properties of the experimental setting.
   a) Reflection and reverberation.
   b) Absorption efficiency of surroundings.
2. Influence of other stimuli, e.g., light.

References

1. Stevens, S. S., and Davis, H. *Hearing, its psychology and physiology.* New York: Wiley. 1938.
2. Wever, E. G. *Theory of hearing.* New York: Wiley. 1949.

Experiment 11. Audition: The Discrimination of
Pitch and Loudness of Tones

Introduction. The psychological dimensions of sound are those of pitch, loudness, and timbre. Some investigators add a dimension of "volume." The basic dimensions, however, are usually considered to be pitch and loudness; these are the aspects of sound which are most directly involved in auditory theories. The understanding of the auditory mechanism entails an understanding of what it can and cannot do with various frequencies and intensities of a sound stimulus. The lower and upper limits of frequencies and intensities to which responses can be made are presumably set by the auditory apparatus of each organism.

Such terminal thresholds are not the only significant factors: difference limens are just as important. An auditory theory must account for the capacity of the organism to respond discriminatively to the total number of separate frequency-intensity combinations which can initiate separate responses. If an organism, for example, could respond to five separate tones only, then the sense organ involved must be such as to handle just these five. If, on the other hand, it can respond to 100,000 different tones, then the auditory system must be such as to provide for the discriminative reactions to that number. To appreciate the responsibilities of an auditory theory, we must have a knowledge of the total number of separate tones which can be heard; this is primarily a question of difference limens. It is the purpose of this experiment to determine the *DL* for pitch and intensity in a limited range of tones and thereby to get acquainted with the scope of the problem.

Apparatus and Procedure. Any device that will provide tones of different pitch in a graded series, which can be compared with a tone of a standard pitch, can be used for purposes of calculating a *DL*. One commonly used arrangement consists of a pair of differential tuning forks, one of which is provided with movable weights which can be raised or lowered on the prongs of the fork. Raising the weights slows the vibrations and lowers the frequency. Lowering the weights has the reverse effect. The heavier a vibrating object, the lower its frequency. A similar result can be obtained by lengthening or shortening a vibrating string or setting a hairpin into vibration along the edge of a table. In these cases, the longer the vibrating object, the lower its frequency.

A more convenient method of presenting tones of different pitch is to use a standard set of tones recorded on phonograph discs. The tones can be presented in pairs with fixed frequency differences between them. The subject has only to report on the second of a pair of tones. He can judge it as louder or higher than the first of a pair. Half of the time (in random order) the standard tone appears first, the comparison tone second; this arrangement is reversed in the remaining trials. Such a procedure involves a number of undesirable experimental features, but it is convenient for obtaining data from many subjects at the same time.

A series of records prepared by Seashore (1) for testing "musical talent" serves the purposes of the present experiment reasonably well. In this series, each record contains 100 pairs of tones (50 on each side) in groups of 10 pairs. A short pause follows each group of 10 pairs. In the record, presumably testing pitch discrimination, the two tones of a pair vary in terms of frequency of vibration. The subject records in Table 16 his impression of the second tone. If it seems higher, he writes the letter H in the appropriate block. If it seems lower, he writes L. The subject fills out the *columns* in sequence. For the "intensity" record the same procedure holds except for writing W (for weaker) or S for stronger in Table 17. In each set of 10 pairs, the tones differ by the same degree, but this degree of difference varies from set to set. The experimenter will inform you concerning the degree of difference after you have recorded your judgments, and after he has announced the correct status of the second stimulus for both records.

Table 16. *Seashore Musical Talent Test for Pitch. Results of One Subject.*

Trials	A	B	C	D	E	F	G	H	I	J
1										
2										
3										
4										
5										
6										
7										
8										
9										
10										
Percent correct										

Score on total test____. Percentile on total test____.

Table 17. *Seashore Musical Talent Test for Intensity. Results of One Subject.*

Trials	A	B	C	D	E	F	G	H	I	J
1										
2										
3										
4										
5										
6										
7										
8										
9										
10										
Percent correct										

Score on total test____. Percentile on total test____.

Results. From Tables 16 and 17 plot a curve showing the per-cent of correct responses at each frequency and intensity differ-ence.* Arrange your frequency and intensity values on the ab-scissa and your percentage values on the ordinate. What are your *DL's* for pitch and intensity at the 75 percent level? Remember that your chance score in this experiment is 50 percent correct. What was your percent correct for the total test for pitch and in-tensity? To what percentiles do these correspond?

Discussion

1. What psychophysical method is approximated in the Seashore records?
2. What are the limitations of this procedure for determining the *DL?*
3. What sources of error enter into this experiment? Which of these were controlled? Which uncontrolled?
4. In what respect would the experiment be improved by using differential tuning forks in which the standard fork emitted a tone of 256 vibrations per second?

References

1. Seashore, C. E. *The psychology of music.* New York: McGraw-Hill Book Co. 1938.
2. Woodworth, R. S. *Experimental psychology.* New York: Henry Holt. 1938, chap. 21.

* Correct answers and percentiles are listed in the manual accompanying the Seashore records.

11

The Chemical Senses

UNDER THE GENERAL HEADING of the "chemical senses" we distinguish taste, olfaction, and what for want of a better term is called the "common chemical sense." The three varieties of response are intimately related to each other, and each interferes to some extent with attempts at experimental study of the others. The student is already familiar with the significance of smell in connection with taste. A head cold, with its accompanying anosmia, makes cigarettes "taste like hay," and makes food tasteless. In the results of biting into a juicy red apple we have an example of complex stimulation of eyes, ears, nose, and throat, as well as of taste buds. When all other sources of stimulation are accounted for, our apple turns out to be merely sweet or sour, or a combination of these.

Odors are the chief disturbers in the analysis of taste, and experimental work with taste involves, as a primary control, the effective blocking of smell. This can be done by plugging the nostrils, prevention of swallowing, which allows for some olfactory stimulation "by the back door," or by, in animals, severing the olfactory nerve.

The "common chemical sense" is the next most important variable to consider. The mucous membranes of the nose, mouth, and throat are responsive to various types of chemical agents which cause inflammations or other irritations of these membranes. Such
208

irritations are often confused with either odor or taste, and are an obvious source of error. The factor of the "common chemical sense" is a useful experimental control, however, especially in deciding questions as to the possible existence of tastes other than the traditionally accepted sweet, salt, sour, and bitter. It is well established that the different regions of the tongue are differentially receptive to stimulations of these four types (tip: sweet; sides: sour and salt; rear: bitter; central area: none).

The fact that the central area of the tongue is presumed to have no taste buds and, hence, that it apparently cannot be stimulated to evoke a taste response, makes it possible to use this area as a check, or control, area. If some substance is alleged to have a taste different from the traditional ones, the experimenter can stimulate the central area with the substance. If any reaction is obtained, it can be then classified as a "common chemical sense" reaction and not a taste.* A different type of procedure must be used in handling the "common sense" control in odor experiments. In these cases the olfactory nerve must be blocked by drugs or severed. If reaction remains, it can be attributed to the "common" sense.

The study of the chemical senses has not arrived at the same stage of development as has the study of vision and audition. There is no obvious physical correlate by which we can identify, on a scale, just what a "sweet" stimulus amounts to, or what a "goaty" smell is. In vision or audition we can relate a hue or a pitch to wave length or vibration frequency. In olfaction and taste we are still forced to talk about cheese or sugar.

In the olfactory area of study, there is some possibility of quantification in terms indicated by the work of Miles and Beck (2). These investigators claim, on the basis of work done on bees, that infrared rays are being continuously discharged into the atmos-

* For an excellent illustration, see: Kloehn, N. W., and Brogden, W. J. The alkaline taste: a comparison of absolute thresholds for sodium hydroxide on the tip and mid-dorsal surfaces of the tongue. *Amer. J. Psychol.*, 1948, *61*, 90–93.

phere from the olfactory organs, and replacements are continuously returning from the environment to establish an equilibrium of heat balance. If some substance, say honey, is in the environment, this substance absorbs certain infrared rays, and the equilibrium is lost. The bee reacts to the difference between output and return just as does the bat which finds its way around in the dark on the basis of echoes from the supersonic sounds it emits. By measuring the infrared-ray absorption of honey with a suitable spectrometer, the value of honey odor as a wave length in the infrared spectrum can be determined. Eventually, all odoriferous substances might be so calibrated; at least this is the hope of Miles and Beck.

For the present, however, we must be content with describing olfactory stimuli either in terms of the chemical constitution (usually of an organic compound) or of a standard commercial product. Some use is made of so-called subjective scales such as those of Henning or Crocker (1) which attempt to describe odor stimuli (or responses) as "flowery, fruity, burnt, putrid, resinous, and spicy" (Henning), or "fragrant, acid, burnt, and caprylic" (Crocker). A check of Crocker's scales by Ross and Harriman (3) showed them to be highly unreliable. Their report, by the way, is a good example of methodology in olfactory experiments.

In the area of taste, we are still limited to the verbal descriptions of sweet, salt, bitter, and sour. The only attempt at quantifying the description of stimuli in taste has been in terms of identifying the fractional components of each type of stimulus in complex solutions. For instance, the taste of lemonade might be reported something like $\frac{3}{15}$ sour, $\frac{1}{15}$ bitter, $\frac{11}{15}$ sweet. The possibility of some eventual reduction of taste stimuli to some form of wave energy awaits future investigation.

In the light of the above remarks we can now proceed to a listing of the methods and sources of error involved in gustatory and olfactory experimentation. The methods in both instances are still relatively primitive and "indirect" in that the findings are open to various interpretations.

Taste

The essential factor in testing taste stimulation is to reduce the substance to be tasted to some soluble form. This is necessary because of the structure of the taste buds, which cannot be stimulated unless the substance involved is in solution. The use of solutions has the advantage of permitting a description of the comparative strength of the stimulus in terms of solution strength. Once the solution is available, it remains to apply it to the tongue, either in quantities which can be sipped and allowed to remain in the mouth before they are expectorated, or by specific application to selected areas by use of small camel's-hair brushes, hypodermic needles, or medicine droppers. In general, some psychophysical method is used in arranging the order of stimuli. Usually the method of constant stimuli is employed, although the "method of absolute judgment" is sometimes followed. In the latter method, the subject reports, on the basis of some arbitrary scale, that the substance does or does not taste one way or another, and sometimes uses modifiers like "mild," "strong," "very strong," etc.

In working with taste, it is obvious that the olfactory sense and the common chemical sense must be excluded either through mechanical means (such as plugging of the nostrils), by drugs, or by surgical interference. The temperature of a substance is usually kept at room temperature because of variations in taste thresholds due to that factor.

The following variables must be taken into consideration:

In the subject:

1. Individual differences (habitual use of seasonings, tobacco, etc.).
2. Time since last meal (aftertastes of food often cause difficulty).
3. Adaptation and contrast effects (the mouth is usually rinsed with distilled water to overcome the relatively rapid adaptation of the tongue, and the possible loss of response to components of a complex substance).

4. Area of tongue stimulated (the latest evidence suggests that there are specific sense organs for at least three of the tastes (none for sugar) as well as specific areas of special sensitivity.

In the stimulus:

1. Concentration of each component in the mixture or of a single component in a solution.
2. Temperature of the solution.
3. Rate of stimulation (aftertastes, adaptation, sensitization effects).
4. Method of presentation (large or small quantities) and order of presentation of successive stimuli.

Olfaction

In experimenting with odors the basic necessity is to provide gaseous or vaporous stimuli, preferably in known concentrations. Three common methods are used:

1. The open-bottle technique. In this method, a bottle containing some substance is held under the nostrils, and the subject is instructed to sniff actively until the bottle is removed. Sniffing is essential in this procedure as, with minute concentrations, an odor may not be reported if the substance is not sufficiently volatile.

2. The olfactometer technique. An instrument consisting of one or two glass tubes with curved ends for insertion into the nostrils is used to bring the odor to the subject. A hollow cylinder containing the odor substance on its inner walls is then slipped over the free end of the tube(s). The concentration of odor is then varied by the distance to which the cylinder is allowed to project beyond the tube. If the cylinder is halfway on the tube, then air coming through the cylinder and the tube cannot pick up as much concentration of the stimulus as it would if the cylinder were at the extreme end of the tube. The distance along the tube to which the cylinder extends is graduated in "olfacties," units of odor strength invented by Zwaardemaker.

3. The blast-injection technique. This procedure makes use of a tanklike container (a liter jar, e.g.) in which the air pressure can be altered by an external pump (a hypodermic syringe can serve the purpose). From the tank, tubes lead to the nose of the subject; these tubes are "stoppered off" until the appropriate pressure has been built up. The pressure is then allowed to escape through the tubes, thus bringing a blast of charged air into the nose of the subject. This procedure has the definite advantage of quantifying the stimulus concentration and pressure, eliminating the troublesome variable introduced by variations in sniffing.

These are some of the variables in olfactory experimentation:

In the subject:
1. Physical condition (such as anosmia).
2. State of adaptation (time since smoking and eating, for instance).
3. Monorhinic or dirhinic stimulation.

In the stimulus:
1. Concentration of the stimulus.
2. Pressure.
3. Purity of the stimulus. (This is especially difficult to control because of the "clinging" quality of odors. To get rid of odors from previous stimuli, new containers must be used for each odor. It is almost impossible to wash out odors. Electrostatic methods must often be employed to prevent contrast and masking effects.)
4. Rate of presentation. (Adaptation occurs rapidly.)
5. The "common chemical sense." (Surgical interference is the only sure way of eliminating this variable.)

6. Clearing of the nose by fresh air supply following each stimulation. (This is difficult to achieve in a room where odors
cling to walls and furniture.)

References

1. Boring, E. G. A new system for the classification of odors.
Amer. J. Psychol., 1928, *40,* 345–349.
2. Miles, W., and Beck, L. H. Infrared absorption in field studies
of olfaction in bees. *Science,* 1947, *106,* 512 (abstract).
3. Ross, S., and Harriman, A. E. A preliminary study of the
Crocker-Henderson odor-classification system. *Amer. J. Psychol.,* 1949, *42,* 399–404.
4. Woodworth, R. S. *Experimental psychology.* New York: Henry
Holt. 1938.

Experiment 12. The Chemical Senses: Olfactory Adaptation

Introduction. It is commonplace knowledge that some time after exposure to an odor we are no longer able to report its presence. We say that we "got used" to it. The concept of adaptation which is referred to by these words is an extremely significant one in the appreciation of various other psychological problems besides those involved in the sense organs. You will come across it again in connection with the activity of the nervous system and in discussions of learning, extinction, and forgetting. A thorough understanding of the nature of sensory adaptation as it exhibits itself in various sense organs will enable you to judge the limitations that must be imposed on speculation about the role of adaptation in other fields. The present experiment in olfactory adaptation has been selected because it strikingly demonstrates the process of sensory adaptation.

NOTE: In this experiment the student is asked to prepare his own apparatus because it is desirable to get practice in the mixing or blending of odors, and materials are readily available. It is expected that the first attempts at blending odors will be instructive failures and that final approximations will be equally instructive successes.

Procedure. In Woodworth's (2) chapter on the olfactory sense you will find a discussion and listing of "odors" that blend well. Using this information, prepare bottles containing odoriferous substances from the variety of materials you will find in your own home or chemistry laboratory (medicines, spices, flavoring extracts, etc.). You will need three bottles. Each of the first two will contain a very small amount of one of two substances; the third will contain a blend of the first two. Be sure to prepare your mixture slowly and carefully so as to achieve a blend without a dominant odor. In selecting your odors, consider your subject, and provide him with reasonably pleasant stimuli. Label your bottles in code.

In performing your experiment, present your subject with the blend, and ask him to identify the components if he is able to do so. Record his remarks. Then select one of your stimuli, and ask your subject to hold the bottle to his nostrils and inhale the odor. The subject should actively sniff at the bottle and continue to do so until he can no longer detect any odor. The subject should be careful to report any changes in the odor stimulus during this adaptation period. Your substance may contain several components which "adapt out" at different rates. When the subject has "exhausted" the odor, allow him to rest one minute. Take the time of adaptation in seconds. Repeat this procedure 10 times. Again test the subject with the blend, and record his remarks. Now repeat the above procedure with the other odor, and again test with the blend. Can your subject identify the components in the blend after a sufficient rest? The subject need not know the names of the stimuli.

Results. Record your adaptation times for the two odors in Table 18, below. Summarize the subject's reports concerning the blend and changes in the separate stimuli. Plot your data in graphical form. Which odor resisted adaptation longer?

Table 18. *Adaptation Time in Seconds for Ten Successive Adaptation Trials for Two Odors, Odor A ____ and Odor B ____, for One Subject.*

Odors	Trials									
	1	2	3	4	5	6	7	8	9	10
A.										
B.										

Discussion

1. What sources of error, controlled and uncontrolled, did you encounter in this experiment?
2. What were the independent and dependent variables?

3. What other method of presenting stimuli could you suggest that would improve the procedure?
4. What effect would eating, smoking, or the presence of other odors in the experimental room have?

References

1. Postman, L., and Egan, J. P. *Experimental psychology*. New York: Harper and Brothers. 1949, chap. 5.
2. Woodworth, R. S. *Experimental psychology*. New York: Henry Holt. 1938, chap. 21.

12

The Study of the Skin

ALTHOUGH not generally thought of as such, the skin is an organ of the body, and scientifically one of the most important of the many organs and organ systems. The skin is a form of "iron curtain" between you and the rest of the world. In one sense it divides private from public experience in that, generally, only you can react to stimuli which are effective in initiating impulses in your cutaneous nerves. Only one person can sit on a particular tack at a given moment.

Although the following statement is not strictly true, it can be said that a large number of individuals can see the same light or hear the same sound at a given time. The skin senses seem to be more a matter of individual reaction. It is much more difficult, because of apparatus complications, to stimulate a number of people at the same time with the same "pain" or "touch" stimulus.

As a matter of fact, it is difficult to define a pain, a touch, or, for that matter, a temperature *stimulus*. Lights and sounds are describable in physical terms and can be readily reproduced, although there are difficulties even there, as we have seen. The stimulus for pain, however, is no simple matter of manipulation of some physical object emitting a measurable form of energy. Almost any form of energy, including light, sound, and *temperature,* can be used as a pain stimulus. The isolation of stimuli for the several skin senses is a problem to which we will return later.
218

Our present concern is with the general status of the scientific study of the skin.

Because of the relatively more private nature of the results of skin stimulation, not much information concerning skin sensitivity is currently available in comparison with that about the "distance receptors." What information there is, is in many instances of dubious quality and open to argument. There are many reasons for such a state of affairs, and an examination of them will help us appreciate the more general implications of the study of sense organs for psychology.

In the first place, the skin is no specific, localized organ. It encompasses the body and varies in its efficiency with respect to discriminating stimuli. It becomes necessary, therefore, to relate any acquired data to the specific area from which the data were obtained. To do this, the area must ordinarily be described in terms of distances from prominent bony structures or other permanent features of the body if such scientifically vague terms as the "back," "nape of the neck," etc., are to be avoided. The lack of well marked boundaries on the skin forces the psychologist to study anatomy if he is to make comparisons between individuals in collecting data for a general understanding of skin sensitivity.

In the second place, it is difficult to arrange a situation wherein relatively isolated stimuli can be presented, as can be done with vision and audition. It is possible to arrange a light-free chamber and control the amount of light to be used for visual stimulation; it is also possible to have a relatively quiet room into which sounds can be introduced. But, try to arrange for freedom from pressure. This may not be important because of adaptation, and might be quite simple for a given area, but the customs of civilization involving the wearing of clothes, including gloves, shoes, and neckties, subject us to continual skin stimulation. The ardors and labors of this same civilization, which include such items as digging ditches, washing dishes, and counting currency, have their varied effects. We are constantly subjected to skin stimulation in our feet when standing, in more generalized areas while sitting; and, depending on our clothing, girdles, ties, and other apparel, we are constantly adjusting and adapting to skin stimulation. To achieve a skin condition comparable to silence in audition, or darkness in vision, appears impossible. Investigators of the skin senses have their difficulties.

The apparent privacy of cutaneous reactions is the most important experimental factor responsible for the doubts and uncertainties in our knowledge of the skin senses. Actually, such reactions are no more and no less private than those of other senses. It is only the lack of an *immediate* social check that makes them seem so. A flashing light can be witnessed by a multitude of observers. A tickle or an itch is a more intimately individual matter. Being such individual affairs, the reactions of the skin are not easily comparable from person to person. Since the experimenter, normally, does not apply the stimulus to himself, he must depend on the subject's reports and is unable to have similar reactions himself at the same time.

This lack of common experience results in a language difficulty in that no mutual corrective interplay is possible, such as is the case when an adult corrects a child who mistakenly uses an incorrect color term. As a consequence, there is no commonly accepted set of terms by which definite communication can be obtained in an experimental situation. We have no spectra or audibility curves in the skin senses, no hues or pitches by which to report responses. Consider your difficulty in trying to describe the feeling of "pins and needles" when your leg "falls asleep."

The language difficulty has turned many psychologists away from an interest in the skin. As a consequence, we know next to nothing about the one sense without which we could scarcely survive: pain. Our knowledge of other skin conditions and reactions of organs within the body cavity is equally poor, and represents a challenge which few investigators seem willing to take up. The apparent "subjectivity" of such responses seems to deter some psychologists, although, as we have seen, they are no more subjective than the reactions of any other sense organ. The importance of the skin and its components should not be undervalued in comparison with that of the eye and the ear, as is the case with most elementary texts, whose chapters on vision and hearing contain more pages than there are paragraphs on the skin.

Traditionally, the skin senses have been divided into those of temperature (warm and cold), pressure (surface and deep), and pain. This by no means exhausts the variety of reports descriptive of reactions to stimuli applied to the skin, although some psychologists have tried to reduce all reactions, such as those of tickling, itching, roughness, oiliness, vibration, etc., to a combination or pattern of the temperature, touch, and pain responses.

Our own purposes will be served with an account of the basic methods of studying the above allegedly fundamental senses with an indication of the sources of error involved in the analysis of each. It should be remembered that the progress in the study of the skin is most meager, and that the methods now in use will eventually give way to more productive techniques when and if the significance of the skin senses, those of the internal organs, and those of the muscles, tendons, and joints, is more widely recognized.

For our present purposes, we shall consider the more common methods of studying skin sensitivity in connection with the senses of temperature, touch, and pain. Our primary interest is in the nature of the instruments used to provide stimuli, the methods of presenting stimuli, and the appropriate controls.

1. *The temperature sense.* Laboratory study has generally made use of "punctiform" stimulation in the study of temperature reactions; that is, the stimuli used consist of one device or another with a pointed tip which can be warmed or cooled and applied to some area of the skin. The reason for using such stimulus points lies in the traditional belief in the existence of tiny sense organs under the skin which are alleged to be the media for the sensations of warmth and cold. Other than the dubious "spot" theory, there is no special rationale for limit-

ing the stimulation to a square millimeter of skin except that
of custom. It is presumably easier to "control" such a minute
area, and problems of control would certainly arise if one attempted temperature studies on larger areas, or on the whole
body at once, by enclosing the subject in a refrigerator, oven,
ice-bath, etc. In view of the relatively unsupportable "spot"
theory, however, it might be desirable to extend the stimulus
aspects of skin study to take in more area.

The basic controls in applying a temperature stimulus to the
skin include the following: (1) The unstimulated skin temperature and the rate of stimulation must be known (adaptation is a
significant variable here as it is in vision, audition, olfaction, and
taste). (2) The temperature of the stimulus object must be known.
(3) The area of skin covered and the location of the area on the
body must be stated (the cornea, for example, cannot detect
warmth or cold). (4) The pressure with which the stimulus is applied must be known and, presumably, held constant.
Instruments have been constructed which include devices for
circulating warm or cold water around the stimulus point, and
which work from a type of balance beam which permits any desirable pressure to be used. Such instruments are refinements over
the traditional temperature "cylinders," which consist of pointed
brass rods which are cooled in ice-water or warmed in heated water. When such cylinders are dipped in water, the experimenter
must be careful to dry them before applying them to the skin,
otherwise the water will adhere to the skin and change both the
duration and temperature of the stimulus as the water approaches,
or drops below, room temperature in evaporating. Evaporation,
itself, is a cooling process. Less elaborate instruments, such as
common nails or knitting needles, can be employed for temperature stimulation if they are treated as are the cylinders. A relatively recent innovation in skin stimulation is the use of a temperature "grid," which consists of fine hollow tubes. Alternate
tubes are heated and cooled simultaneously. Application of such
a grid to the skin usually elicits a report of "hot."

To avoid the problems of pressure, moisture, and touch in studying temperature, use is sometimes made of radiant heat (infrared rays), concentrated by a lens, and beamed at an area of the skin. Such a procedure does not permit the study of cold sensitivity, however; and for the latter, resort has been had to the use of rapidly evaporating liquids (ether, alcohol, etc.).

The possibilities of movement of the skin or of the stimulus must be considered. The skin's elasticity permits some degree of movement; emotional reactions and other stimulus conditions may involve a "tightening" of the skin, "goose-flesh," or other skin activity. Circulatory changes, involving contraction and expansion of blood vessels, also cause changes in the disposition of the skin and are considered by some workers to be the basic variables in the senses of warmth and cold. When all of the above variables are under control or accounted for, one is ready to apply a temperature stimulus. In general, one reports his stimulus temperature in degrees centigrade, and also determines the "physiological zero" of his subject under the conditions studied. This is normally about 33° centigrade, and represents the temperature at which a stimulus is reported neither "warm" nor "cold."

2. *The pressure sense.* The pressure sense is usually divided into two sub-senses: surface pressure, or "touch," and "deep" pressure. The latter is to be thought of in terms of reactions to relatively broad and heavy pressures which distort muscles, as well as the skin, out of position. There are nervous diseases and drugs which eliminate responses to surface touch but do not eliminate deep pressure, so that a subject might, for example, report one but not the other.

As with the temperature sense, laboratory study of the pressure sense has been largely confined to punctiform stimulation, in this case by means of pointed light wooden sticks (skewers, tooth-picks) or stiff horsehairs. Von Frey selected a series of horsehairs which were graduated in terms of the pressure necessary to bend each, and used these for plotting pressure "spots" on the skin.

The important variables are: (1) amount of pressure; (2) area stimulated (hairless areas like the lips and fingertips are very sensitive to pressure; in other areas, the presence of hair facilitates a touch response. Shaving the area is often resorted to, but this introduces other variables resulting from the shaving process, as it involves the removal of some skin surface along with the hair); (3) movement, which is perhaps the most significant variable (it appears that unless there is an actual depression of the skin, no report of touch will be elicited; further, unless movement continues, adaptation sets in. Movement is especially significant in studies on varieties of touch sensitivity, such as smoothness, roughness, hardness, etc.); and (4) pain and temperature stimulation, which must presumably be excluded.

Two types of experimentation in the sense of touch require special mention: (1) localization of stimulation points, and (2) two-point discrimination. In the first, the subject is "touched" on some skin point and is asked to name, point to, or duplicate the stimulation with a pointed instrument of his own. In such experiments care must be taken to prevent the subject from getting cues from the appearance of the skin, which might be marked by the experimenter's instrument. The experimenter must have an exact map of the skin area on which to record his stimuli and the responses. Usually (and this applies to all punctiform stimulus situations) the experimenter stamps a cross-patched, grid-like square on the subject's skin and uses a similar squared area for his record. The rate of stimulation becomes an important variable in this type of study, the subject becoming confused between current stimuli and aftereffects of the previous ones if the rate is too rapid.

In two-point discrimination studies, the experimenter tries to determine how far apart two points must be, when placed on the skin simultaneously, before the subject can report them as two. Because the two points must be applied simultaneously, the experimenter must be extremely careful in setting his instrument (an aesthesiometer) on the surface being tested. This is not always simple, because the human body presents relatively few flat areas. The two points must be presented with equal pressure as well as at the same time, or the subject may respond in terms of two different touch intensities instead of in terms of two spatially separated stimuli. It is also necessary to maintain a constant axis (lengthwise or crosswise) on a given area, because results will differ with axis changes, presumably due to nerve distribution.

Because the subject knows two points are applied, he may permit himself some generous guesses. This type of unreliability can be checked by occasionally applying only one point (the subject usually wears a blindfold or is otherwise kept from seeing the stimulus). Under such conditions the subject is best instructed to respond with "two" only when he is "certain" that he feels two, and to respond with "one" in any case of doubt. Such a criterion will lead to more consistent results. Usually a modification of the method of limits is used in determining such two-point sensitivity. The student recognizes the problem as one of determination of the *DL*.

3. *The sense of pain.* There is no reason, of course, to confine the study of the pain sense to the skin, as we are all familiar with pain arising from a variety of other organs. Toothaches, headaches, and heartaches are deserving of the psychologists' attention. Traditionally, however, the psychologists' study of pain has been largely restricted to the laboratory, where the experiments have, to a large extent, consisted of applying sharp, pointed instruments (algometers) to a minute skin area for the detection of pain "spots." The variables of movement, pressure, stimulus size, and skin area are again important. The fact that subjects report "pain" from practically all parts of the skin is an interesting, although not astounding or otherwise rewarding, finding.

Besides being tested with needle points, pain has been studied as a response to other forms of stimuli, such as electric shock, extreme temperature and pressure variations, high intensity sounds, etc. The use of these stimuli involves separate variables which cannot be considered here in our discussion of the skin as a sense organ.

The use of electric shock in stimulation of animals is usually not associated with the study of pain. It is thought of primarily as a method of arousing other types of activity, such as escape or avoidance, the pain being taken for granted, or considered immaterial or irrelevant, depending on the systematic orientation of the experimenter.

The above account has paid little attention to the subject. He is usually treated as a necessary evil, whose participation is to be limited to monosyllabic utterances, such as "warm," "hot," "now," "yes," "two," etc. Attempts to enlarge his vocabulary, for example, by introducing various scales of intensity, have not been successful; and methods of this sort are not commonly used at present.

The lack of physical continua (such as the spectrum in vision), the relative size and the differential sensitivity of the skin, and the relative "privacy" of the reactions to skin stimulation, have resulted in our own current lack of knowledge concerning even elementary facts about cutaneous sensitivity. The unrewarding study of the skin does not arouse much interest or activity among present-day psychologists; yet it is, with the kinesthetic sense, the one most called on in our daily adjustments and, if pain is considered a skin sense, in our learning and survival.

References

1. Postman, L., and Egan, J. P. *Experimental psychology*. New York: Harper and Brothers. 1949, chap. 3.
2. Woodworth, R. S. *Experimental psychology*. New York: Henry Holt. 1938, chap. 19.

Experiment 13. The Cutaneous Senses: Two-Point Discrimination

Introduction. How far apart must you place two points on the skin of a subject for him to report there are two points and not one? Determining an answer to this question will introduce the student to a number of variables which are common to the experimental study of the skin, at least of the traditional "skin senses" (temperature, touch, and pain). The control of these variables is often difficult, and has obstructed progress in the understanding of cutaneous functions. The experiment you will perform should serve as background for a general orientation of your psychological thinking about stimuli, "sensation and perception," and "subjective" experience.

Apparatus and Procedure. Any device that will permit you to apply two points to a skin area at the same time, with equal pressure, and with a reasonably efficient method of measuring the distance of separation, can be used. In its most simple form, such a device is approximated by a draftsman's compass or dividers, a mechanic's calipers, or even two toothpicks. The usual form of instrument consists of a millimeter scale with a fixed point at one end and a movable point which can be set at any desired distance from the first. Such a device is called an aesthesiometer. Various additional features are incorporated in several varieties in attempts to control the pressure variable. One such device is a sliding grip on a handle fixed so that the experimenter allows only the weight of the instrument itself to rest on the skin.

In your procedure, you will select two areas on the skin (one on the back of the hand and one on the back of the neck) and determine the *DL* for each area by the method of limits.

On each area draw a line approximately two inches long (in ink) along the axis of the arm and of the neck. Ask your subject to extend his arm along the table, resting his head on the other arm, and closing his eyes. Then, starting with your aesthesiometer points far apart, apply both points to the skin along the line with an even pressure, and ask your subject to report whether he feels one or two points. Starting with a distance sure to elicit a "two-point" response, continue applying the points with gradually diminishing separation distances (in steps of 1 mm.) until the subject reports "one." Enter this distance in Table 19. Then start with a smaller distance of separation (certain to elicit a "one"), and gradually increase the separation in 1-mm. units until the subject reports "two." Enter this distance in the table. Now do the same for the neck area for one descending and one ascending series of measurements. Return to the hand, and repeat. Continue alternating between neck and hand until you have secured 10 readings for each ascending and descending series. Average the series separately, and finally average the two means for your *DL*. From time to time apply only one point to counteract guessing. Instruct your subject to report "one" unless he is certain of his report of "two" (your data will be conservative). Observe the usual precautions of the method of limits, such as avoiding constant starting points, etc.

Results

1. Is the back of the hand more sensitive than the back of the neck? How do your *DL's* compare with those of the class?
2. Were there any significant changes in your thresholds as the experiment continued?

Discussion

1. What cautions would you cite before making comparisons with other subjects? Consider this question carefully before answering.
2. Describe your subject's attitudes in the course of the experiment. Did he have difficulty in concentrating? Did he show signs of "conditioning," afterimages, sensitivity changes, irritability?

Table 19. *Threshold Distance in Millimeters at Which One Subject Discriminated Two Points Applied to Skin on Back of Hand and on Back of Neck*

Location of Test	Trials										Mean	DL
	1	2	3	4	5	6	7	8	9	10		
HAND Ascending series												
Descending series												
NECK Ascending series												
Descending series												

3. Is this experiment a sample of "introspection"? of "subjective experimentation"? Can the results of such experiments be generalized upon? Can you suggest any practical applications?
4. What is epicritic and protopathic sensitivity?

References

1. Postman, L., and Egan, J. P. *Experimental psychology.* New York: Harper and Brothers. 1949, chap. 3.
2. Woodworth, R. S. *Experimental psychology.* New York: Henry Holt. 1938, chap. 19.

Part 3

The Study of Responses in Psychological
Experimentation

13

The Study of Behavior

PSYCHOLOGY is usually defined as the study of behavior. This innocent definition is customarily glossed over as self-explanatory, and the student proceeds to a consideration of the gamut of psychological topics from innate behavior to senility. In the laboratory study of "behavior," however, we cannot advance so briskly. We are brought up short immediately, when we set out to experiment, by the realization that we cannot study "behavior" in general, but must select samples, and only such samples as are socially permissible and feasible.

The laboratory approach requires that the behavior under scrutiny be measured and, if possible, recorded. These restrictions further limit the selection of samples. The samples often become, for these reasons, pale and sometimes poor reflections of the life they are supposed to mirror. The practical man, and even the practical psychologist, points a scornful finger at the "ivory tower" (more likely a damp cellar or stuffy attic) that houses the experimentalist at work on his trivial problems, while the world cries for help for its neurotics, its salesmen, its politicians, its educators, and its reformers.

Too often the experimentalist yields to the demands of the world and attempts to show the practical implications of his studies. In this attempt to alleviate the world's woes, there is a great danger, the danger of forgetting the limitations imposed by the laboratory, and of stretching and trimming laboratory findings to fit a variety of practical ends. The same "facts" can be, and have been, used to argue, for example, both for punishing and for not punishing children who displease their parents, for advocating and for denying social security, for progressive and for standard education, for more and for less freedom for prisoners, etc. The difficulty involved in such paradoxes can be avoided if the experimentalist is fully oriented in what he is actually measuring and recording.

In his selection of samples of behavior, the psychologist has tried to work with miniature systems or units which presumably illustrate a type of behavior that exists on a more complicated and involved level. In the process of analysis of behavior, it was more or less inevitable that some attempt would be made to discover a behavioral unit, a building block or element, which, when thoroughly understood, would provide many answers to the nature of the total structure. The physiologists, from the time of Descartes, had such a unit in their construct of the *reflex*, and early behavioristic psychologists grasped at the "reflex" gratefully as a basic behavioral unit. Pavlov and Behkterev had shown the potential psychological usefulness of the "reflex" in their publications on *Conditioned Reflexes* and *Reflexology*. Watson, Holt, and Weiss carried the conditioned reflex bodily into psychology and set about the task of building up behavior from an assortment of innate reflexes, from which they thought all the rest of behavior developed through the process of conditioning.

The choice of "reflex" as a behavioral unit proved an unwise one. As indicated above, the "reflex" of the physiologists was a hypothetical construct which Sherrington appropriately described as a "convenient abstraction." The traditional "reflex-arc," with its divisions of sensory receptor, sensory nerve, central synapse, efferent nerve, and effector, is a fiction. The physiological description of the most simple behavior involves many more complications. Many parts and activities of the nervous system and of the body generally contribute to the simplest knee jerk or eyelid blink.

John Dewey, in 1896, pointed out the impossibility of separating out functionally any reflex from the behavior which precedes and follows it. Dewey preferred to think of behavior as a continuous process of adjustment in which stimuli contributed to responses, which in turn created stimuli, and so on. Watson ignored the cautions of Dewey and Sherrington and continued his theorizing on the basis of a limited physiology. He was attacked as a "muscle-twitch" psychologist by those observers who saw difficulties and complexities in the application of Pavlov's conditioned reflexes to an explanation of behavior.

The critics of Pavlov claimed that his picture was too simple, that he did not give a complete account of the behavioral changes and the differences between the original unconditioned reflexes and the conditioned reflexes that resulted from simultaneous presentation of adequate and irrelevant stimuli. The critics suggested that the term "reflex" was too narrow, that a more useful term, "response," would permit inclusion of items of behavior that Pavlov ignored. The term "response" was rapidly accepted and assimilated into the psychologists' jargon; so strongly, in fact, that most psychologists think of the study of behavior as a matter of describing the relationships that hold between stimuli and responses. The basic formula of modern psychology is that a stimulus always leads to a response (we have seen before that stimuli are usually defined in terms of a response).

It is true that not all psychologists accept a straight S—R formula as a basic principle. Some, like Woodworth (8), would include an additional, intervening factor, the organism, or O, and its "sets," W. Others would modify our notions of the *stimulus* in terms of its "functions," and still others emphasize the fact that the stimulus is really an abstraction from a greater "stimulus complex." Still others, especially the Gestalt psychologists, would deny the validity of the formula altogether, as far as any significant psychological role is concerned, and place the burden of accounting for behavior on the "dynamic" action of the personality.

Our present concern, however, is not with the stimulus or the formula as such, but with responses. If we scrutinize the term closely and ask for a definition, we are likely to encounter difficulties and receive vague and over-generalized answers. We can dismiss such obvious suggestions as "a response is that which follows a stimulus" because that will leave us a bit weak when we try to define the stimulus as "that which elicits a response." The trouble comes from the fact that the term "response" is used to describe anything and everything that an organism does, from awakening to falling asleep. This inclusiveness, however, is only part of the trouble, and the lesser part. The greater difficulty is the *interpretation* placed on the response.

Take, for example, such a response as opening a door. What could be simpler? A person opens a door. Are we content to leave it at that? In general, we are not. We immediately begin to attach meanings, interpretations, goals, purposes, ends, and ideas to the response. Why did he open the door? He must have a reason, or he has a motive, or a drive, or a "sign-significate." Perhaps he has all of these. What if the door happens to be on a puzzle-box and is opened by a cat, rat, or dog? Do they have reasons, ideas, motives, means-ends? "Perhaps," again. A rat in a Skinner box presses a little bar. This performance is followed by the arrival of food in a little dish. The food is eaten promptly. Now, what did the bar-press mean? That the animal was hungry, that he *knew* he could get food by pressing the bar if he *chose* to do so, and that he *decided* to do so? Sounds a little dangerous, doesn't it?

In one of *Life Magazine's* photographic scientific essays there were some pictures of a rat named "Pliny" which Professor B. F. Skinner trained to pull a chain. When the chain was pulled, a marble dropped into the rat's cage. The rat placed the marble into a receptacle. The marble then set off a contact which released food into a tray. The captions in the article contained these statements: Pliny "works for a living." He "hoards the marbles" (when the receptacle is covered) and he "squanders his savings" (when the cover is removed). The readers of *Life* got a photographic story which presented Pliny as an educated, hard-work-

FIGURE 11. *A RAT IN A SKINNER BOX*. This rat took its own picture. At the moment it pressed the bar, a camera shutter was closed by a solenoid wired to the bar. After some early variability, rats often settle down to a stereotyped set of movements and press the bar in the same way for trial after trial.

ing rat that knew "his" business and proceeded rationally in "his" encounters with psychologists. Was Pliny "hoarding"? Did he "squander" his "savings"? Such language describes Pliny in a picturesque manner but leaves much to be desired from a scientific point of view. How far are we legitimately entitled to go in describing the "behavior" we study? Let us forget Pliny, the Super-Rat, and consider one of his less-educated cousins learning to press a bar in a simpler Skinner box. If we trace the course of his training briefly, we may get a hint of an answer to the questions we are raising.

The usual procedure in training a rat to press a bar involves a complete reversal of the routine of events from those that will be engaged in by the trained rat. The rat must first be allowed to investigate the box and to find food in the dish (and in no other place in the box). After a day or two of such "habituation," the rat is placed in the box, but no food is in the dish. As the rat approaches the dish, the trainer drops some food into it. This presentation of food is usually accompanied by some slight sound. After twenty or thirty such presentations, the rat comes to the food dish from any part of the box when the food drops into the dish. On the next day, the rat is again placed in the box, and again there is no food in the dish.

Now, for the first time, a bar or lever is introduced into the box. The rat, in its wanderings about the box eventually pushes the bar in some manner. As soon as the bar is touched, a mechanism automatically releases food into the dish, with an accompanying noise. The rat leaves the bar and goes to the dish and eats. This sequence is repeated time after time, with the intervals between bar-pressing and eating growing shorter. After thirty or forty such sequences, the rat performs with apparent "know-how," and the spectator witnessing the performance of the trained rat is convinced that the rat "knows" what to do, how to do it, and is, in general, a "capable little fellow."

The spectator, and many a psychologist, is willing to put all kinds of "behavior" into the rat (drives, purposes, means-ends, intelligence, decisions, and what not). He may not consider sufficiently the fact that the whole performance was learned backwards, step by step—perhaps, in a rat's case, quite blindly and mechanically—and that the rat is functioning strictly in accordance with its training. If we move the bar to another part of the cage, the rat may have to learn a part of the performance all over again. Guthrie and Thorndike have, for a long time, claimed that the "behavior" indulged in by their cats "meant" nothing to the animals. Many of the writer's rats, when learning in Skinner boxes, make "passes" at the bar, without actually touching it, and then go to the food dish. Spectators say the rats "expect to find the food because they think they hit the bar." The writer does not know what the rats "expect" or "think," and so he says merely that "they go to the dish."

Now, let us get back to the point. We have looked at Pliny and other animals and watched their performance. That is a great deal more than many psychologists do when actually performing experiments using rats in such boxes. A common laboratory procedure is to place a rat in a box with its automatic feeder, hook-up a recording device which will register the time and frequency of bar presses on some continuous tape, and then ignore the rat until it is time to take it out. Some experimenters sit and watch the record, others prefer to study the record later. Now we are ready for the question. What are these psychologists studying? Behavior? Reflexes? Responses? It seems quite obvious that they are studying nothing of the sort. They are studying *records*. But the record *means* that some sort of behavior went on. That is probably true enough, but that merely raises the question of the meaning of the record. And herein lies the danger. Records have to be interpreted; inferences must be drawn. What these inferences shall be depend to a considerable degree on the maker of the inference.

Some psychologists, like Skinner, claim that the records are enough and speak for themselves; whatever inferences are drawn should be extremely limited in scope. Nothing should be put into the animal that is not in the record. Others feel that this approach is too limited and narrow, and insist on interpretation. As soon as they make an interpretation, however, someone makes an alternative interpretation. An example or two might make this difficulty more apparent.

In reasonably identical situations, Professors Hull and Leeper trained rats in a T maze to turn to the right when hungry and to the left when thirsty with no other cues than the "drives" involved. The facts are plain enough. The rats performed as they should, but Leeper attributes the correctness of choice to a perceptual appreciation corresponding roughly to a sort of "understanding" or "insight," while Hull claims that the turns were made on the basis of conditioning-to-drive stimuli. The argument is still alive, although the discriminating rats have long since passed beyond.

Perhaps the student may infer that such controversies occur only in the field of learning, and only with animal subjects. He has but to look around a bit into other areas of psychology, or for that matter into any of the arts and sciences. Sticking to psychology, however, consider the heredity-environment controversy in all of its ramifications. Are some races inferior to others in intelligence? The *records* are quite clear. Test results are facts that are the same for all observers. The answer to the question, however, is far from clear. Is feeble-mindedness inherited or a product of the environment? Consider the theories of audition, vision, the temperature sense, and any other sense. The *facts* are there, the same for all interpreters. Yet a variety of theories exists. Consider Rhine and his extrasensory perception. No one denies his facts, yet his *views* do not find ready acceptance by any great number of psychologists. In the fields of abnormal behavior and clinical practice, the same facts invite various interpretations by Freudians, Adlerians, Rogerians, etc. Consider electric-shock treatment for psychotics, Rorschach tests, hypnosis, Gallup polls, maturation, audiogenic seizures, the nervous impulse, perception, personality, or any other psychological topic, and you will find the same situation: The facts, the records, are stable, unshaken, the same for everyone; but the interpretations are diverse.

We can return to the argument and consider again our original question. Are psychologists studying "behavior"? We have seen or will see them studying records of wave patterns on an oscilloscope coming from the eighth nerve of the carp or cat, intelligence-test scores, blood-pressure and breathing rates, rates of depressing bars in Skinner boxes, numbers of errors in mazes, number of trials to learn lists of nonsense syllables, etc., but it is a pretty question as to whether we will see them studying "behavior." The mental tester appears to be no more interested in the

individual taking the test than the learning psychologist is in his
unseen rat in his soundproof, light-proof box. Both of them are
interested primarily in the *scores*. They will both talk about "responses" and "behavior," but the student must continually inquire into just what they are talking about.

One additional difficulty should receive our consideration. The
term "response," as we have seen, is a general one, and usually
is used to refer to some selected activity of an organism. Thus,
walking is a response, so is talking, hitting a baseball, drinking
a cocktail, etc. But all of these "responses" are only parts of what
the organism as a whole is doing. An individual can be walking,
talking, smoking, and holding hands with his girl-friend all at
the same time. What "response" is he making? We note that
response generally can be translated as an *act* of some kind. Previously we referred to the act of closing a door, and recognized
that a variety of inferences could be drawn concerning this act.
We have noted that the inferences might well be contradictory
to other inferences drawn by equally astute observers.

It is well, then, to point out that we are *not* observing the alleged operations that are inferred by the theorists. When someone
shuts a door, we do not see his "desire" to shut the door, or his
"decision," or his "knowledge" of how to do so. We observe only
his *movements* in shutting it. Guthrie (2) has made the distinction between acts and movements a major principle of his psychology. We need not concern ourselves at present with Guthrie's
special theories, but it is well to observe that in any experimental
procedure, the experimenter is *at best* recording and observing
movements, whether they be of nervous impulses, muscle fibers,
or muscle systems. Often enough he is not even observing these,
but only representations of these in terms of his recording devices
with their own special limitations and sources of error. So long
as the experimentalist realizes that he is observing and/or recording movements, and usually only an extremely limited number of these, and that he is not observing "learning," "insight,"
"perception," or "behavior," he is on safe experimental ground.

From this point on, the experimentalist has his choice as to what to do with his records. He can take one of two courses, depending on his philosophy and tastes. If he is so inclined, he may stay on the record level and present his results in the form of empirical relationships between his stimulus conditions and his records. In effect he can attain the scientific aim of prediction by being able to state: "Given these conditions, these records will be obtained." If he is more "theoretically" inclined, he may begin to infer the nature of unobservable or unobserved intervening variables, and try to construct a theory which will account for not only the current relationship between stimulus conditions and records, but also for untried stimulus conditions and their consequences. As long as he is in the laboratory, he must resign himself to the fact that he is observing only movements or their symbolic reproductions, and must recognize that "behavior," like the "reflex," is "a convenient abstraction." The student interested in examples of these approaches can consult the chapters dealing with the theories of B. F. Skinner and C. L. Hull in Hilgard's *Theories of learning* (3).

The Observation of "Responses" in the Laboratory

As we have just seen, the term "response" has never been defined in a satisfactory manner, although it is perhaps the most commonly used word in the psychologist's vocabulary. We cannot hope to read it out of the dictionary, and so we must attempt to find out what is meant by the term. Our approach can be considered an operational one, as we shall use the "pointing definition" technique and examine the types of events that are referred to as "responses." The exercise should prove of some interest and allow us to keep from stumbling too awkwardly in our interpretations of laboratory records.

Several broad classes of events have been categorized as responses, and we can, perhaps, profit from a consideration of these classes. The following list of kinds of "responses," although not completely inclusive, will provide a framework for our discussion. It should be noted that the various terms used are by no means mutually exclusive. A single response can be thought of as reflex, involuntary, conscious, and innate.

Responses described in terms of the *degree of participation* by the various muscles, organs, and systems of the body:
1. Muscle twitch (of isolated muscle fibre).
2. Nerve-muscle contraction, e.g., of the quadriceps muscle of frog dissected out of the body with its nerve.
3. "Reflex," or sensorimotor responses, e.g., knee jerk (involving the central nervous system).
4. Movement of some selected part of the body, e.g., eye-movements, hand or foot withdrawal, capillary constriction, eye-hand co-ordination, etc.
5. Act—a response considered in terms of end-results, regardless of the parts of the body involved.

Responses described in terms of the *types of tissue* or effector involved:
1. Smooth muscle, e.g., pupillary contraction, visceral activity.
2. Gland secretions, e.g., lacrimation, adrenal secretions.
3. Striate muscle, e.g., contraction of arm muscles.
4. Action currents (nerve or muscle).
5. Other electrical responses, e.g., brain waves, cochlear microphonic, psychogalvanic responses, etc.

Responses described in terms of *their efficiency* from the observer's viewpoint:
1. Random ("trial and error") and vicarious trial and error (VTE).
2. Generalized (undifferentiated and unintegrated).
3. Specific (differentiated, e.g., contraction of a toe to stimulation on the foot in contrast to arm-waving, which might occur in new-born babies or in the foetus).

4. Goal responses (consummatory) and sub-goal responses. Sub-goals are objects or events closely associated with goals. A dinner-bell or praise might serve as examples of sub-goals.

5. Anticipatory responses (preparatory to goal responses), e.g., salivating before food is in the mouth.

6. Directed or "intelligent," as opposed to "disorganized," emotional, etc., responses.

Responses considered from the *developmental or genetic viewpoint:*

1. Native, innate, instinctive, or unlearned responses.

2. Responses that are native but that do not occur for some time after birth, perhaps not till puberty, and that are usually classified as resulting from maturation.

3. Learned, conditioned, or "trained" responses.

Responses considered in terms of their *determiners:*

1. Involuntary responses (external, or uncontrollable internal, stimulus required, e.g., pupillary contraction, hiccups). *Evoked* responses.

2. Semi-voluntary, e.g., eyelid blink (cannot be completely "controlled").

3. Voluntary, choice, or "willed" responses (e.g., tying a shoe lace, refusing dessert). Emitted or *operant* responses.

Responses considered in terms of their *relation to "consciousness":*

1. Unconscious reactions (automatic responses, responses in sleep, in delirium, etc.).

2. Semiconscious, preconscious, foreconscious responses (reactions to peripheral stimuli or responses that are relatively available).

3. Conscious reactions, discriminating "awareness."

It is obvious that we cannot consider every one of the types of responses mentioned above. To do so would require a rather complete text in general psychology and would take us too far afield, as many of the types must be studied by research methods

other than those used in the experimental laboratory. That is
not to say that one type of experimental program or another cannot be developed to study the problems involved in the classes
of events mentioned. We have already seen how a physicist handled the homing "instinct" of pigeons in an experimental manner. Many experiments on maturation have been performed.
Experiments on sleep, hypnosis, "states of consciousness," etc.,
indicate that "conscious" responses are not unassailable by laboratory technique. Our primary concern, however, is with getting
some appreciation of responses from the viewpoint of the experimenter stimulating his subjects, human or otherwise, and observing their "behavior." With this concern before us, we cannot
engage in a philological controversy in dealing with such terms
as "the unconscious," which, as J. G. Miller (6) has pointed out,
has at least sixteen different interpretations.

We have already seen that, as far as the experimenter is concerned in his laboratory activity, the nature of the response in
which he is interested reduces to the measurement of the symbolic
representation of movements of effectors. If we interpret "measurement" broadly, we can include such items as verbal reports,
which can be recorded phonographically or otherwise for leisurely study. The inclusion of verbal reports in our measurements
complicates the experimenter's work tremendously, and involves
us with a host of variables which are difficult to handle operationally. The experimenter handling verbal reports as his data
must steer carefully to avoid the difficulties arising from the philosopher's concepts of conation and consciousness.

An appreciation of the experimenter's problem can be obtained
if we examine his actual procedure. In effect he introduces a subject into a situation, the features of which are under his control.
Into this "stimulus complex" he introduces his "stimuli." The
subject then "responds" to the stimuli, and these "responses" or,
as more usual, a selected portion of them, are recorded by one
means or another on photographic, waxed, or smoked paper, or
on phonographic records, wire or tape, or simply in protocol form

by pencil checks. The "responses" are then analyzed for their features. In general, most laboratory-studied responses have the following characteristics:

1. Frequency. This can be represented as either a "yes" or "no" matter indicating that a response did or did not occur, or in terms of a percentage of the times that the response occurred out of all of the trials.

2. Amplitude. This can refer to actual physical extent of some movement or to various other kinds of measurement for which acceptable scales must be at hand, such as the degree of activity (e.g., running behavior, amount of secretion of saliva, electrical resistance of the skin, etc.).

3. Time relationships. A variety of time measurements might be available. The time interval between the onset of the stimulus and the beginning of the response is one of the most commonly employed measures. This interval is what has been known as "reaction time," or more generally as "latency." The *duration* of a response is also often of interest. The *rate* of response is a measurement employing both frequency and time measures, and is commonly used in learning, work, motivation, and other experiments.

4. Direction. The above characteristics of response are frequently combined to take account of the fact that often experimental observations take the form of a series of waves, or can be represented as indicating positive or negative values from a zero point. Occasionally, special emphasis is laid on direction of response more directly, as in left or right choices, in vectors resulting from combinations of stimuli, or in "field forces."

The measurement of responses in space and time is only a part of the experimenter's task. He must also describe his stimulating conditions and agents in equally appropriate fashion, and try as nearly as possible to record them as well as he does his responses.

With the above general schema before us, let us consider, for illustrative purposes, an actual experimental situation which involves a great many of the aspects of response which have been listed previously. A suitable demonstration experiment might be that of conditioning the eyelid response in a human subject.

In the typical conditioned-eyelid experiment, it is necessary to arrange the stimuli to elicit the response, record their occurrence, and record the response. The eyelid will close or "blink" in response to instructions, to a sudden loud noise, a bright flash of light, a puff of air on the cornea, an electric shock, a blow on the cheek, or a threatening movement in the general direction of the eye. Any one of these stimuli might be chosen.

Suppose we settle for the loud sound. This can be produced by any of a number of methods; a simple procedure is to allow a mousetrap spring to snap on a sounding board. To record the onset of this stimulus, a system must be devised for translating the vibration of the sounding board into a movement of some kind which can be recorded. If we choose to use photographic methods of recording, a light, slender rod might be attached to the board in such a way as to project in front of a camera lens. If the rod interrupts a beam of light, any vibration of the rod will photograph as a moving shadow.

Once the "unconditioned" stimulus is arranged, a "conditioning" stimulus is required. The only restriction on this, if we are using a photographic technique, is that its onset must be such that it will affect the photographic plate or film. We might choose a light of an intensity that will not elicit the wink by itself. This light can be arranged so that it, too, will enter the camera lens, possibly by reflection from a suitably placed mirror. To record the response, it is necessary that the movement of the eyelid be photographed. This can be arranged by pasting a light, stiff piece of paper onto the eyelid and placing the subject's head in a fixed position so that the artificial eyelash also projects across the lens. Now, both stimuli and response can be recorded.

It is now desirable to arrange for presenting the stimuli and timing the intervals between stimuli and response on the record. The stimuli can be presented in their proper sequence by any of a number of timing procedures. As simple a way as any is to have a pendulum bob with a tripping device swing past a set of switches, each of which controls an electromagnet. The electromagnets, in turn, control the stimuli. As the switches are tripped by the pendulum, the conditioning stimulus comes on, followed at a suitable interval by the loud sound. The intervals can be adjusted by separating the switches by greater or lesser distances in the arc of the pendulum. The pendulum bob may also serve to carry the photographic plate, and swing this past the lens, thus operating as a motion picture camera as well as a stimulus-release mechanism. A device which does all of this work is the pendulum photochronoscope of Dodge (1).

To record and measure the time interval, a constant-speed motor can be placed in front of a "wash" light, which will also serve to create the shadows of the artificial eyelash and vibrating rod. The motor can rotate an "episcotister," or disk with sections cut out of it, forming, in effect, a many-bladed fan. As each blade comes before the light source, it will also be recorded as a faint vertical shadow on the plate. The distance between one shadow and another will represent time intervals whose duration depends on the speed of the motor and the number of blades. The time between the stimuli and the response can be read directly in terms of the number of vertical lines on the picture. If the lens is divided by equally spaced fine wires in a horizontal series, the shadows of the wires can be used to measure the amplitude of the wink.

With the arrangement described above, we are able to study the eyelid blink in terms of frequency, amplitude, and time relationships either as a reflex, a conditioned, or a "voluntary" response. Since our original program was based on a conditioning procedure, we can consider that first. All that is necessary to go about the business of conditioning is to present the light stimulus and follow this by the sound stimulus, taking the picture of both of the stimuli and the responses thereto. In about forty or fifty trials we will note *in our record* that the wink starts to occur before the sound comes on. The response has been "conditioned." Since the time interval is so short, the subject is unable to discriminate or report that he is conditioned. Also, since the sound comes on after the response, it is unnecessary to test for response to light alone, thereby risking the possibility of "extinction of the conditioning." For this last reason, the eyelid blink is an ideal "response" for conditioning purposes.

If we wish to use the eyelid blink as a "reflex" sample, we need to use only the sound stimulus. If we care to study the inhibitory or facilitatory action of other stimuli, they can be presented in adequate intensity and at suitable intervals for such results. There is hardly as aspect of "reflex" activity to which the arrangement described cannot be adapted.

To study "voluntary" responses, we have merely to instruct the subject to blink at stated intervals or to certain selected stimuli. It will be noted that we are here equating "voluntary" activity and "responses to instructions." As far as the laboratory is concerned, that is the only operational procedure that has been devised. As Hilgard and Marquis (4, p. 257) phrase it: "In the laboratory voluntary behavior may be identified as actions which are evoked, without repetitive training, by instructions given to the subject."

In this connection it is desirable to point out that even when the experimenter does not issue specific instructions to the subjects, the subjects will proceed to instruct themselves and act accordingly. Such self-instruction, or "set," is likely to interfere greatly with the nature of the action of the subject. As J. Miller (5) discovered, many of his subjects who received no specific instructions from him adopted either facilitatory or inhibitory "sets" when serving as subjects in eyelid conditioning. The interpretation of the "responses" of a subject whose "sets" are not specifically known is likely to be extremely insecure. Before Miller's study, dozens of experiments on eyelid responses were performed and conclusions drawn on the basis of the records. How many of such conclusions are completely or partially invalidated as a result of the subject's sets cannot now be known.

If the same response can be used for reflex, conditioned, and voluntary studies, it seems likely that whatever differences exist among these terms are created, not by the subject, but by the experimenter's arrangements and instructions. If we try to find rigid demarcations by studying the frequency, amplitude, and latency characteristics of the responses themselves, we shall find, as did Peak (7), that there are no such dividing lines; that, on the contrary, there is a continuum of each type of measurement from "reflex" through "voluntary behavior." *

Although we have taken the simple eyelid reflex as our sample of laboratory "response," the student will realize on reviewing the classification presented earlier that, as far as his experimental procedure is concerned, he will be measuring the same four features of frequency, amplitude or amount, time relationships, and direction whether he is working with a nerve-muscle preparation of a frog or the amatory behavior of an elephant. Whatever else he *chooses to say* he is studying, e.g., "insight" or "purpose" or "conflict" or what not, his measurements and the validity of his study will depend on these four factors. It should be most painfully obvious, then, that if the experimenter is going to dress his data so as to have them appear as "frustration," "emotion," "spatial orientation," "hypotheses," etc., these terms must be rigidly defined in terms of the measurements on which they are based, and such definitions must be clearly phrased so as to be acceptable to the scientists concerned.

Because of the wide possibilities of the eyelid blink for future experimental purposes, as well as its already distinguished history,

---

* The finding that a continuum exists for one or even several measurements does not exclude the possibility of segregating types of responses on the basis of other criteria or conditions.

it is appropriate to begin our experimental study of responses with the eyelid reflex in Experiment 15.

References

1. Dodge, R. A. pendulum photochronograph. *J. exp. Psychol.*, 1926, *9*, 155–161.
2. Guthrie, E. *Cats in a puzzle box*. New York: Rinehart. 1946.
3. Hilgard, E. *Theories of learning*. New York: Appleton-Century-Crofts. 1947.
4. Hilgard, E., and Marquis, D. *Conditioning and learning*. New York: Appleton-Century. 1939.
5. Miller, J. The effect of facilitatory and inhibitory attitudes on eyelid conditioning. Abstr. in *Psychol. Bull.*, 1939, *36*, 577–578.
6. Miller, J. G. *Unconsciousness*. New York: Wiley. 1942.
7. Peak, H. Reflex and voluntary reactions of the eyelid. *J. gen. Psychol.*, 1933, *8*, 130–156.
8. Woodworth, R. S. *Psychology*, 5th ed. rev. New York: Henry Holt. 1945.

Experiment 14. Motor Responses: The Reflex; The Eyelid Blink

Introduction. Although the term "reflex" is now generally conceded to be a "hypothetical construct" and cannot be construed as an independent system of receptor, sensory nerve, central connection, motor nerve, effector, nor as a "unit" of behavior, it is still commonly used to denote a variety of relatively simple responses not obviously involving many muscle systems. In studying behavior, it is convenient to make use of this "convenient abstraction" because of the general identifiability, stability, relative uniformity, and, frequently, relative freedom from control by self-instruction. The more commonly studied "reflexes" or samples of behavior are the knee jerk, the galvanic response, the pupillary reflex, and the eyelid blink. The last of these is peculiarly suited to the needs of psychological experimentation because it is easily elicited and does not present too many difficulties in recording.

This response can be elicited in many ways (by air puffs, electric shock, tap on the cheek, threatening gestures, loud noises, bright lights) and can be recorded photographically or mechanically. It also has the virtues of appearing as a "reflex," a conditioned response, or as a self-initiated (voluntary) response. Familiarity with this behavior sample is a requirement for the student who expects to follow experimental literature. In this present experiment you will examine some of the features of behavior in terms of four fundamental measures: latency, amplitude, frequency, and direction, or wave form, as part of an experimental approach to the problem of adaptation or "habituation."

Apparatus and Procedure. The apparatus requirements involve the presentation of a stimulus, recording its occurrence, and recording the occurrence and form and amplitude of the response. Because you will use a mechanical recording procedure, and because the eyelid is not a powerful organ, the apparatus must be relatively light.

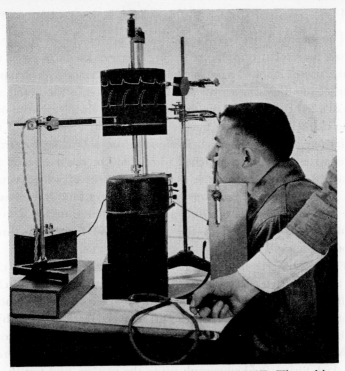

FIGURE 12. *THE EYELID-REFLEX EXPERIMENT*. The subject sits with his head supported by a chin rest. A fine thread is attached to a strip of adhesive tape $\frac{1}{8}$-inch by $\frac{1}{2}$-inch. The adhesive is fixed to the lower edge of the eyelid just above the lashes. The other end of the thread is attached to a light celluloid marker, which works like a lever and rides on a pin bearing. The thread is attached to the marker when the eye is open. A stop is provided so that the marker traces a steady line on the smoked paper of the kymograph when the eye is open. Closing the eye results in raising the marker and thereby tracing a rising curve on the kymograph paper. A stimulus for eyelid closure is provided by smartly squeezing a bulb (an ear-syringe will do) and forcing air through a tube which leads to a glass Y. One end of the Y is connected with another tube which leads to a point just below the subject's eye. The other end of the Y is connected with a tube leading to a tambour which carries a marker on its membrane (the cellophane from a cigarette package serves well as a membrane). When the bulb is pressed, some air strikes the subject's eye, and some displaces the membrane of the tambour. The tambour marker is agitated and leaves a record of the occurrence of the stimulus.

253

The essential need is to translate a movement of the eyelid into a movement on some recording surface. To do this you will make use of smoked-paper revolving on a kymograph drum. A marker mounted on a ring stand and attached to the eyelid will make a light scratch on the smoked paper when the eyelid moves. The marker should be a narrow strip of 6-inch-length light material (e.g., celluloid) which is mounted on a bearing to form a lever-system. A thread attached to one end of the marker is also attached to the base of the eyelid by a strip of adhesive tape (½ by ⅛ inches). Make sure that the adhesive tape is as close to the subject's lashes as possible, and allow some time for it to become securely attached to the lid after you loop your thread around the tape.

Fix the subject's head in a head rest, or have him rest his chin on a table with a slight backward tilt. Adjust the thread attached to his eyelid by raising or lowering the marker on a ring stand so that the thread is taut when the lid is open. Instruct the subject to blink voluntarily while you observe the marker, which should move freely up and down. When you are satisfied that there is no slack, bring the kymograph up to the marker, and test the action of the marker. It should rest lightly against the smoked paper. Arrange the marker so that it rides with, not against, the rotation of the drum. You are now ready to record the response.

To record the stimulus (an air puff, for purposes of this experiment) attach a length of rubber tubing to an ordinary ear syringe. At the other end of the tubing insert a piece of glass Y tubing. Now attach additional rubber tubing to the ends of the Y, one end going to a point just under the eye, the other to a tambour which carries a marker that is placed against the smoked paper of the kymograph. Pressure on the syringe will direct a stream of air against the cornea and at the same time operate the marker resting on the tambour, thus presenting and recording the stimulus at the same time. Adjust the tambour marker just under the lid marker, and test it for proper action.

Before beginning your recording, inscribe a time line on your smoked paper by using an electrically driven tuning fork or other time-marking device. If none is available, you can later make a time ruler by obtaining the speed of the kymograph and dividing a strip of the paper into millimeter units, each representing a fraction of a second.

Now start the kymograph and begin your recording. Present 50 stimuli in succession at 2-second intervals. Mark the last response with a suitable symbol. Now ask your subject to blink voluntarily several times and record these blinks. Stop the drum. Lower the kymograph drum on its support to provide a new surface, and try to "condition" the eyelid response in the following manner: Announce to the subject that you will signal each air puff by the word "now." Start a series of puffs, each preceded by "now." After about 15 or 20 such paired stimuli, say "now" in the usual manner, but do not present the puff. Repeat several times without the puff. Remove the adhesive tape from your subject's eyelid gently. Label all your situation types by writing directly on the drum. Fix your record by passing it through an alcohol and shellac mixture (10 percent shellac). In handling the drum be careful not to allow it to touch anything but your markers.

Results

1. Present your results on adaptation by (a) including the original kymograph record in your report, and (b) measuring the amplitude of each blink and presenting a table showing the means of every five successive blinks. Plot these means. Do the means indicate any trend?

2. What was the average height of the voluntary blinks? Were they greater or smaller than the first five reflex blinks?

3. Does your subject show any conditioned responses? What was their mean amplitude?

4. Were there any changes in latency of response in the adaptation series? Compare the first five with the last five for latency.

5. Were there any changes in the *form* of the responses in the

adaptation, voluntary, and conditioned series? Comment on this question in terms of the appearance of the record.

Discussion

1. How would you measure the latency of a voluntary response, a conditioned response?
2. What procedure would you use in photographing the eyelid reflex?
3. What sources of error were you able to control? Not able to control?
4. What feature of the eyelid did you note which makes it unsuitable for some "reflex" experiments?

References

1. Woodworth, R. S. *Experimental psychology*. New York: Henry Holt. 1938, chap. 5.

NOTE: The next chapter and the next three experiments deal with the subject of "motivation." Experiments 15 and 16 should be completed before Chapter 14 is read because they provide illustrations of phenomena discussed in the chapter and, also, because it is desirable not to reveal the point of the experiments before the student has a chance to do them.

Experiment 15. Motivation I: Work Decrement

Introduction. The concept of "fatigue" is of major importance to scientific workers in the areas of economics, physiology, and psychology. No satisfactory definition of the term has acquired general acceptance, as there are complex physical, physiological, and psychological aspects to consider in any situation involving activity and energy expenditure. A subject engaged in some activity may be willing to work, but unable to do so, and vice versa. His work may or may not suffer from "monotony," "boredom," and other reported personal feelings. His output is a function of a large number of variables such as rest, difficulty of the task, repetitiveness, physiological condition, motivation, etc.

Because "motivation" can keep a subject at work long beyond ordinary (standard) motivating conditions, the course of energy expenditure in a human subject is a problem of great interest for the psychologist. The study of work and effort is attracting considerable attention from "learning" psychologists in their attempts at understanding such phenomena as extinction and inhibition. In this experiment you will have an opportunity to observe the relationship between a number of variables and what Robinson has called "work decrement" for lack of a better operational term to use in describing "fatigue."

A work situation also appears suited to investigate the meaning of "motivation." When a subject is working, we have a chance to observe behavior which may provide inferences for answering such questions as: (1) What factors determine the course of his work, the ups and downs, changes in efficiency, etc.? (2) What factors lead the subject to cease working? (3) What are the influences of rewards, goals, incentives, environmental and social stimuli? After the experiment is finished, try to develop an operational definition of motivation based on your observations of a subject at work.

FIGURE 13. *A FINGER ERGOGRAPH.* The subject holds the bolt firmly with his hand. The index finger grasps the loop in the wire and pulls against the weight attached to the other end. The metal marker records the extent of each pull on wax paper driven by a polyograph. The working parts are mounted on a piece of 2 inch by 4 inch lumber. The slide for the marker can be manufactured in a number of ways. The method shown is simple and satisfactory. The bolt handgrip is a painless substitute for former methods of restricting hand and arm movements. The amount of weight should be adjusted for each subject, depending on his strength. Window sash-weights are convenient. Heavy cable cord is advisable to avoid breaks during experimental trials.

Apparatus. "Fatigue" or "work decrement" experiments generally require some work situation calling for regular and consistent energy expenditure over a period of time sufficient to bring about a change in performance level from some standard. In the laboratory it is difficult to arrange natural situations calling for useful work, such as shovelling coal or building houses, etc. Such tasks immediately introduce factors of skill, previous associations, and so on.

The Italian physiologist, Mosso, devised an instrument which he called the "ergograph" to eliminate some of the difficulties associated with normal activities. In using the ergograph, a limited number of muscles is used to pull up and lower a weight, usually in time with a metronome. See Figure 13. The extent of each pull is recorded and later measured. Bills (1) and Robinson (2) devised a number of tasks, such as naming colors, repeating words, or writing letters, for their studies of work decrement. In the present experiment you will use a modified Mosso ergograph and a letter-writing task.

Procedure. Part 1. Ergograph. The subject will work at the ergograph task twice, with a 10-minute rest interval. While he is resting, the experimenter will change places with him and perform the same duties. The experimenter will instruct the subject to work with one finger only (the index finger of the right hand), and to pull the weight up as far as possible with each stroke until he can no longer do so, i.e., until he is unable to bend the finger sufficiently to move the marker which traces a record of his work. He is to keep in time with a metronome beating 60 times per minute, and is not to fall behind in time. The subject should watch the metronome wand and pull back against the weight when the wand comes toward him, and release the weight when the wand returns. The weight is to be *let* back, not dropped. A weight of about 14 pounds is adequate. Lighter weights can be provided for weaker subjects. The record of work will be recorded on a polygraph or kymograph. The subject is not to see his records until the experiment is finished. The subject should practice a few strokes without the weight until he has the rhythm and technique mastered.

Part 2. *Letter writing.* The instructor will serve as experimenter and will instruct the subjects to write the letters *p* and *q* in rapid succession, thus: *pqpqpqpqpq,* etc. The subject will be supplied with plenty of lined paper and writing implements. At 30-second intervals the experimenter will say "now." At each "now" the subject will skip a space of about 1 inch and continue without pause until the experiment is over. The subjects *will not be told* how long they are to work, and are instructed to work at maximum speed throughout the experiment, with no restraint or other inhibitions. When the experimenter calls "time," there will be a 10-minute rest and another work period like the first, although the time will be different. The times will be known only to the instructor.

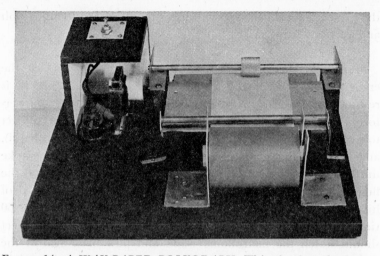

FIGURE 14. *A WAX-PAPER POLYGRAPH*. This simple polygraph is constructed from parts costing about $10.00. A 1-RPM Telechron motor is used to drive a mimeograph roller which pulls the waxed (or any other type of paper) tape over a writing table. Another roller rests above the paper and provides the necessary resistance. To obtain the best efficiency, the motor must be securely mounted in alignment with the shaft of the roller which rides in roller bearings. To connect the motor to the roller, fit the shaft of the motor with a tubular shaft. Compress the end of the shaft until it resembles the tip of a screw driver. This tip is then inserted into a slot filed in the roller shaft. Markers indicating occurrence of events are fashioned from electromagnets stripped from doorbells or any other source. Wax paper is obtainable from the Stylograph Corporation, Rochester, New York.

Results

1. Present a drawing and description of your apparatus and your two ergograms suitably mounted and described.
2. Graph the amount of work done per 30-second period in the letter-writing experiment by counting the number of *p's* written. How do your two curves compare in shape, subjectively considered? What work-curve characteristic can you point out? Is there a "warm up" in each curve? Is there an end-spurt?

Does the second curve in either task show a practice effect? Apply the same analysis to your two ergograms. Plot your ergograms by taking the median height of each fifteenth of the curve.

3. Are there any similarities between the ergograms and the letter-writing curves? Which curve shows the greater decrement? Why?

4. How can practice effects be controlled in work decrement experiments?

Discussion

1. What factors influenced the work of yourself and your subject?
2. Did you follow the instructions, or did you modify them either before or during the work sessions? State the instructions you were given and those you actually followed.
3. What suggestions can you make relating your work activity to motivation? To personality?
4. Can you suggest other tasks by which energy expenditure and work decrement could be studied profitably?
5. In the light of your work experience, how would you define "fatigue"?

References

1. Bills, A. G. *General experimental psychology.* New York: Longmans, Green. 1934. See chaps. 21, 22.
2. Robinson, E. S. Work of the integrated organism. In Murchison, C., *Handbook of general experimental psychology.* Worchester: Clark University Press. 1934.
3. Underwood, B. J. *Experimental psychology.* New York: Appleton-Century-Crofts. 1949, chap. 16.

Experiment 16. Motivation II: Mental Set—
A Demonstration Experiment

TO THE STUDENT: *Do not read any part of this experiment until instructed to do so.*

Introduction. The nature of the instructions given the subject in a psychological experiment is a major influence on his performance and can often be a strongly biasing factor, a primary source of error. This is often apparent in complicated test procedures, e.g., the Rorschach test. In a more simple experimental situation, where the subject is told to do some one specific thing, e.g., press a key at a given signal, it might appear that anyone with a simple knowledge of English would comply adequately. This is by no means true, as even the most simple instructions are often perverted, twisted, and complicated by the subject's previous experience, expectations, desire to be helpful or to outwit the experimenter, etc.

A typical control procedure is to read instructions verbatim, thus assuring that at least all the subjects were instructed with the same words. This, of course, does not insure uniform understanding. It does little good to ask, "Do you understand?" as obvously the subject who *mis*understands does not realize his failure to comprehend. It is probably true that you can never be sure of the attitudes or "sets" adopted by any specific subject to a given set of instructions.

One might even raise the question whether some of the higher animal species do not disturb experimental procedures by their own "sets" or reactions to what amounts to "instructions" in some animal experiments. Thus, animals who have previously learned several mazes can go about the business of learning a new one with some efficiency. They are "maze-wise," as compared with "naïve" animals. They may be enjoying the benefits of "positive transfer" of reactions to identical elements, i.e., they meet the new situation with useful habits. It is possible to interpret this greater efficiency as an indication that the maze-wise rat faces the new maze as a path to master, whereas the beginner may have quite other "sets."

The present experiment is designed to demonstrate how sub- µ jects will instruct themselves and behave in a particular manner in spite of *no* instructions to do so. The experiment will probably show, in some instances, that the subjects were not even aware of the instructions they gave themselves. Instructions presumably result in a reaction or adjustment to respond in a certain way. Such an adjustment is called a "set." Sometimes the expression "mental set" is used when the behavior involved is relatively restricted in an overt, physical, sense. If, as suggested above, some subjects react in accordance with a self-imposed instructional "set" which they cannot describe, there is some justification for speaking of "unconscious mental sets."

Apparatus and Procedure. Two groups of subjects—experimental and control—will solve 30 five-letter anagrams.* The anagrams can be presented in mimeographed columns on ordinary sheets of paper, so that each subject receives a single sheet and has no way of knowing that there are two different sets of materials, one set for each group. Of the 30 anagrams to be solved, 15 have only one solution, that is, only one English word can be made up of the five letters involved. Thus, the letters "khalc" can be rearranged to spell "chalk" but no other word. The remaining 15 anagrams have two or more solutions.

The arrangement of the anagrams differs for the two groups. For the experimental group, the anagrams are arranged so that the first 15 have only one solution, the remainder (16 through 30) have at least two common-word solutions. All of the 30 anagrams for this group can be solved by following a simple formula: the last three letters are the first three of the solution, and the first

* The two lists of anagrams are included in Appendix 2.

and second letters are reversed to form the fourth and fifth letters. Numerically, the order of the letters is 54123. For example, n-e-l-i-n becomes "linen." The subject going through the list can solve the first 15 only in the 54123 manner. This practice tends to carry over, and he continues to solve many of the remaining 15 in the same fashion, even though other solutions are possible.

For the control group, only those anagrams which comprise the last 15 of the experimental group can be solved by the formula. These "test" or "key" anagrams are intermixed at random with 15 other anagrams which have only one solution, but this solution does not follow any formula. (The same words which make up the first 15 of the experimental group are used, but the order of the letters is scrambled at random.)

The experimenter instructs both groups to solve the anagrams as rapidly as possible and in consecutive order (without returning to any missed). One minute is allowed for each anagram, although subjects may go on if they finish before time is called for the next anagram. The subjects note the time of finishing the task, and report this later. A sheet of paper with a narrow slot in one edge is used as a screen, permitting work on only one anagram at a time and serving as a record sheet. As soon as the subject finishes the anagrams, he is asked to attempt the solution of a fairly difficult puzzle. The puzzle, prepared by the experimenter, can be included on the record sheets or written on a blackboard, although the former method is more suitable.

The subjects are not informed until the experiment is over that they were members of different groups or that they worked on different materials. At the end of the thirty-minute work period, the experimenter questions members of both groups in a manner calculated to bring out the answers called for under "results." The questions should be informal and nondirective, and should develop the degree of information about the nature of the anagrams and the experiment that the subjects obtained. Particular emphasis should be placed on such questions as: "Why did the members of the experimental group work as they did?"

Results

1. How many of the subjects knew that some of the anagrams could be solved by a "system"? How many knew that all of the experimental ones could be so solved? When was such information acquired, i.e., after how many solutions?

2. How many subjects knew that *several* solutions were possible in the last 15 experimental anagrams? This is a crucial question, as it reflects a type of "set," a "one-track mind" or "falling-in-a-rut" factor. Which group finished first? Why?

3. How many subjects can accurately describe the system without reference to the words?

4. How many subjects had a preponderance of "formula" solutions without knowing that there was a formula?

5. What is the critical ratio of the difference between the percentage of test anagrams solved by formula between the two groups? In calculating this percentage, add all the 54123 solutions for the test anagrams in each group separately. Divide this by 15 N where N is the number of subjects. Then use the formula below for the "standard error of the difference." Note that $N1$ and $N2$ in the formula are also obtained as above and amount to 15 N. The p's represent the percentage of formula solutions, the q's represent 100 p. The p's and q's are reported as decimals, e.g., 0.58.

Standard error of the difference between 2 percentages =

$$\sqrt{\frac{p_1 q_1}{n_1} + \frac{p_2 q_2}{n_2}}$$

Discussion

1. Why were you asked to work on a puzzle after solving the anagrams?

2. How does this experiment demonstrate the nature of "sets"? How does it fit your concept of motivation?

3. Why is a control group used in this experiment? Did the control group use the formula often? If so, why?

4. Can you work up a set of anagrams in which the solution of the first few can be obtained only by using animal names, and then check the effect of an "animal-name-set" by providing anagrams which can be solved as animal names or as some other common terms?

References

1. Rees, H. J., and Israel, H. E. An investigation of the establishment of mental sets. *Psychol. Mono.*, 1935, *46*, 1–26.
2. Underwood, B. J. *Experimental psychology.* New York: Appleton-Century-Crofts. 1949, chap. 6.

14

The Control of Motivation in Experimentation

Do not read this chapter until after you have done Experiments 15 and 16.

WHENEVER ONE SPEAKS of conditions within the organism which alter the behavior from what would be expected without such conditions, he is dealing with the variable of motivation. This variable is, perhaps, the most important, and at the same time, the most complex factor in behavior. We cannot hope to consider all the significant aspects of motivation in this text and must confine ourselves to appreciating the role of motivation in experimental work.

The discussion to follow, therefore, is not offered as an exhaustive or even satisfactory treatment of the concept of motivation. For our present purposes we can concern ourselves only with recognizing the problems involved in the manipulations of the environment which eventuate in behavior. To achieve this end we must first consider how motivation is involved in laboratory work, and then try to arrive at methods of describing this variable operationally and of controlling, or at least appreciating, its nature. Before we consider motivation from this operational and laboratory viewpoint, we might benefit by a brief general consideration of the problem of motivation, to which we now turn.

The concept of motivation is basic to modern psychology. It

occupies a central place in learning theory, in clinical practice, in interpretations of all manner of individual and social behavior. In view of its singular importance, it is certainly necessary, even vital, for psychologists to be in agreement about the nature of this concept. It is strange that no such agreement exists about so widely used a concept. In every text the significance of motivation is stressed but left unexplained and undefined. Following a practice popularized by Dashiell (1), the usual writer plunges into "tissue conditions," which he terms "drives," indicates that he appreciates the fact that drives such as hunger, thirst, pain, etc., do not account for the activity level of the successful banker who refuses to retire, and plunges with equal facility into a discussion of social motives which take care of the banker. The transition between tissue activity and social activity is assumed to take place by learning, or through "mechanisms" becoming "drives," or through some process of becoming "functionally autonomous," whereby historical antecedents drop out of the motivational picture. The average student struggling with these mysteries gradually comes to accept one position or another—he must, if he is to survive as a student—and often feels that failure to understand is the fault of his own inadequacy. Surely these writers of texts must know what they are talking about.

Leeper (3) has reported that writers on emotion are not necessarily logical or consistent and may not even contribute positively to an understanding of emotional behavior. Following his lead, the present writer is inclined toward similar conclusions concerning the treatment of the topic of motivation in the average text. Some authors have approached what the writer regards as a reasonably correct position, but have failed to draw the necessary conclusions, and since it appears that a reasonable position can be worked out, the following analysis is presented. It should be noted that this analysis does no harm to any current system of psychology and, in fact, could be adopted by almost any system without modification of views already commonly and widely held. Actually it says nothing new. On the contrary, it is merely setting down what others have perhaps considered too radical a view.

It appears wise to start with motives rather than with drives. The other approach has been tried and found wanting. The reverse might prove more profitable. Starting with motives allows us to consider the human organism immediately without trying to jump from rats in an obstruction box to motives for war, professional approval, racial supremacy, etc.

Let us also take a simple experimental situation: Supply a human subject with a number of problems involving the solution of anagrams, as was done by Israel and Rees (6), or the solution of a series of mathematical problems (Luchins, 4). The experiments just mentioned were procedurally the same, but Luchins' is simpler to describe. A subject is asked to indicate how he would use containers of various sizes to get a specific amount of water in a larger container. In each problem, the solution can be arrived at by only one method (use one container twice, another once, and a third once for emptying). After a number of such problems are solved, a test problem is presented in which the practiced solution is unduly cumbersome and unnecessary, though possible. The average subject continues to follow the routine, failing to notice the simpler solutions. When other test problems are submitted in which the routine solution does not work, the subject keeps trying it, and often fails to solve the problems even though they are outrageously simple. Why does he persist? Does this persistent behavior involve motivation? As Rees and Israel have demonstrated, a subject will solve a series of problems using a method which he cannot describe, which he denies having recognized, and which he is surprised to hear about. Was he "unconsciously" motivated? Rees and Israel do not go so far as to say so; they conclude that an "unconscious mental set" was demonstrated. In the mathematical problems the same findings appear; they are likewise described as involving "mental sets."

The term "mental set" retains a degree of acceptability among psychologists which has long been denied any other phenomenon even faintly suggesting a "mental" operation. There appears to be no more logical ground for retaining the adjective "mental" in conjunction with the term "set" than in any other area of discourse, and it is proposed that it be dropped and the term "set" alone be retained, at least temporarily, as a descriptive agent for discussing such findings as described above.

When we consider the nature of this "set" in anagram solution or problem solving, and ask how did this set develop, we readily recognize the learning factor and tend to concentrate on it. But the learning factor is present only as an artifact of the experiment. It could easily be reduced or omitted by the simple expedient of instructing the subjects on the method of solution, either in whole or in part. Learning of a one-trial nature would still be present, but this type of learning is generally ignored *as learning* and left out of consideration because it is accepted as a normal understanding of instructions. When the experimenter fails to instruct the subject, he should not be surprised if the subject gradually pieces out the instructions *that might have been given* and proceeds to instruct himself. This process of self-instruction seems to be what goes on in the types of experiments cited as far as the writer can determine after repeating both experiments dozens of times with classes in experimental psychology.

In the two situations cited, the motivational factor has been reduced to "mental set," and the latter term to self-instruction. Since a subject can instruct himself incorrectly, in whole or in part, or since he can mistakenly overemphasize some features of a situation at the expense of others, he may find that he has been responding to some features or stimuli which are actually irrelevant to the solution of the problem and which keep him from looking at other aspects of a situation. A person with a strong racial prejudice, for example, may be unable to perceive obvious virtues in an individual of a race he dislikes. His "sets" or habits of perception blind him as much as love blinds a lover.

Methods of solving problems, or any habitual responses, may develop without the subject ever recognizing the relevant aspects of a situation. If he does not stop and talk to himself about them, that is, if he does not engage in self-instruction, he may not be able to tell us about how he reacted. When a subject is unable to describe the sequences in some response system verbally, we usually describe his behavior as "unconscious." You can readily think of many responses which you are perfectly capable of performing but which you cannot easily describe verbally: tying shoe laces, for example. In some types of problem-solving situations, the solutions come quickly and easily and may be repeated so rapidly that you do not stop to verbalize. This seems to be what happens in the Luchins and the Rees and Israel experiments. The subject is finished with the task before he knows, in a verbal sense, how he did it. In that case we may be justified in speaking of "unconscious motivation" in describing some of the factors directing his behavior.

The development of likes, dislikes, and fears may have similar controlling factors. Stimuli may be present which become associated with the reactions without being verbalized. This is most likely to occur in childhood before verbalization is strongly developed. An individual might come to fear some object or go through some pattern of responses and be unable to give a verbal description of the relation of the stimuli present to the responses in which he is engaging. Because of his "set," he may ascribe his behavior to completely irrelevant or incorrect relationships. A few successes associated with irrelevant stimuli may force a subject into a rut from which he may never extricate himself. The reluctance with which people, even the young, accept changed circumstances is an obvious example.

The importance of self-instruction should not be overlooked by the experimenter who may feel that reading a set of typed instructions to his subject is all that is necessary. The writer used to use the question "Do you understand?" when explaining some matters or giving instructions to a class. Because no hands were raised, it was assumed that understanding prevailed. The occurrence of errors, or failures to follow instructions, should have brought the essential stupidity of the question to the writer's attention long ago, but it was slow in coming. It seems that subjects thought they understood and therefore did not report failure to comprehend. From the subject's viewpoint, either he understands or he doesn't. Since he is the sole interpreter of the meaning of words to him, he can understand anything that the words mean to him. In short, the experimenter does not instruct subjects. They instruct themselves. All that the experimenter can hope for is that the self-instruction parallels his desires in the situation. (He should always check this by preliminary tests or trials, and usually does.)

A striking example of how self-instruction can modify the results of experimentation has been reported by J. Miller (5). In his studies of eyelid conditioning, Miller found that the frequency and amplitude of responses was to some extent controllable by the subjects. When subjects were asked to do nothing to prevent blinking, more blinks were recorded than when only routine instructions were given. This finding clearly indicates that, under routine instructions, the subjects were *instructing themselves* in some fashion to prevent blinking. Since numerous studies of eyelid responses had been published before Miller's discovery, there is considerable reason for questioning the validity of many of the results accumulated by experimenters who did not take account of the subjects' tendency to inhibit the blink response.

Another sample of self-instruction in a simple experimental situation may not be amiss. In work with a Mosso ergograph, subjects are usually instructed to pull up a weight by flexing a finger as much as possible with each beat of a metronome. These instructions seem to cover the needs of the experiment. A "fatigue" curve usually results. The shape of this curve, however, varies from individual to individual, although it retains a reasonable similarity from day to day for any given individual.

When various instructions are given subjects in this work situation, however, the appearance of the curve alters radically. Suppose a subject has been working regularly for about two minutes per day, not knowing the exact length of time. Ask him to work "for two minutes" some day, and his work output changes, his work habits change, all semblance of similarity to previous activity disappears. What does this mean other than that his conception of "two minutes" enters into his self-instruction? Or ask him on each pull to reach a certain standard which he normally but unknowingly has achieved in daily practice. Immediately his behavior alters. He instructs himself in terms of his understanding of the situation. Or have him work in a social situation when he has formerly worked in isolation. Again the work curve changes.

In every case, the subject demonstrates that the original instructions mean a certain kind of adjustment or response to him. This adjustment is highly individualized for the particular subject and cannot be appreciated by the experimenter until he can determine what new responses may emerge. Behavior changes with self-instruction, and self-instruction is a resultant of a combination of circumstances, including the subject's previous history, the demands of the external situation, and only partially the actual overt instructions of the experimenter.*

To carry the matter a step forward, consider what happens when a financial reward for more output is offered a subject who is approaching complete decrement. What changes if the subject begins to put forth more effort? His motivation? That is too vague and general a term. His behavior is determined by his interpretation of the financial reward to him, then and there, in the specific circumstances; and such interpretation will modify, at least, his self-instruction. If the subject works harder, we might loosely phrase the result as due to "telling himself to do so." If he does not work harder, then we are left with the possibility either that he does not tell himself to do so, or that he cannot respond to his own instructions.

The matter of subjects' understanding of instructions and their reaction thereto has been discussed at some length because it

* Kinesthetic and pain stimuli are considered here as part of the pattern of stimuli determining the subject's self-instruction.

opens the question of motivation to an operational attack. It is customary to consider motivation as a *cause* of behavior. This view appears to be founded on a historical, moralistic, legalistic, and linguistic background and does violence to any deterministic type of psychology. In trying to comprehend man as a rational creature, the causes or reasons for his behavior were the primary preoccupation of our classical psychologists.

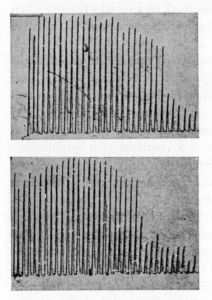

FIGURE 15. *SAMPLE WORK CURVES FROM ONE SUBJECT*. These records were obtained on two successive days and indicate the degree of similarity in successive performances on the finger ergograph. Other subjects produce curves which differ in pattern from those of this subject, but which are also similar from day to day under standard instructions.

As the biological influences replaced the mentalistic rationalism of the eighteenth and nineteenth centuries, instincts, genes, drives, glands, and other biological constructs or tissues received attention as sources of reasons or causes of behavior. In our law courts, motives (in terms of conscious premeditations, intents, purposes, etc.) are still of major concern in establishing the degree of seriousness of crime (e.g., first-degree murder implies premeditation or intent; manslaughter is a lesser crime, even though the victim may be much less neatly dispatched).

Voluntaristic, mentalistic, and rationalistic psychologists were intent upon equipping man with causes for his acts. Such causes he supposedly carried about with him, consciously, unconsciously, or autonomously. Any attempt to take such causes away from man is still regarded with suspicion, not only by students brought up on the folklore of centuries and on current mystery novels, but also by professional psychologists. Because it is obvious that man reacts differently in many situations and at different times, it is necessary that he carry about with him a wide variety of motives. This makes the situation a bit awkward when the variety of responses an individual is called on to make on any day or any hour is considered.

A man has social, economic, political, sexual, nationalistic, prestige, scholastic, and other motives; at least he appears to exhibit these from time to time. It is obvious that he cannot exhibit these all at once, and so it is generally assumed that only one is functioning at a time, the rest being held in abeyance, or even repressed into an unconscious "something" or "somewhere." These "repressed" motives may then carry on an apparently independent struggle for power (if one cares to go along with certain psychoanalytic views).

The necessity for pushing all but one or two motives out of the active sphere at any given moment has given rise to a series of strategic retreats. Various terms have been invented, all of which mean the same thing operationally, although literally they may have nuances of some merit. Hilgard,* for example, in one sentence lists the following: "sets," "attitudes," "readiness." Other terms such as "wish," "desire," "intent," "purpose," "interest," "attention," "ambition," "end," "goal," and like are often used as if they had some real meaning and private existence of their own. In fact, various painfully elaborate definitions have been constructed for some of these, but in effect they consist of attempts to endow the organism with causal agents or mechanisms, to put "motives" or motivation into the individual. Sometimes other varieties of phenomena are given motivational, driving, or "dy-

* *Theories of Learning.* New York: Appleton-Century-Crofts, 1948.

namic" significance (anxieties, conflicts, fears, worries, frustration, and emotion generally).

The present writer feels that all such attempts to equip the organism with causes or reasons are misguided. There is no special objection to any of the terms mentioned above if they are deprived of their causative functions and are properly used as descriptive generalizations in a specific framework. To get along verbally without recourse to some of these would drop the content of even basic English a measurable amount. The writer proposes a reorientation of our thinking in the problem of the causes of behavior. It is suggested that psychologists have not tried to make stimulus-response psychology work.* Woodworth, for example, starts out with an S-O-R psychology that appears suitable, but he leaves it when he gets to motives. He is not as guilty as most, and the writer hastens to acknowledge a debt to Woodworth which the latter may disavow.

Perhaps we have not given S-R psychology a chance. We have too readily attempted to endow man with a variety of faculties, capacities, drives, and mechanisms, many of which we could do well without. The writer is not proposing an empty-organism psychology, as there are, in his opinion, a number of potentially useful constructs assumed to exist within a behaving organism which are gradually submitting to analysis (such as the stimuli from "fractional anticipatory goal responses" of Hull and the "movement-produced stimuli" of Guthrie). But it should be noted that the above "constructs" have to do with the nature of *stimuli*. There are other constructs that deal with neural activity, such as stimulus traces, spontaneous neural action, neural interaction, refractory phase, etc., which can be thought of as *responses* of an internal nature whose presence or activity determines the nature of overt behavioral responses; these too can be admitted for purposes of analyzing the dynamics of behavior. The question remains whether a stimulus-response psychology which includes in-

* The term "response" is to be interpreted broadly as including not only overt behavior in the form of muscle contractions, but also, following Hebb (2), as central-nervous-system reactions. Stimuli, too, can be central processes.

ternal stimuli and internal responses (glandular or muscular activity, neural states resulting from prior activity, or bio-chemical changes such as result from failure of the organism to maintain adequate amounts and kinds of food, water, oxygen, temperature, etc.) is enough to account for behavior. The remainder of this chapter will be concerned with suggesting that it is.

It is first proposed that the distinction between "drive" and "motive" be dropped as irrelevant and meaningless, tending to perpetuate a problem which does not exist (the transformation of physical drives into social motives). Both terms basically indicate the same kind of answer to the question: "Why did this organism react in this particular fashion to this particular stimulus situation?" It is just as easy (or as difficult) to formulate the same general type of answer to a question concerning the reason for a rat's crossing a grid to a prospective mate, as to explain a woman's desire for, or purchase of, a new Easter bonnet.

Next it is proposed that the concept of "set" be considered as a broad general principle to cover all motivational situations. "Set" is to be thought of in terms of a response, basically a learned, habitual response. It is to be remembered that certain sets are adopted so readily (one-trial learning) that the learning process is often overlooked. A typical and obvious example is the sprinter in his starting blocks awaiting the starter's pistol shot. The quality of the sprinter's set is fundamental to his making an adequate response to the stimulus. That such an obvious example of "set" is a matter of the physical response of practically the entire muscle system hardly needs mention. The sprinter is ready, tense, attentive, "set." Dashiell long ago identified such muscular contraction as a basic ingredient of attention with his happy choice of words: "a tension." The behavior of individuals other than sprinters is not qualitatively different in other situations.

A particular stimulus (internal or external) evokes a response. This response may be of a preparatory nature, a tentative, adjustive response, preparing the organism for future stimuli which in the past have regularly followed. The response may be in the nature of a central nervous process which we can not at the moment observe, but for which we have reasonable support from current neurophysiological evidence (2). Such responses which prepare the organism for reacting in specific ways to specific stimuli are just as much learned, or "habits," as are the more direct and overt moves normally classified as responses or "behavior." The rat in the Skinner box is generally trained to come to a food dish at a sound. Later he makes the sound himself by tapping a bar. The sound "sets" him for "eating behavior" as is evident from his behavior when, in training, the sound and food are omitted for a while and the animal "extinguishes." Reinstating the sound, but not the food, "re-sets" the animal. He is again "motivated," whereas a minute before he stayed away from the food dish.

That a "set" can influence perceptual responses is well known, although the mechanisms involved are not understood or even open to effective examination. The writer has found that subjects can report more units in tachistoscopic perception when they are told what kinds of objects are to be exposed. Thus, when told that they will see letters on a screen, they are able to identify more letters than when they are told that numbers will appear but instead are shown letters. Seeing numbers when letters are "expected" results in some sort of disturbance, frustration, or conflict. What elements are in conflict has not yet been discovered. No specific muscular set appears to be present. The type of set involved may be a purely central-nervous-system activity. Interrogation of subjects has not produced helpful hints. The subjects are not able to describe any action taken in assuming a set for numbers or letters. They report, typically, "I just visualized numbers (or letters), said them over to myself," etc. Whatever the essential mechanisms are, there is no question about the effectiveness of the set and its preparatory, facilitatory nature.

Next it is proposed that motives, as "sets," are strictly temporary, momentary, and continuously changing, although the changes may be immeasurably minute at any one time. In other words, motives do not exist in the individual as such. They are created as responses to given stimuli when, and only when, stimuli for such responses are present. The rat in the Skinner box leaves his bar-pressing motives behind when not in the box. The student who "is highly motivated for study" has no such motives when at the theatre with a favorite girl friend. The student who has an intention, ambition, motive, or what not to be a doctor has none of these things when preparing to dive into the water from a springboard or when playing chess or basketball. Certainly he does not go about chanting, "I want to be a doctor, I want to be a doctor." The anti-Semitic person is not anti-Semitic when he is asleep or admiring roses or even praising Hitler. Attitudes *develop* upon occasion. They are not carried about, any more than other habits, learned responses, or memorized poems are carried about *in something*.

An analogy to photographic procedures might illustrate the point. When the photographer snaps his shutter, he may speak of "taking a picture." Actually he has no picture in his camera and will have none till he subjects the exposed film to proper chemicals (stimuli) which will bring out the picture (response). So with the organism: in the past it has been exposed to certain stimuli and altered in certain ways. If the proper stimuli are presented, a response of a certain type occurs. It may be an "attitude," an emotion, a desire, or what not, depending on the stimuli and the previous exposure. The organism must be regarded as a rather complicated collection of exposed (and, therefore, altered) negatives, any of which may be "developed" at a given time.

From an experimental point of view the essential feature of motivation is that the experimenter arranges a situation so that the subject's freedom of response is strongly restricted to a limited number of possibilities, and that responses to certain of these possibilities are encouraged. An animal is deprived of food so that food-taking and food-seeking responses will predominate in his behavior. Stimuli from non-food sources, e.g., sex partners, will lose effectiveness The runner in a race is made ready by his instructions to respond to the sound of a shot in a specific manner (the spectator may be startled). Motivation then serves to limit the range of behavior to those features the experimenter wishes to observe. If the experimenter is interested in observing the number of times a rat will press a bar, he must arrange conditions so that bar-pressing is a likely occurrence. A well fed rat is not likely to press often. He is receptive to other stimuli, perhaps those which initiate sleep responses. Even the well fed rat, however, can become a bar-presser if he is shocked until he presses. He has been made receptive to bar-pressing stimuli.

Finally, it is proposed that "sets" as learned reactions are no more autonomous or free to act than any other type of response, but must occur to stimuli. The historical continuity in a particular attitude may be hard to trace, especially if there have been many changes over the years, and if the habits involved were learned in childhood in prelanguage states or under circumstances where the real verbal cues were disguised or misrepresented to children by parents who gave superficial verbal explanation for situations where stimuli to emotional behavior were the actual conditioning agents. This type of learning situation may account for many alleged motives of fear, likes and dislikes, appetites, ambitions, etc., whose historical continuity is lost for an individual.

In summarizing, it is suggested that the concept of motivation be reconsidered in its cause-effect aspects. Motivation is a response to stimuli, and therefore an effect of stimuli, not a cause of behavior. Motivation can be thought of as a preparatory response of a habitual nature in certain stimulus situations. As such, motivation is equivalent to what is generally identified as set or readiness or attention. "Attention" is to be thought of as a certain type of readiness to react in a certain way, whether to perceive (react to) some types of stimuli, as in the typical reaction-time experiment, or to facilitate the movement of a specific muscle group, as in the "motor-set" in reaction time. The type of set adopted by the individual in terms of the wide variety of behavioral situations ordinarily included under "motivation" will vary with each individual and with each situation. To give a general operational definition of a noncircular variety may be extremely difficult, although practical and feasible for any specific situation.

Sets are considered to be momentary, although some aspects of a given act may be present as component parts of a series of succeeding sets in some general situation. For example, in a series of problems of the same kind, such as a series of mathematical exercises involving multiplication, a general set to multiply can be inferred from the difficulty of switching to other types of operations.

The choice of the term "set" as a substitute for "motivation" may not be the best, but it has the advantages of usage and familiarity in situations which, when the term came into wide usage, should have been recognized as involving the basic aspects of motivation.

For human organisms, instructions from without, or self-instructions (responses to stimuli from within, or as individual habit responses), are of major significance in establishing sets. The possibility of broadening the category of instructed behavior (including self-instruction) to animals need not be denied. The "principle of expectancy" of Tolman may well be worked out in terms of self-instruction through experience and habit formation as a matter of preparatory response or set. The role of Hull's $rg's$ and stimuli therefrom in the formation of set-responses is basic for a consideration of the possibility of "self-instruction" (on a behavioristic basic) in animals.

The proposals made above are already standard and accepted usages in the psychological laboratory. "Motivation" is a recognized variable, but no attempt is ever made to control motivation directly. When animal subjects are used, the *state* of the animal is described in terms of hours of deprivation of certain stimuli (*food, water, mates, etc.*). It is assumed that animals in such a condition are ready (set) to respond to other stimuli manipulated by the experimenter. The deprivation procedure is used as a substitute for instructions, which are of little use in the average experiment with animals. A trained dog, however, can be "set" by instructions which consist of words or suitable signs. When human subjects are studied, not much can be done beyond the statement of the instructions given. When experimenters go beyond the description of instructions and describe the state of their human subjects in terms of desires, ambitions, etc., they are no longer working operationally. The operational reduction of some of these descriptive terms, like "level of aspiration," amounts to an account of self-instruction.

Fortunately most problems in the laboratory do not depend upon the subject's "motivation" in any primary respect. "Motivation" may be a serious preoccupation of the *subject,* but it can often be ignored by the experimenter if the problem permits. In a nonsense-syllable experiment, for instance, where the experimenter is concerned with the order of learning of the syllables, he need not concern himself too seriously with the subject's complaints of boredom or lack of interest; as long as the subject continues to learn, that is all that the experimenter has any right to demand. As a matter of fact, the experimenter is in no position to evaluate the influence of the subject's mood in such an experiment, and would be at a loss to explain why the subject *should* be happy about the whole thing, or anything but bored.

The student in experimental psychology is often anxious to be sure that his subjects are equally "motivated." Such anxiety represents a phantasy which has no chance of realization. Certainly money and food rewards or praise and punishment cannot be equated for different individuals without protracted preliminary experiments. The great Knute Rockne could not inspire his men equally by pep talks; neither can the best psychologist. As far as the laboratory control of motivation is concerned, the experimenter will have to be content with his instructions and the reactions of his subjects to their own interpretations of these instructions.

References

1. Dashiell, J. F. *Fundamentals of general psychology*, 3d. ed. New York: Houghton Mifflin. 1949.
2. Hebb, D. O. *The organization of behavior*. New York: Wiley. 1949.
3. Leeper, R. A motivational theory of emotion to replace "Emotion as disorganized response." *Psychol. Rev.*, 1948, *55*, 5–21.
4. Luchins, A. S. Classroom experiments on mental set. *Amer. J. Psychol.*, 1946, *54*, 295–298.
5. Miller, J. The effect of facilitatory and inhibitory attitudes upon eyelid conditioning. Abstr. in *Psychol. Bull.*, 1939, *36*, 577–578.
6. Rees, H. J., and Israel, H. E. An investigation of the establishment of mental sets. *Psychol. Mono.*, 1935, *46*, no. 210, 1–26.
7. Woodworth, R. S. *Psychology*, 5th ed. rev. New York: Henry Holt. 1945.

Experiment 17. Motivation III: Level of Aspiration

Introduction. The level of aspiration is one's estimate of his future performance in a given task. This estimate varies with many conditions and modes of measurement, but it is basically limited by one's knowledge of his past performance in the same or similar tasks. Experiments on levels of aspiration are of great interest to social psychologists and students of personality. From an experimental viewpoint they are interesting in that they show strikingly some of the effects of *knowledge of results,* an important source of error in many experiments with human subjects.

The average college student who volunteers, or is otherwise procured for service as a subject for experimentation, refuses to part with his "personality" and to do simply what he is told to do. He tries to "figure out" the purpose of the experiment, and then, as often as not, he will try to help the experimenter along, or, if otherwise inclined, he will try to frustrate the experimenter. We have already seen the importance of self-instruction in connection with many experiments. The "level of aspiration" situation brings the factor of self-instruction into the open.

Apparatus and Procedure. The ordinary experimental technique involves the use of some partially practiced skill which can be measured readily. Such skills as horseshoe pitching, dart throwing, broad jumping, etc., can be used. The subject is asked to estimate how far he can throw a baseball, for example. After he guesses, he is allowed to throw, and the result is compared with the guess. Another guess follows, and another throw, and so on. The changes in aspiration as they are affected by the results are compared and interpreted.

In the present experiment, the experimenter will instruct the subject to sort 52 playing cards according to a particular system. He will time each trial in seconds. Before each trial, including the first, the subject will estimate the number of seconds he will

your observations of your subject's behavior and his scores.
What type of information can you obtain about your subject's "personality" from this form of experimentation?

References

1. Chapman, D. W., and Volkmann, J. A social determinant of
   the level of aspiration. *J. abn. & soc. Psychol.*, 1939, *34*, 225–
   238, or selections from the above in Newcomb, T. M., and
   Hartley, E. L. *Readings in social psychology*. New York: Henry
   Holt. 1947.
2. Lewin, K. Levels of Aspiration. Chapter 10 in *Personality and
   the behavior disorders,* J. McV. Hunt, ed. New York: Ronald
   Press. 1944.

15

Experimenting in Learning

THE SUBJECT of learning has received and is now receiving more attention from psychologists than any other topic of psychological interest. Woodworth (4) devotes a third of his *Experimental psychology* to this area. Guthrie considers the field of learning (and motivation) the basic research area of psychology and implies that until the problem of learning is solved, psychology will be virtually marking time. In no other area of psychology is there so much argument and theorizing, with rival systems advanced in competition with each other. In *Theories of learning*, Hilgard (1) presents ten different theoretical views, each of which has strong proponents.

Although the theoretical aspects of learning are fascinating, we have no time for considering them here, as our problem is to become familiar with ways of studying learning. The specialized apparatus and procedures used in learning-studies are not difficult to comprehend, even if the results obtained are open to ten different interpretations. Each of the prominent theorists has tended to make use of some special device or technique, and it will be our immediate business to become acquainted with the commonly used pieces of equipment and the procedures, special precautions, and measurements obtained in the use of these experimental stand-bys.

Before proceeding to an examination of apparatus and procedure, we should at least consider some definition of learning. It
288

is interesting that this term is not usually defined specifically by most writers; it is as if the theorists assume that everyone knows what learning is. We shall not get involved in too much difficulty if we accept the definition suggested by McGeoch (3): "Learning is a change in performance as a result of practice." The student will observe that this definition has definite operational possibilities. It is, of course, necessary to indicate how the change, performance, and practice are measured. Presumably the change will be in some positive direction of greater efficiency in order to eliminate such results of practice as "work decrement," "staleness," etc. The practice, too, must be specifically distinguished from mere repetition. The type of "performance" involved must be specified. Other definitions might be considered, but in general they reduce to some equivalent of McGeoch's statement, and so they need not occupy us at this time.

A variety of approaches might profitably be pursued in describing the different methods developed for the study of learning. We might, for example, proceed historically, or in terms of the types of subjects employed, or the types of theories evolved. None of these is especially logical, and we shall follow, instead, a program of describing the learning apparatus and procedures from the simplest to the most involved.

1. **Classical conditioning.** The simplest method of studying "changes in performance as a result of practice" is the technique of conditioning. This has already been described to some extent in a previous chapter. In general, conditioning procedure of the "classical" or Pavlovian type amounts to presenting a *conditioning* stimulus (which can be any irrelevant stimulus such that it does not at first evoke the response in which we are interested) and following this by the presentation of an *unconditioned* stimulus. The latter stimulus is one that *elicits* the desired response as a usual consequence. The stimuli should follow each other closely, so that there will be some temporal overlap between their presumed neural effects. In

general, if the conditioned stimulus precedes the unconditioned stimulus by about one second, conditioning will occur;
the optimal interval should be determined for each of the stimulus combinations used. The occurrence of a conditioned response can be tested by omission of the unconditioned stimulus. (In conditional eyelid technique, described in Chapter 13,
it is not necessary to omit the *Unc. S.* because the response
occurs before the *Unc. S.* as a temporally anticipatory reaction.)

Once the response is conditioned, it is sometimes possible
to use the conditioned stimulus in the role of unconditioned
stimulus, and condition the response to a new stimulus. Thus,
once a subject is conditioned to react to a bell, the bell can be
paired with a light. The light will then evoke the response
after it has preceded the bell a suitable number of times. Such
conditioning is called "second-order conditioning." Additional
"orders" have sometimes been reported. Whether or not a response is "reflex," "conditioned," or voluntary depends largely
on its latency as measured from the onset of the conditioning
stimulus. Lacking a reaction-time measure, occurrence of a
response in the absence of the *Unc. S.* is usually accepted as
evidence of conditioning.

It is often argued that the conditioned response and the original response are not the same. This argument is sometimes
advanced as a devastating criticism of conditioning principles.
It should be pointed out, however, that even unconditioned
responses vary from trial to trial, and are rarely exactly alike
in all characteristics. If a dog is shocked repeatedly, he will
eventually respond with a relatively abbreviated movement,
even though his first responses were gross, agitated, and generalized attempts at escape. If control observations are taken,
it will be seen that animals which are forced to respond to the
Unc. S. alone will also vary their responses. The latter type of
control is rarely attempted, but should be considered an experimental obligation.

Once a conditioned response is established, a number of different experimental procedures may be employed to observe its nature, functions, and characteristics. One such *procedure* is that of *experimental extinction*. The student will note that this refers to a laboratory procedure, and not, as some writers appear to imply, a process in the animal. It amounts to stimulating the animal repeatedly with the conditioned stimulus, but with omission of the unconditioned stimulus. As a general consequence, the CR tends to diminish in frequency and amplitude, and eventually to disappear. If the CS is now omitted for some interval and reintroduced some time later, the CR may reappear; such a reappearance is called "spontaneous recovery."

Conditioning, extinction, and spontaneous recovery are the basic aspects of conditioning experimentation. From these a wide variety of additional phenomena can be produced. For many studies concerning sense-organ functions, conflict, reasoning, etc., the processes of *generalization* and *discrimination* are important. Generalization refers to the fact that, along with the original CS, a whole range of the stimulus continuum involved may evoke the response. Thus, if a tuning fork is the original CS, other forks of different frequencies may be effective in eliciting the response. Discrimination, on the other hand, refers to a process of extinguishing the CR to any but the original CS, which itself is constantly followed by the *Unc. S.* The above description of conditioning procedure and its results must serve, at the moment, for the classical or Pavlovian type. Another type will be considered later. It might be mentioned, in passing, that Guthrie is perhaps the most prominent psychologist who makes use of the classical type of conditioning in theoretical writings, although his experimental work is confined to another type of learning experimentation.

2. The runway or experimental "alley." A somewhat more involved method for "learning" experimentation makes use of an alleyway in which an animal's activity is watched or recorded. The alleyway can be of any convenient dimensions, usually 3 to 6 feet in length, although alleys 40 feet long have been used for some purposes. The alleyway need be only high and wide enough to permit the animal to move freely. The floor may be of grillwork so that shock can be administered to the animal's feet at any or all points in the alley. Usually a starting box is set up at one end and a goal box at the other.

The animal may be observed in terms of the time or rate of progress from one end to the other when there is food in the goal box, or a shock in the starting box, or whatever other conditions may be set up. A barrier of some kind, perhaps shock, might be arranged at various positions in the alley, and the animal's "drive" might be measured in terms of number of crossings or amounts of shock he will "accept." The spatial movements of the animal can be recorded mechanically by attaching a harness to the animal, so that as he moves he pulls against a marker which leaves a record on waxed or smoked paper. It is customary to "habituate" animals to an alley by leaving them in it over night or for some regular time period before the experiment proper is to begin. A type of experiment in which the alley is specifically useful is one wherein the animal has learned to find food at one end and has also been (later) shocked at the same end. The animal may be placed in the alley at any point and his "positive" and "negative" responses recorded. Many experiments of this type have been performed by N. Miller.*

3. The T maze. The alley may be changed to a T maze by the addition of another alley at right angles to the first with access from one to the other. The T was originally developed by Watson and Yerkes for studies of sensory discriminations of animals. It provides the experimenter an opportunity to make

* See Miller's chapter, Experimental studies of conflict, in *Personality and the behavior disorders*, J. McV. Hunt, ed. New York: Ronald, 1943.

one end of the T positive (rewarded) and the other end negative, or punished.

In the study of color vision in dogs, for example, lights of different colors could be presented at the two ends, say red on the right and green on the left. The dog might be fed for choosing the green-light end. In running the trials, the dog would be placed in a starting box at the base of the T and allowed to proceed to the intersection, which is generally called "the choice point." The green light would appear on the left on some trials and on the right on others, in random order. The percent of correct choices would be the datum to consider. Obviously, it would be necessary to make sure in any given instance that only one variable, say "greenness," was operating at a time.

In other experimental uses, animals might be fed on the right and given water on the left for a series of trials. If they are always hungry and never thirsty when they are trained, they could be tested for any "latent" learning if they are put in the box when thirsty. In such studies, it is necessary to force the animals to select each side of the T equally often. Tolman and Spence are prominent users of the T maze for a wide variety of problems.

4. The Lashley jumping-stand. This is a modification of the T which introduces the animal to the choice point without bothering with the preliminary run up the base of the T. The animal is placed on a stand about a foot away from a screen. The screen has two doors, each bearing some visual stimulus, e.g., a black cross on a white background and a white cross on a black background. One of these stimuli is made "positive" in that the door bearing this stimulus will fall backward onto a feeding platform as the animal jumps to it and knocks it down. The other door is held closed by a suitable latch. The positions of the stimuli are altered from left to right in random order for the successive trials. If the animal jumps at the wrong door, it does not open, and the animal falls to the floor or into a basket placed below the screen. The percent of correct choices is taken as a measure of learning. The time to make a "choice" and the number of "vicarious trials and errors" (*VTE*), that is, stretching toward one or the other stimulus without actually jumping, might also be used as an indication of performance change.

It should be noted that in preliminary training the stand is placed right up against the screen so that the animal walks up to the door. The stand is then gradually moved back until an air gap separates the stand from the screen. A common use of the jumping stand is in so-called conflict experiments where the difference between the stimuli is steadily reduced until the animal begins to stay on the stand instead of jumping. He is then, in some instances, forced to jump by shock or by the application of air pressure under his tail. Such experiments have already been alluded to earlier in our work.

5. The double-alternation box. This is an additional complication on the T in that it consists of two boxes placed side-by-side inside a larger box with sufficient space between the adjacent boxes and the walls of the outer box to permit an animal (or human) free locomotion. The situation can be so arranged by the experimenter that an animal must travel up the middle alley to a "choice point," proceed around the box on the right, return to the middle alley and repeat the performance; then he must again go to the choice point, turn left, and come around once more to the choice point for another left turn. Such a pattern could be represented as a right, right, left, left or *RRLL* pattern.

The significant feature of this type of T is that on the third trip up the middle alley, the animal arriving at the choice point has *no differential* cues to stimulate him to make the now required left turn. To succeed at all, he must depend on internal or "symbolic" cues, if he has them. Since it is a 50–50 proposition, a large number of trials must be run to eliminate the possibility of chance turnings.

It is also necessary to consider the possibility of some spontaneous alternation in turnings which might be involved in some of the choices. Such spontaneous alternation has been observed frequently in animals, and success in the box may mean no more than the functioning of some alternation process, the nature of which need not concern us at this point. It should be recognized by the beginning experimenter that it is quite impossible to get the animal to follow such a pattern by simply putting the animal into the situation and rewarding the final left turn. It is necessary to force the animal around the box by strategically placed doors which prevent entrance into wrong alleys and retracings of correct ones. The doors are left open only on test runs. Hunter has claimed that he trained racoons in the *RRLL* pattern, but successes with animals lower than humans have not been reported frequently or with convincing data.

6. The maze. For most beginning students the "maze" is the identifying symbol of the psychologist. Psychologists are people who "run rats in mazes and stuff like that." In this view the student testifies to a culture lag, as the formal maze is no longer extensively used in laboratories, although it still has its uses for special problems. The type of mazes now in use, however, bear little resemblance to the common notions about what mazes should look like, as they are constructed for highly specialized investigations.

In general, a maze is only a series of T mazes joined together and represents, therefore, a multiplication of the problems involved in the T. The length of the legs in each T may be varied and their geographical orientation arranged for the purpose at hand. A maze could be constructed with all left or all right turns or any combination thereof. The floors, sides, and roofs of the maze can be constructed of various materials depending on the needs of the experiment. The floor, for example, might consist of water, so that the animal has to swim through the maze. For some purposes, the floor might be made of opal glass and lighted from below so that the animal's progress might be observed through a glass roof as a moving shadow. Other floors of wood, sawdust, shock grill, etc., can be used as desired. Mazes can be built with no sides or roofs, consisting only of narrow strips of wood representing a floor. Such strips are then elevated on stilts or supported by tables or platforms. A maze of this sort is called an "elevated" maze. The animal is free to look about and move from one strip to another. An elevation of three feet is enough to discourage jumping to the floor.

In the ordinary maze all blind alleys, or *cul-de-sacs,* and correct turns are screened by little curtains or doors that the animal has to push through before it "discovers" whether it is in a blind alley or on the "true" path. In use, all external cues or lights in the room, waterpipes and walls which conduct sound, animal cages containing either animals or their odor, the position of the experimenter, etc., usually must be controlled if the animal is to be considered as learning to respond to the cues in the maze and not to some external orientation point. One method of such control is to vary the compass position of the maze and its starting point by turning the maze around from trial to trial or day to day.

The "learning behavior" of the animal is interpreted from records of the *time* it takes him to arrive at a goal box after release from the starting position, and the *number of errors* he makes. The *time* record is open to serious misinterpretation, especially in the early trials, because the animal, even if "habituated" to the maze by being placed in the maze for several hours or overnight, may spend considerable time in washing, grooming, sleeping, or otherwise "wasting" his time. How to separate nonlearning time from learning time is a difficult problem. The error record is usually kept in terms of the number of each error made and in terms of reversals or retracings of the path. The order of elimination of errors is an important theoretical problem. As with all other learning devices or procedures, some criterion is established for the specific problem as to when the maze is "learned." Two errorless trials in an arbitrarily fixed time might be one criterion.

The maze has been used extensively in one modified form or another by Tolman and Hull. One of Hull's modified mazes might be described as an indication of the fact that the "maze" is only a general term to describe multiple-choice arrangements. In this modification Hull uses a long alley about a foot wide. The alley is compartmentalized into a series of chambers with connecting hallways. The animal proceeds from a starting box to a "room" with four doors on the far wall. If he pushes at the correct door, it opens; the rest are blocked off. The correct door leads into another small chamber and another hallway, which opens onto the next "room" with its four doors, and so on. This arrangement allows Hull to feed the animal after each choice or after the complete run, and provides an opportunity for studying the learning of the several sections.

7. The multiple-choice situation. In a sense the T maze is a true-or-false test; the regular maze is a longer such test. Some problems are more easily handled by presenting more than two alternate stimuli or routes to the organism under study. No arrangement has become popular enough to receive a label or serve as a standard, but the general principle is a simple one, that of placing the organism at the center of an enclosed circle with any desired number of true and false goal boxes or paths arranged to point toward the center. The experimental subject can then proceed toward any goal box, and its "choices" are recorded.

A typical problem making use of such a situation is one studied by Tolman: A rat is trained to select one of two paths arranged in the form of a V with the apex of the V at the center of a circular starting stand. Suppose that the right-hand leg of the V leads to food for an animal that has been deprived for some specified time, say 24 hours. When the animal has "mastered the problem," the correct path is blocked off at some point before the goal, and a whole series of additional paths is attached to the starting platform in the form of radiating strips of wood or alleys like spokes in a wheel. If the animal goes up the pathway on which he has been trained, he cannot reach the food and must return to the starting platform, where the array of possibilities faces him. His selections can then be recorded over a series of trials.

There is no limit to the variations possible in the multiple-choice situation. The higher animals (monkeys and apes) may be given the opportunity to press one of a series of levers that protrude into the cages or to point to one of a series of drawers, boxes, symbols, or what not. The variations that can be used depend on the ingenuity of the apparatus designer, the needs of the problem, and the capacity of the organism. Since the multiple-choice situation is only an elaborated T maze, the precautions pertaining to mazes must be observed in the multiple-choice situation equally stringently.

8. *The puzzle or problem box.* The problem box came into popular psychological use with the studies of animal intelligence initiated by Thorndike in the 1890's. In Thorndike's experiments, an animal, usually a cat, would be placed inside a cage-like box from which it could "escape" if it performed some movement decided upon by the experimenter. The movement could be a "logical" one, such as pushing against a latch which held a door shut or pulling on a string which raised the door. The animal that solved this problem would appear to the casual observer as a rather knowing little beast, since it could be, with sufficient trials, allowed to develop a "know-how" of great efficiency and impressiveness.

FIGURE 16. *A CAT IN A THORNDIKE BOX*. Such a box is easily constructed. Any kind of device within the cat's scope can be used to open the door. By shifting the position of the opening device, the experimenter is able to test the nature of the cat's learning. Although food is placed outside the door, the student experimenter should not be surprised if the cat ignores the food upon escaping and must be pursued for the second trial.

On the other hand, the experimenter might decide to make the door open only when the animal made some irrelevant movement, such as scratching its left ear with its right rear paw. To have the animal learn to get out of the box, the experimenter would simply wait till the desired movement was executed and would then open the door. The learning would follow the same course in terms of the measurements employed (usually time to get out) regardless of the "logic" of the movement involved.

One consideration should be inserted here as a technical fact, even though we are not concerned at this time with learning theory: If the latch or loop of string is placed at some other, though equally obvious position, the animal will ignore it and continue making the original movements in the original place. The previously intelligent and ingenious animal now looks a little ridiculous. This consideration is emphasized because of the danger of the naïve observer, and sometimes even of the trained psychologist, forgetting that the "logic" and "intelligence" demonstrated by the animal has been inserted into the situation, if not into the animal, by the experimenter.

The puzzle box has been used as a standard type of experiment by E. R. Guthrie. In his version of the box, the door of the box is made to open by any displacement of a vertical pole placed somewhere in the box. The pole is mounted on a weighted rocking base which stands on an electrical contact. If the pole is pushed by an animal, it rolls off the contact, allowing the magnetically held door to open. The base and pole then settle back into position like a child's roly-poly toy. In Guthrie's experiments, a cat is allowed to enter the box from the rear. In its progress around the box it eventually dislodges the pole in one way or another, and leaves. To attract the animal to the front of the box, a sardine or other suitable lure is placed in front of the box. The sides of the box can be of glass or grillwork to permit the animal to see the lure. The term "lure" is used in deference to Guthrie's insistence that *rewards* do not function in learning in any way except to direct the animal to the proper situation and to keep it from *unlearning* what it has just learned by removing the stimuli to which the experimentally desired responses have been conditioned.

The usual measurement employed in puzzle boxes is "time to escape." Since the animal may spend much time in grooming or sleeping, we have the same problem of separating out "learning" time from total time as in the maze situation. Guthrie has introduced another type of measurement which is difficult to reduce to numerical terms. He keeps track, photographically or otherwise, of the specific movements made by the animals, because it is his firm conviction that animals learn to make certain movements and not acts. We have already considered this problem before and need only mention it now as one of Guthrie's major emphases. The analysis of behavior into movements, however, is a complicated task that has just barely been begun.

9. The Skinner Box. One of the most widely used pieces of apparatus in psychology today is an interesting variation on the Thorndike box developed by B. F. Skinner. In the Thorndike box, the animal learns how to *get out* of the box. He is usually offered some form of food reward as he emerges; this food, as Guthrie points out, is often rejected or ignored. In the Skinner box, the animal *stays in the box,* and food is presented to him either by the experimenter dropping it in or by having the animal do something (anything) which can be arranged to release a small amount of food or water into a receptacle from which the animal can obtain it. The usual procedure is to insert into the animal's living cage, or a specially constructed box, a small bar or lever which serves as a switch to operate some electrical device that delivers the desired amount of "reward" whenever the bar is depressed. The fact that the animal remains in the box is a great timesaver, as once it is in the box it need not be disturbed, and a large number of learning trials can follow one another in rapid succession. The food appears in the form of small pellets, of which the animal can eat a great number before satiation.

In the Skinner box, the animal is not specifically forced to respond to some stimulus, as it is in the classical or Pavlovian conditioning situation. In Skinner's language, the animal "emits" the response. Skinner's view is that the actual stimulus for bar-pressing is unknown, or at least not observed; what counts is the response. This is observed, and is the only feature of the experiment with which we should properly concern ourselves. For this reason, Skinner claims that the bar-pressing represents a different kind of learning. He thinks of it as still describable in conditioning language, and calls it an "operant," or *R-type*, of conditioning in contrast to the Pavlovian, or *S*-type, where the experimenter concentrates on the conditioning stimulus.

Although we will not argue the case here, it is interesting to note that both Guthrie and Skinner employ essentially the same experimental situation (as did Thorndike long before them), yet Guthrie maintains that the Pavlovian type of conditioning is fully adequate to account for his cats' learning, while Skinner claims just as strongly that it is not, and that a new type of learning must be postulated. We might add that Hull is ready to claim them both wrong in that only one type of learning need be assumed which would account for both the Guthrie-Pavlov view and Skinner's two types on the basis of a modification of Thorndike's *law of effect*. The procedure followed in training animals in the Skinner box has already been described in connection with the discussion of Pliny, the Super-Rat, but some additional details might be in order. The animal is usually allowed some period of habituation in the box before the lever is introduced. Under ordinary conditions, an animal that has not been fed for 24 hours will be somewhat active. In its wanderings around the box it will investigate the food dish from time to time. As it does so, the experimenter may drop it some food from outside the box. The sound of the dropping food usually is enough to bring the rat on the run to the food dish.

After this preliminary training, the bar is inserted, and the experimenter waits for the animal to press the bar. When it does so, food is dropped either by the experimenter or automatically. At the same time, a signal marker is displaced from its course on a kymograph drum or moving tape, indicating the time of the response. As the animal continues to press the bar, the marks on the recorder accumulate. The animal keeps pressing the bar until it meets the experimenter's arbitrary criterion of learning, which can be expressed as a given number of total presses, or in terms of rate (e.g., number of presses per minute).

The phenomena mentioned in the discussion of Pavlovian conditioning (extinction, spontaneous recovery, generalization, and discrimination, etc.) can all be studied in the Skinner box. Skinner himself introduced a number of interesting variations. One of these he calls *P.R.* or "periodic reconditioning." In this variation the experimenter arranges the electrical connections so that some food is dropped into the box at certain time intervals, e.g., at one-minute intervals, regardless of the number of bar presses made; or every second or tenth bar press is followed by food. This arrangement has proved useful for the study of several theoretically important problems. In another situation Skinner introduces some additional stimulus, e.g., a light at certain intervals. When the light is on, bar presses are followed by food. When it is off, no food appears after a press. If the animal learns to work only when the light is on, the light becomes a "discriminated stimulus" or S^D.

In the above discussion we have been careful in the use of the word "reward" and have usually substituted the word "food." This has been done because the term "reward" is objectionable due to the difficulty of reducing it to an operational interpretation. The term "reinforcement" has been popularized by Hull and Skinner as a less objectionable substitute. It refers to anything which strengthens a habit. Such strengthening can be defined in terms of frequency, of amount or latency of responses, or of an additional type of measurement strongly favored by Skinner, the resistance to extinction. In this latter measurement the rate of response is observed after reinforcement ceases. The stronger the habit, the more often will the animal continue to respond, according to both Hull and Skinner.

Recapitulation

The above description of the various types of apparatus and procedures in learning is not intended to be complete. For one thing, no mention of verbal types of learning has been made; this type of learning will be our next concern, and it warrants a separate section in itself. The types mentioned, however, represent a reasonable sample of the work of "learning" psychologists, especially of those who are prone to work with lower animals. It might be valuable to recapitulate somewhat at this point and review the various points of significance brought out in our survey. The schema of Hilgard and Marquis (2) appears to be a useful framework for such a review. Hilgard and Marquis, although favoring no special view themselves, point out that "learning" psychologists are divided into two broad camps: The Classical or Pavlovian conditioned-response school, and what they call the "instrumental conditioning" group. The former has already been described. The latter requires only a brief explanation in addition to what the reader has already been able to infer. According to Hilgard and Marquis, instrumental conditioning includes the whole area of studies of responses of the Skinner Type R variety, wherein the *response* is the important feature; the response is *instrumental* in effecting some change for the animal, usually in the form of some reinforcement or other. There are supposed to be four subtypes of "instrumental" learning:

1. **Reward training.** This includes such responses as are involved in Thorndike, Guthrie, or Skinner boxes, mazes, T mazes, multiple-choice situations, etc.

2. **Secondary reward training.** This includes the study of responses which are not followed by any tangible "reward," such as food or water, but occur only for less apparent "reinforcements," e.g., praise, money, or its symbolic substitutes. Stimuli which occur in the presence of a "primary" reinforcing agent are said to take on reinforcing potentialities. A rat, for example, might continue to press a bar if the sound that formerly accompanied the food continues to occur, but he will work less if no such sound occurs. Almost any of the devices described can be used for secondary reward studies.

3. **Escape training.** This type of training usually makes use of punishment by shock in an alley situation. The animal is forced into activity by the shock, and eventually learns to "turn it off" by doing something that the experimenter arranges for him to do. A rat, for example, might be shocked until he raises his right paw to his ear in the form of a salute, or he might be required to do something "logical," like stepping onto a platform which controls a switch for turning off the shock.

4. **Avoidance training.** This type resembles the classical conditioning situation closely in that an unconditioned stimulus, e.g., shock, forces a given specific response. A conditioning stimulus is presented at the same time, and the response eventually is made to it. In the typical "avoidance" experiment, a dog might be shocked in the hind foot. He thereupon raises the leg. An accompanying buzzer will eventually evoke the leg-raising response in time to *avoid* the shock. Since the shock is avoided, the resemblance to the classical situation appears to break down; and because the response is thus "instrumen-

tal" in preventing pain or annoyance, Hilgard and Marquis regard it as a special type of learning.

The theoretical ramifications of the results of experiments using the techniques described in this section are too involved to warrant our present attention. For our purposes we must be content with learning how to use the techniques with reasonable understanding of what we are doing. Before we can start arguing about the results and their interpretations, we must first learn to get the results. In this section we have tried to emphasize the importance of appreciating what our results *actually are* in scientific terms. The student who appreciates the fact that our results are frequencies, amplitudes, latencies, and extinction rates, and not insight, trials and errors, laws of recency, or anything else of the sort, will be on reasonably safe ground.

References

1. Hilgard, E. *Theories of learning.* New York: Appleton-Century-Crofts. 1948.
2. Hilgard, E., and Marquis, D. *Conditioning and learning.* New York: Appleton-Century. 1940.
3. McGeoch, J. *The psychology of human learning.* New York: Longmans, Green. 1942.
4. Woodworth, R. S. *Experimental psychology.* New York: Henry Holt. 1938.

Experiment 18. Learning I: Conditioning an "Operant" Response *

Introduction. In the attempt to comprehend the basic mechanisms of learning, psychologists try to reduce various types of learned behavior to their simplest terms or components for purposes of orderly and controlled observation. You will work with several such reductions in your laboratory study of learning, and you must constantly appreciate the fact that the laboratory situation is deliberately simplified in order to facilitate observation. Generalizations beyond your data must be made with extreme care, as the field of "learning" theory is one of the most strongly debated in psychology. There will be three or more explanations of reasonable plausibility for your observations of the most simple learned performance. It is your function as experimenter to make your observations correct and *complete,* if your interpretations are to be of any value.

The present experiment involves the observation of the development of a seemingly simple response in a seemingly simple organism, the albino rat. You will observe the rat learn to depress a bar which you insert in its cage. The apparent simplicity of this situation is most misleading. You will find enough questions to raise about the rat's behavior to fill a book. In fact, a rather long book has been filled with such questions and suggested answers by B. F. Skinner (1), who originated the learning situation described here. Skinner calls this type of behavior "operant," because in this situation an organism operates upon its environment. Sometimes this type of behavior is called "instrumental," because the behavior of the organism is instrumental in bringing about some consequent event, such as the arrival of food.

According to Skinner, this behavior should be distinguished from "respondent" behavior in which the organism reacts to some

---

* The writer is indebted to Dr. Donald H. Bullock for introducing this experiment and developing the apparatus and procedures as herein described.

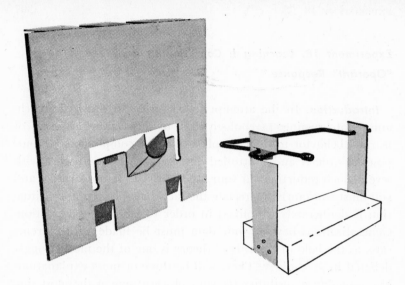

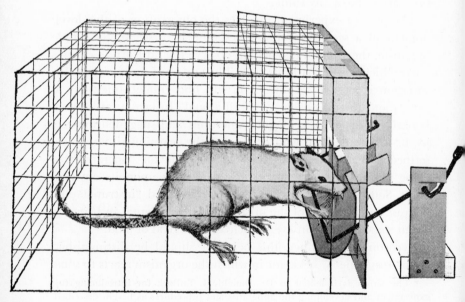

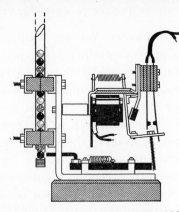
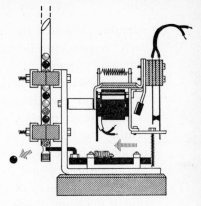

FIGURE 17. *THE SKINNER BAR-PRESSING APPARATUS.* The living-cage of a rat is used as the experimental box. A metal door, slotted as shown, is inserted in place of the regular door, which is swung out of the way. The slots in the new cage front permit the insertion of a wire bar, fashioned from coat-hanger wire, into the cage. On the inside of the false front there is a small trough which serves to catch food pellets as they are dropped into the funnel soldered to the out-side. When the rat presses the bar, the ex-perimenter drops him a pellet of food.

A simple solution for an automatic feeder is shown at the right. Pellets are loaded into a plexiglass tube, one on top of another. The bottom of the tube is sealed off. Just above the bottom, a hole is drilled through the tube. A metal pin is now attached to a mag-net so that when the magnet operates, the pin projects into the hole and ejects a pellet. When contact is broken, the pin retracts and allows the next pellet to descend into posi-tion. The magnet is wired to a switch that is arranged to function when the rat presses the bar. The switch can also be wired to a magnetic marker, which records the bar press on a moving tape. Pellets of uniform size are obtainable from P. J. Noyes, Lancaster, N. H.

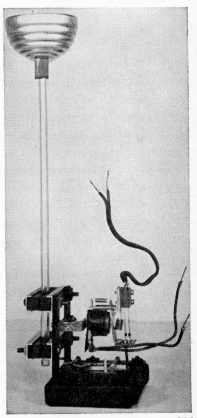

stimulus presented by the experimenter. You are familiar with such "respondent" behavior from your eyelid-reflex experiment. When a "respondent" reaction is associated with some irrelevant stimulus, Skinner calls the ensuing conditioning "Pavlovian" or "respondent conditioning," or "type *S*" (because the *stimulus* is important in *eliciting* the response). When the organism "emits" the behavior, as it appears to do in the Skinner box situation, Skinner speaks of "operant conditioning," or "type *R* (because the *response* is important). Accepting Skinner's terminology for purposes of this experiment, and without consideration of the many disputes raging about the nature of the learning involved in this situation, you will attempt to "condition" an operant response in a rat according to the procedure described below.

Apparatus and Procedure. You will work with an already-caged rat so that there will be no need to handle the animal. The cage is so constructed that the animal can be viewed from above through a screen. The door of the cage has been replaced by a metal panel with slots so cut that a bent wire "bar" can be inserted into the cage just above a small chute through which food can be dropped to the animal. The bar will rest on slot-bearings and operate like a lever. When the animal presses the bar downward inside the cage, the ends of the bar outside the cage will rise and hit against a stop.

Three students will work together. One will observe the rat; one will drop a pellet of food to the animal whenever it presses the bar enough to hit the outside stop, and the third will record the time of every bar-press in seconds. (Start timing by minute and second from the moment the bar is inserted). The specific procedure follows:

1. Insert the bar and note the time. When the rat depresses the bar to the criterion point, drop it a pellet of food. (Make sure it eats the food before giving it any more.)

2. Allow the rat to depress the bar 20 times, "reinforcing" each response with a food pellet. Record the time of each response.

3. After 20 reinforcements, stop dropping food pellets to the rat even though it presses the bar. Continue recording times of responses until the animal does not press the bar for 2 minutes. This will be considered an "extinction" to a 2-minute criterion.

4. Remove the bar and wait 5 minutes. Replace the bar and record the time of the first response. Reinforce this, and the next 4 responses. If the rat presses the bar after the 5-minute interval, it can be said to have shown "spontaneous recovery." After the 5th reinforcement, remove the bar.

4. Throughout the training process, one student, acting as observer, will make notes on the behavior of the rat. He will especially watch for such items as the way in which the rat strikes the bar (with teeth, paws, head, etc., and any changes therein), how it responds to the food, and any routines or patterns of response engaged in by the rat.

Results. You will have in your record the times of response during reinforcement, extinction, and spontaneous recovery. Plot these times of response in a "cumulative" learning curve. Such a curve is easily drawn on graph paper where number of responses is indicated on the ordinate and time is on the abscissa. To plot your record, make one vertical square represent one response, 2 squares, 2 responses, etc. Then after the first response is recorded, draw a horizontal line parallel to the base line to the point indicating the time when the 2nd response was made. Continue this procedure for each response. The final curve will be step-like, with longer or shorter distances between the steps, depending upon the rate of response. Label all sections of the curve (learning, extinction, recovery, relearning, etc.). In addition to your learning curve, present a rough-draft description of your observations, and summarize the response data in a suitably constructed table.

Discussion

1. Did your rat "learn" to press the bar? When did he do so? What criterion of learning could you suggest?
2. What happened during the "extinction" period? Was the rat "frustrated"? What changes took place in the curve as the response was learned? During extinction?
3. Why is this an example of "operant" behavior? Did the rat have to learn to press? Or did he already "know how" to press bars? In what does the learning consist? Can you define "learning" in this situation?
4. How does this type of response differ from the conditioned-eyelid response you studied in Experiment 15? (3).

References

1. Skinner, B. F. *The behavior of organisms.* New York: Appleton-Century. 1938.
2. Underwood, B. J. *Experimental psychology.* New York: Appleton-Century-Crofts. 1949, chap. 11.
3. Woodworth, R. S. *Experimental psychology.* New York: Henry Holt. 1938.

Experiment 19. Learning II: Maze Learning.
The Punchboard and the Stylus Maze

Introduction. The response conditioned in the Skinner box can be thought of as a single response in a given situation. Actually, as you observed, it is not the result of a single movement of a single effector (a condition approximated in your eyelid experiment), but a complicated series of movements involving reaching, pressing, releasing, getting to the food, eating, returning to the bar (or elsewhere), and repeating. There is some evidence that under certain conditions the movements of the animal may be highly stereotyped. Under other conditions considerable variation may be introduced.

The question arises whether we are dealing with a movement, a series of movements, or an "act." No definite answer has been agreed upon by "learning" psychologists. In the maze (animal or human) the subject is required to go through a *series* of responses (movements?) which terminate at a "goal." The nature of this goal depends upon the organism involved. In its simplest form the maze would consist of a starting place and a straight pathway leading to a "choice point," where the subject must turn either left or right. How an animal comes to make a consistently correct response in such a simple T maze is by no means settled, and we might well begin our study of maze learning with such a simple situation. By adding successive "choice points" to the original, we complicate the problem tremendously, and raise a number of additional questions.

If we use human subjects in a T maze situation, the problem is mastered so readily that we have little opportunity to make observations which might enable us to interpret the underlying mechanisms. By complicating the "T," we may be able to obtain data not only about behavior at one choice point, but also about a more involved and patterned form of behavior from which we may be able to generalize to other forms of serial response.

Apparatus and Procedure. The type of maze to be used varies with the purpose of the experiment and the nature of the organism. A wide variety of mazes have been devised for special problems. Mazes with all left or all right turns have been tried; circular mazes, endless mazes, water mazes, etc., have been used for special problems. For humans, the maze can be built up in relief of wire or wood sections; such mazes are "traced" out with a finger. The maze can consist of a slotted pathway in a wooden or metal plate with suitable *cul-de-sacs* or blind alleys (See Fig. 18). In the use of such mazes the subject generally wears a blindfold or is otherwise prevented from seeing the maze as he traces the path with a pencil or stylus.

A type of maze coming into common use consists of a pair of hinged boards with a series of holes drilled through the top piece (See Fig. 19). The holes are drilled in pairs (or a greater number in a row), and one of the holes in each row of the top piece has a corresponding hole in the bottom section. The experimenter places a sheet of paper between the two sections. The subject inserts a pencil into the holes in the top section. If he happens to choose a hole which is just over a hole in the lower section, his pencil will penetrate the paper. If he tries the other hole first, he will be unable to penetrate, and will leave a pencil mark on the paper, thus marking an error. His problem is to find his way from the first row to the last without making errors. The experimenter may use such mazes for a variety of problems, and arranges his conditions according to the needs of the problem.

In the present experiment, one subject will learn a stylus maze, the other will learn a punchboard type. In both cases the time and errors per trial will be recorded in Table 21. The subject will be instructed to go from the start to the end of the maze as rapidly as possible, and to continue practice until either 25 trials have been made or he makes two errorless trials in less than 10 seconds. Allow 30 seconds rest between trials. In both cases the experimenter will take notes on incidental observations concern-

FIGURE 18. *A STYLUS MAZE.*
This is a plan view of a pencil
maze. The indicated outline is
cut out of any durable material
(linoleum, plywood, metal, plastic) on a jig saw. Suitable dimensions are 2-inch slots (¼-inch
wide) with ¾-inch distances between the horizontal slots. This
maze was designed by Warden
(see Woodworth, R. S. *Experimental Psychology,* p. 147, for an
account of the results obtained
with its use). In using the maze,
the subject tries to get from S to
G by following the pathways
with a pencil. A sheet of paper
placed beneath the maze retains
a record of each trial. The errors
are numbered, and a record is
kept by the experimenter of the
frequency with which each error
is made. A blindfold can be worn
by the subject. If a blindfold
makes the subject uneasy, a
screen can be erected between
the subject and the maze with an
opening for his hand and arm.

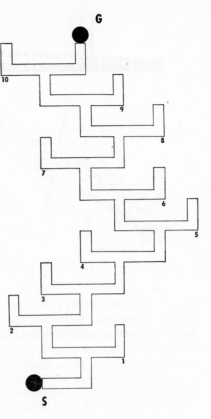

ing the subject's behavior. The following special instructions per-
tain to the separate mazes:

1. *The stylus maze.* The subject is not to see the maze at all until
   the experiment is over. After the criterion has been met, the
   subject will try to draw a diagram of the true path, first with
   his blindfold in place, and then without a blindfold. The experimenter will compare these freehand drawings with the true
   path as traced directly from the maze. Before each trial the
   experimenter will place a fresh sheet of paper under the maze

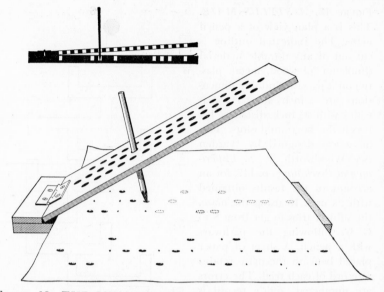

FIGURE 19. *THE PUNCHBOARD MAZE.* Two pieces of wood are hinged at one end. Holes are drilled in the top piece as shown. As many rows and columns of holes can be provided as desired. Holes are drilled in the bottom piece to correspond with certain of those in the top. In the bottom piece, however, only one hole is drilled in each row. The arrangement of corresponding holes is randomized. When using the maze, the experimenter places a sheet of paper between the two sections. The subject is directed to insert his pencil in the starting hole at the top. As he does so, he penetrates the paper into the corresponding bottom hole. He then chooses a hole in the first row. If he fails to penetrate the paper, he leaves a record of his error, and continues choosing until he finds the correct hole, when he is allowed to proceed to the next row. If desired, the maze can be made of cardboard with holes cut out by a paper punch. The paper maze can be hinged with adhesive tape and will serve adequately, although it will be less durable.

so that he can have a direct record of all errors made. Errors will consist of every entry into a blind alley when the subject is going in a forward direction. If the subject starts to reverse his path, the experimenter will count each such reversal as a "reversal error," but will ignore *cul-de-sacs* until the subject starts going in the correct direction again.

2. *The punchboard maze.* The subject is timed from the moment he inserts his pencil in the starting hole. He is instructed to insert his pencil firmly so that he will either tear the paper or make a mark. The maze you will use will have three holes in each row, two of which will be errors. Count each error made per row per trial. Insert a sheet of paper between the two sections, and move this along an adequate distance between trials for your permanent record. Label each trial. Be sure to prevent your subject from seeing former trial records by covering these with a screen. Instruct your subject not to mark the top board in any fashion.

Results. Report your results to the instructor for group tabulation. Present your learning data in graphical form for both time and errors.

Discussion

1. Describe the form of your learning curves. Are they negatively or positively accelerated? Are there any plateaus? Which curve do you think better represents the progress of learning, the time or error curve? Are time and errors good measures of learning?
2. What cues did the subject use to learn the mazes? Were kinesthetic cues basic to the learning of the stylus maze? Did the subject work according to any plan, hypotheses, or "cognitive map"?
3. Did the subject learn a series of movements, or did he learn the maze as a generalized response or total behavior pattern?

References

1. Postman, L., and Egan, J. P. *Experimental psychology.* New York: Harper and Brothers. 1949, chap. 18.

2. Woodworth, R. S. *Experimental psychology*. New York: Henry Holt. 1938, chaps. 6, 7.

Table 21. *Time and Errors per Trial of One Subject in a _____ Maze*

Trial	Errors															Reversals	Total	Time
	1	2	3	4	5	6	7	8	9	10	11	12	13	14	15			
1																		
2																		
3																		
4																		
5																		
6																		
7																		
8																		
9																		
10																		
11																		
12																		
13																		
14																		
15																		
16																		
17																		
18																		
19																		
20																		
21																		
22																		
23																		
24																		
25																		
Total																		

Experiment 20. Learning III: Transfer of Training

Introduction. What is the effect of practice of some skill or activity on itself, on the retention of some previously practiced activity, and on future activities? These questions summarize the problems arising from a wide variety of "learning" situations. It used to be thought, for example, that students who studied classical languages and mathematics would benefit from these courses in future and unrelated subjects. If such effects could be established, we would speak of *positive* transfer. On the other hand, we find that learning some things may prevent effective future learning of other things, or interfere with recall or use of older information or skills. Such cases are labeled "negative transfer."

In the present experiment you will have an opportunity to examine some of the variables in a transfer situation which will aid in appreciating the "learning" principles involved. You will also have an opportunity to consider the complex problems in the measurement of "learning" progress and thus be in a position to evaluate studies wherein the problems of measurement were superficially analyzed before "learning scores" were reported.

Apparatus and Procedure. The skill chosen for practice is that of mirror drawing or mirror tracing. You will view a six-pointed star in a mirror and try to draw a pencil track around the star, keeping within the double lines outlining the star. Direct view of the star will be prevented by a screen attached to your drawing board. All drawings will be made in a counterclockwise direction, starting at the point nearest the subject. You will start by making several tracings with your left (or unskilled) hand, to determine an "untrained" score. Following these trials you will make 15 tracings with your right (or skilled) hand. Then another test of the left hand performance will be made to determine the practice effect or "transfer." (See below for details of trials.) As an additional control measure, you will compare the scores of those stu-

FIGURE 20. *MIRROR-DRAWING APPARATUS.* Two slotted metal tubes serve to hold a mirrow. A swivel arm holds a screen to prevent direct view of a 6-pointed star drawn with a double boundary which forms a ⅛-inch track. The same effect can be obtained by pushing a pencil through a piece of cardboard which can serve as a portable screen. The stars are mimeographed.

dents who serve first as subjects with the scores of those who will be experimenters first and subjects later. As experimenters they will have the opportunity to observe the activities of the first performers and possibly will derive benefit from this observation. Each subject will strive to trace the star as rapidly as possible and to make as few errors as possible. An error will be counted for every time the pencil crosses one of the boundaries of the star outline. The subject must always return to the point where he went outside the boundary.

The specific order of trials to be run follows:

1. Experimenter makes 8 runs, the first with his skilled and the next with his unskilled hand, and so on. (The subject times him in seconds, but does not watch his performance.)
2. The experimenter observes the subject as the latter now makes 8 runs, starting with his skilled hand and alternating right and left, so that he will have 4 trials with each hand at the end of trial 8, just as the experimenter did before him.
3. The subject now makes 11 runs with his skilled hand.

4. Immediately after trial 19, the subject makes 4 additional runs
   with his unskilled hand.
5. The experimenter now takes his place as subject, and the procedure from step 3 on is repeated. Remember that the experimenter already has 8 trials.

Results. Tabulate your times and errors per trial in Table 22.
Plot your data for times and errors in curves. In your graphs, plot
the first 4 trials with the unskilled hand first; then break your
curves and plot the 15 trials with your skilled hand; then after
another break, complete the curve with the last 4 unskilled-hand
trials. How much improvement did the subject exhibit in terms
of time? State this as a percentage obtained by dividing the median time of trials 21, 22, and 23 by the median time of trials
4, 6, and 8, and the median of trials 17, 18, and 19 by the median
of trials 3, 5, and 7. How much "transfer" took place or, in other
words, how much did practice with the skilled hand affect the
performance of the unskilled hand? (Compare trial 8 with trial
20.) Was the transfer positive or negative? Did those who served
as subject after first serving as experimenter show any benefit
from the observation of the subject? How can you demonstrate
this? Present a suitably labeled table of the group data. Compare
the percentage gains between trials 8 and 20 for the two groups.

Table 22. *Time and Error Scores for One Subject in*
Mirror-Tracing a Star
(*S* refers to the skilled and *U* to the Unskilled hand)

Trials	Errors	Time	Trials	Errors	Time	Trials	Errors	Time
1 S			9 S			17 S		
2 U			10 S			18 S		
3 S			11 S			19 S		
4 U			12 S			20 U		
5 S			13 S			21 U		
6 U			14 S			22 U		
7 S			15 S			23 U		
8 U			16 S					

Discussion

1. What factors are responsible for the transfer effects?
2. Why were the first eight trials given in alternate order?
3. Consider the difficulty arising from the fact that, if the subject slows down sufficiently, he can proceed without an error and thus have a perfect performance in terms of errors. How do your time and error curves compare? Can you suggest a way out of this difficulty?
4. Can you draw a *true* learning curve for your subject?
5. What features of the traditional "curve of learning" do your curves illustrate?
6. Did you observe signs of conflict in your subject's work? How did your subject get out of conflict?
7. Do your data bear on the questions raised in the introduction?
8. What kinds of activity might profit from "transfer"? What kinds would show a loss?

References

1. Postman, L., and Egan, J. P. *Experimental psychology.* New York: Harper and Brothers. 1949, chap. 18.
2. Woodworth, R. S. *Experimental psychology.* New York: Henry Holt. 1938, chaps. 7, 8.

16

Verbal Learning by Human Subjects

ALTHOUGH HUMAN LEARNING can be studied in part by methods that are commonly employed to observe animal learning behavior, the use of language by humans opens an entirely new avenue of approach to the problems of learning. It may turn out that the same principles are adequate to account for behavior in the Skinner box or maze and for the behavior of the kindergarten or college student. Hull has demonstrated that, in some respects, the rat learning the maze and the college student learning nonsense syllables are both obeying the same "laws" of learning.

The road from rats to men, however, is a long and difficult one, and many investigators prefer to start at the human end of the alleged continuum, assuming, perhaps, that their results will be more pertinent to the understanding of human behavior, which most psychologists regard as their primary responsibility. It certainly cannot be argued that this approach is unsound, unscientific, or unproductive. Whatever facts are discovered concerning human learning must be accepted as facts, regardless of the behavior of rats or cockroaches. Both approaches have their own difficulties and complexities, and it is largely a matter of personal preference as to which approach is selected. It is our business to look into the difficulties and decide whether they are insurmountable or subject to our control.

In the laboratory, the study of human verbal learning must submit to conditions that make observation practicable. In effect

323

this restricts the range and nature of the materials used to such an extent as to make them appear artificial and far removed from normal human language behavior. Until better methods of study are devised, this artificiality cannot be helped; the psychologist must, accordingly, temper his interpretations with considerable modesty and restraint.

In general, the materials used for the study of verbal learning break down into two types: (1) meaningful or "sense" material, and (2) "nonsense" material. In the first group we include the use of samples of poetry or prose of various lengths and degrees of difficulty. The length is easy enough to measure; the degree of difficulty presents an awkward problem. Since most experiments involve the use of "control" selections in one form or another, it is usually necessary to have materials of *equal* difficulty. To say that one sonnet of Shakespeare is just as "difficult" as another sonnet, or that one passage from *Paradise Lost* is equal to another in difficulty, is a decision that should give any psychologist pause. A further source of difficulty frequently arises from individual differences in the reaction of subjects to different passages by the same author and of the same apparent difficulty. One passage catches his fancy, another does not. Because of the problem of measuring difficulty, "meaningful" material is not often used experimentally except for special problems where the form, instead of the content, of the material is of special concern.

The use of "nonsense" material is the logical result of the difficulties arising from the study of meaningful poetry or prose selections. "Learning" psychologists are indebted to Hermann Ebbinghaus for the introduction of the *nonsense syllable* into the learning laboratory. Ebbinghaus was concerned with the development of some unlimited source of learning materials of equal difficulty. He hit upon the device of creating verbalisms which would be meaningless to subjects and, being of equal length, would be of presumably equal difficulty.

The simple arrangement followed by Ebbinghaus consisted of placing a vowel between two consonants, thus forming a three-letter word. If the resulting word had some meaning, either in terms of sound or spelling, it would be discarded as unsuitable. Even this entirely new and artificial language, however, has its difficulties, since it is very difficult to concoct a "nonsense syllable" that is truly without meaning to everyone. The syllable *J-I-K*, for example, which looks innocent enough, is full of meaning to the writer.

As a little exercise the student should make up a list of syllables that are meaningless to him by going through the alphabet systematically. Start with *B*, the first consonant, add *A*, the first vowel, and then add to this combination each consonant in the alphabet. Then change the vowel to *E* and repeat. When you exhaust *B*, go on to *C, D*, and so on. You will find one reason or another for excluding a great many, perhaps the majority of the syllables you create. There is an alarming number of three-letter words. The student with some accomplishment in foreign languages and slang will have shorter lists at his disposal.

Various attempts have been made to alter the original Ebbinghaus formula in the attempt to secure more "nonsense," or less meaning. The device of joining two nonsense syllables into a meaningless six-letter word has been tried. Four-letter nonsense syllables have been suggested. Placing the vowel at the beginning or end, or using no vowel at all, or other variations. Without vowels, the results are only three letters in a combination, and not really syllables. The subject cannot pronounce these combinations, and must resort to spelling. For certain purposes, such specialized "syllables" are suitable. Numbers have also been used in single or multiple form for learning purposes. A subject might, for instance, be asked to learn the series: 176, 294, 375, 860, 117, etc. There is some danger that some combination or other corresponds to, or contains, a well known number, such as the age, address, or phone number of the learner.

In some experiments, lists of ordinary words of about the same length and assumed level of difficulty have been employed. Such words, usually nouns or adjectives, are used for special purposes, as when "similarity" of meaning is under study. It is generally assumed by the experimenter that a word loses its meaningfulness when it is included in a long list with other such isolated words. A list of adjectives, each of which is *equally* familiar to the learner, thus is presumed to eliminate the meaningfulness of the materials as much as would a list of nonsense syllables.

Procedure Employed with Verbal Materials

1. **Preliminary training of the subjects.** Unsophisticated subjects, new to laboratory techniques, should not be used in learning experiments unless one is specially interested in the results of naïve subjects. Such subjects vary their own procedures from trial to trial, hoping to hit upon an efficient method of learning, to such an extent that their results on any trial cannot be interpreted readily. When a beginner is faced with the prospect of memorizing 10 or 20 nonsense syllables, he has varying hopes and misgivings. He may try to learn some specific number of syllables or a particular syllable on each trial; or he may try to recite all the preceding syllables rapidly before the next one is presented. After some practice in learning such materials, he usually settles down to a procedure which he will follow throughout a learning session. A standard technique in the learner's procedure is the first essential control in verbal learning.

2. **Instructions to the subjects.** The "set" of the subjects in learning has been demonstrated by Lester (2) to affect the learning "strength." If the subject is to learn for one occasion only, and does not expect any future recall or other types of learning to follow, his results will differ from those obtained when the expectations of the subject include future tasks or tests. The type of learning also appears to be affected by the *type of test* expected. Students frequently inquire of their instructors whether a quiz will be "objective" or "essay." Such concern

appears to have justification in terms of the study techniques to be employed by the students. Whether the subject is informed about the test of learning to be used, or about events to follow, depends on the experimenter's purpose; the influence of "set" cannot, however, be ignored.

3. Methods of presenting stimuli. The material to be learned can be presented in a variety of ways, depending upon the needs and the material. The experimenter may decide to use a "whole" method of presentation in which the subject studies a prepared list or script which he has before him in its entirety. If poetry, for example, is being learned, the subject might be instructed to read the poem over and over as a unit, in parts learn a section at a time), or in a "part-progressive" procedure, which amounts to learning Part I, then I and II, then I, II, and III, and so on.

With meaningless or semimeaningless materials (adjectives, nouns, etc.) the materials are usually presented separately, that is, discretely, as single items in some fixed time order. Any technique that works can be used to present the units. The simplest method would amount to giving the subject a list of printed stimulus items and asking him to study the list, one unit at a time for some time interval, say 2 seconds, per unit. A metronome could provide a time signal and a paper screen could be used to help the subject to observe only one unit at a time. To help control the time intervals and exposure of one unit at a time, the experimenter could take charge of the materials and expose a printed card at the correct time intervals. A variation on this procedure might involve the experimenter's reading the list of items aloud to the subject. A phonograph record could be made to control the reader's variations from trial to trial.

The most common technique in presenting verbal material makes use of a "memory drum." The memory drum is any form of apparatus which can be arranged to carry the learning material in printed form at a constant rate, usually involving some ratchet device and toothed gear which allow the printed material to remain stationary for some short period per unit.

In the typical case, a drum can be adjusted so that one nonsense syllable appears in an aperture and stays there for 3 seconds, after which it is replaced by the next. This succession continues until the end of the list is reached, when the first part of the list reappears for another trial. A rest interval can be arranged to occur between trials. The length of this rest is an important variable and must be considered specifically in the interpretation of results. In the absence of a regular memory drum, a kymograph can be used as a substitute. A strip of paper on which the syllables are printed at intervals can be pasted on the drum of the kymograph. A screen with a suitable slot can be so arranged that the subject sees only one syllable at a time. It is desirable, when using such an arrangement, to print the syllables vertically rather than horizontally so that the whole syllable appears at once instead of a letter at a time.

The procedure just described applies to what is known as a "serial list." In such a serial list each syllable can be considered both as a stimulus and as a response. Thus, syllable 3 is a response to syllable 2 and a stimulus for syllable 4. Because syllable 1 appears first, it is usually used only as a stimulus syllable, but it can also be arranged to serve as a response to some starting signal, such as an X, which may appear in the aperture before it. This arrangement is desirable because many interpretations of results have ignored the *response* feature of the first syllable, and it is just as well to have the first syllable function in the same fashion as the remainder.

A special precaution must be taken in the selection of syllables for a serial list to make sure that all are of equal difficulty. This is especially true if the interpretations are going to take account of difficulties of learning of the separate items. In one experiment of the writer's, a list which had been described as consisting of syllables of equal difficulty was found to contain some syllables that were twice as easy to learn as were some of the others, regardless of position in the list. Probably the only feasible control is to use many different lists, or to arrange the syllables of one list in many different orders to balance out positional effects. In some instances a particular syllable happens to form a meaningful, or at least a tonal connection, with its successor. The second syllable is then easily learned simply because it "goes well" with the stimulus syllable. Subjects would have no difficulty, for instance, with the following absurd example: *PIC-NIK. NIK* would be sure to appear quickly as a correct response, even with one trial.

The method of serial presentation is only one of a variety of techniques. The most commonly used alternate is the "method of paired associates." In this procedure, two syllables are presented at the same time, the first being the stimulus for the second. As learning progresses, the stimulus syllable is presented alone, and the subject is expected to reply appropriately with the response half of the combination. In this procedure there is an obvious danger that the subject will learn the responses *serially*. The proper control is to vary the order of presentation of the pairs if this can be done. A memory-drum device usually prevents such alterations of order, and some other method must be adopted. One procedure that can be employed is to use projection slides which can be shown on a screen, half at a time. The order of the slides can be altered as the experimenter desires. At any rate, the usual technique is to vary in some way the serial arrangement in the test trials so that any serial learning is useless to the subject.

4. The responses of the subject and the measurement of verbal learning. The type of record kept by the experimenter depends upon his problem and interest. If the subject learns by the *anticipation* method, the experimenter has the opportunity of recording every response made by the subject, as this method requires that the subject try to name the syllable that is next in the list while viewing its predecessor. If the experimenter is interested in partial responses, it is well to have the subject spell out the syllables, so that a record can be kept of responses correct in 1, 2, or 3 letters. For some purposes all that is required is to keep track of the number of correct responses per trial; this can be accomplished by a simple checking system.

One of the immediate needs in record keeping is for the experimenter to decide what criterion of learning he is to follow. The student should concern himself with the question: "When is a syllable or a list of syllables learned?" When it can be repeated correctly once? What if the subject tries again, and misses one or several? Should he be expected to remember for years, for life, or for how long? Usually some arbitrary decision is adopted, such as two successive errorless performances. For some purposes a criterion of 75 percent, or any other percent, correct can be adopted.

Whenever the results are recorded by listing the specific syllables correctly anticipated per trial rather than the total number correct per trial, it becomes clear that one or two syllables are learned quickly and retained thenceforth. Mastery of the list as a whole may be held up for many further trials. All through the additional trials the quickly learned syllables are receiving additional practice and are overlearned. The list is not learned uniformly in any sense. The syllables that are learned last have only a few if any overlearning trials. In future retention tests, only the greatly overlearned syllables may be reported. The experimenter must be cautious in interpreting such data and should not treat his results as reflecting retention of lists as a whole. In the paired-associates procedure, a given pair can be removed from the list when it meets the criterion demanded. The question of what to use as a criterion has no easy answer, and a separate criterion must be established for every specific purpose.

5. *Methods of measuring retention*. The problem of forgetting is so intimately tied up with that of learning—in fact, forgetting is a common measure of learning—that it requires some comment at this time. There are three common methods of measuring retention which we can designate as the three *R's:* recall, recognition, and relearning. *Recall* amounts to requiring the subject to repeat without any cues (except in the *paired associates* method) the original material, and then determining the percent correct that the subject is able to report. This is not a very useful measure in serial-list learning, as the subject may know the syllables, but not in the correct order, and displacements of position are difficult to evaluate. *Recognition* takes the form of a true-or-false test in that the original material is presented along with a suitable number of syllables that are completely new; the subject is required to indicate those he has previously learned. In the *relearning* procedure, the subject is asked to relearn under the original conditions after some time has elapsed. It generally takes fewer trials to reach the same criterion of "learned," and the "savings score" is calculated as the percentage of trials saved as compared with the number required in the original learning.

6. *Typical problems*. Some mention should be made of the variety of problems that have been studied with nonsense and other verbal material. The problem of forgetting has already been mentioned. This problem and a corresponding one of interference of prior learning with new learning will be treated more fully in the next section, "Proactive and Retroactive Inhibition." Such problems as the efficiency of one type of learning over another (whole *vs.* part, space *vs.* crammed, etc.) have been standard preoccupations of "learning" psychologists. The problem of "reminiscence" (better recall some time after the learning than immediately after) has recently received considerable attention because of its theoretical significance.

The whole field of the relation of rote-memory types of learning to the principles of learning as described for conditioning and trial-and-error types has recently been examined. Such an experiment as that of Gibson (1) on the generalization of stimuli in nonsense-syllable learning is an example of this current trend. Experiments on "mediate association" are an interesting application of nonsense-syllable procedures. In this type of experiment a subject learns a set of paired associates, consisting, say, of letter-number combinations, such as A-1. He then learns another set of associates where the former responses are now stimuli for other responses, as 1-X. After learning both series, he is given the original stimuli and asked to respond with the first item he can think of from the second set of responses learned. The results have been interpreted as suggestive of the mechanisms employed in the processes of thinking, reasoning, and problem solving.

The above list of problems is only a small sampling of the vast amount of work done with the nonsense syllable since Ebbinghaus introduced it. Probably nonsense-syllable studies have the longest bibliography in psychology. More than any other single type of tool or technique, the nonsense syllable is the special creation of the psychologist, and through its use many psychologists hope to come to the study of what ordinarily passes for sensible behavior.

Proactive and Retroactive Inhibition

Much of the current literature in the field of learning is devoted to the problems involved in learning consecutive samples of materials. We can think of the problems involved in terms of the question: "What is the effect on learning some material, X, after learning some other material, Y?" And further, "What is the effect on the recall of Y after learning the intervening or "interpolated" material X?" The reader sees at once that these problems are only extensions of the general problem of transfer, but he may suspect that in this case the transfer might be negative, that the learning of some interpolated material might well hamper the recall of some material previously learned. It also appears likely that trying to learn some material after just having learned something else, might, in general, involve some interference or some other form of difficulty with the new learning.

When the recall of some previously learned material is retarded or hampered after the learning of some other material, we attribute the effect to "retroactive inhibition." McGeoch (3) defines retroactive inhibition as "a decrement in retention resulting from activity, usually a learning activity, interpolated between an original learning and a later measurement of retention." When a subject does not learn some new act or material as efficiently as he learned some equivalent previous material, we speak of "proactive inhibition." McGeoch defines proactive inhibition as "a retardation of the rate of learning of a second act or sample of material as a result of the prior learning of some other act or sample of material."

The typical experiments in retroactive inhibition (*RI*) can be diagrammed as follows:

1. Learn some material, *A,* to a criterion.
2. Learn some interpolated material, *B,* to a criterion.
3. Measure retention of *A* by recall, recognition, or "savings" (relearning) methods.

The above steps are usually followed by a group of subjects, working as individuals or as a group, depending upon the experimenter's needs. The validity of the experiment depends upon the performance of a similar group of subjects, matched for learning ability in the first material, who go through only steps 1 and 3. During the time the experimental group is learning the interpolated material, the control group, supposedly, does nothing.

The typical experiment in proactive inhibition (*PI*) involves, similarly, two groups of equated subjects. The steps in the experiment are as follows:

Experimental Group	Control Group
1. Learn material *A* to criterion.	1. Do nothing.
2. Learn material *B* to criterion.	2. Learn material *B* to criterion.

3. Compare efficiency of learning material *B* in both groups.

The student has already thought of numerous sources of error and variables that must be considered in the performance of this type of experiment and the treatment of the results. The following major problems are submitted for consideration and examination or control:

1. The criterion of learning: Will it make any difference if the materials learned, both original and interpolated, are learned to low or high criteria?
2. The length of materials, both original and interpolated: Should the two sets of materials be of equal difficulty and length?
3. Does it make any difference how retention is measured, say, as among the standard methods of recall, recognition, and relearning?
4. The nature of learning materials: Should they be sense materials, nonsense, geometrical figures, numerical combinations, photographs? Should the interpolated material be very like or very unlike the original? How much effect does similarity of materials have? Should the material be presented in serial order, as a simple list, as paired associates? What happens if you use paired associates in both original and interpolated materials, and retain the first members of each pair as stimulus materials, changing only the response side? Suppose, instead, that you retain the response side in the interpolated paired associates, but alter the stimulus halves of the pairs?
5. When is the interpolated material learned? Immediately after the original, immediately before recall or other measure of

retention, or at some intermediate time? How long can you wait and still get retardation effects? A few minutes? A few months? Should there be any time interval between learning of interpolated material by an experimental group and the recall? If so, what should the experimental group do during this unused time?

6. What should the control group do during the "interpolated" activity period of the experimental group? They are hypothetically supposed to do nothing except to suffer the passage of time. The ideal situation would perhaps be something like a quick-freezing process, which would permit suspended animation. Unless some measures are taken to control the control group, they are free to continue practicing the just-learned material. (The usual procedure is to occupy them with the reading of humorous magazines or examination of advertisements.)

The possibility of continued practice by the control group is the usual factor considered as needing control, but there are two other factors which might play vital roles in this situation: (1) The experimental group is getting practice in learning in the given experimental situation, which may be of some assistance to it, especially if a relearning type of retention measure is used later. This additional practice may obscure some retroactive effects, especially if subjects are used who are not at a peak level of practice in the type of performance being studied. (2) The experimental group is undergoing some fatigue effects from continued work. While this effect is possibly negligible in some types of performance, it may be of great influence in tasks which involve eyestrain (as with pied type), rapid writing (as in mathematical problem solutions), rapid talking (as in color naming), etc. Since retroactive inhibition is not supposed to be a simple matter of "fatigue," it is desirable to control this factor. The ideal procedure would consist in having the control group engage in identical physical activity *without learning* anything. How this is to be achieved is extremely difficult to determine.

If the interpolated material is something like writing down solutions to mathematical problems, the control group could be instructed to write down figures from dictation at a rate determined by the average performance of the experimental group, thereby going through the motions, at least. This type of procedure leaves open the question of possible "fatigue" of the experimental group from some "internal activity," and will probably not satisfy the rigid critic. At least, one can consider the problem of possible "fatigue" and additional practice in the experimental group. The latter factor can be eliminated quite easily if the experiment involves considerable delay between completion of interpolated learning and beginning of retention measuring. The possible effects of any kind of allegedly irrelevant activity indulged in by the control group must also be evaluated. It is probably best to have several control groups, differently occupied, to determine the effects of the methods used.

7. What sorts of instructions should be given the subjects? Instructions establish "mental sets," which Lester has shown to be of consequence in the performance. Should the subjects be told that there will be a future recall? An interpolation? Should they be told that interpolated material retards retention of original learning? Should they be urged to try, or not to try, to overcome these expected effects? Should they be held in ignorance of the whole procedure? Should they know what method of retention measuring is going to be used? What self-instruction do the subjects give themselves? What are their own reactions to the interpolation of some new material if this is unexpected? What are their reactions to a measurement of retention? Are they amused, annoyed, perplexed? Do they expect to have trouble?

The experimental work on retroactive and proactive inhibition is the major form of attack on the problem of forgetting. It represents, at the present time, a major preoccupation of "learning" psychologists, and the student of the experimental psychology of learning is obliged to become familiar with the niceties of experimental control in this area of investigation if he expects to appreciate the theoretical difficulties when he eventually meets them.

References

1. Gibson, E. J. Retroactive inhibition as a function of the degree of generalization between tasks. *J. exp. Psychol.,* 1941, *28,* 93–115.
2. Lester, O. P. Mental set in relation to retroactive inhibition. *J. exp. Psychol.,* 1932, *15,* 681–699.
3. McGeoch, J. *The psychology of human learning.* New York: Longmans, Green. 1942, chap. 1.

Experiment 21. Learning IV: Nonsense-Syllable Learning
(Rote Learning of a Serial List)

Introduction. Nonsense syllables are among the most widely used materials in learning studies. The student of experimental psychology must familiarize himself with the problems and variables involved in having subjects learn such materials. One of the most important variables in learning of this type is the experience of the subject. Unless the subject has previously learned five or six lists of syllables, any data you obtain from him are likely to be unreliable.

The reason for this unreliability is that subjects first learning a list are uncertain about their capacity to learn, worry about the possibility of failure to meet a reasonable standard, and fear that they will be considered stupid. In order to learn as rapidly as possible, the "naïve" subject will try first one system, then another, of picking up some of the syllables. He will grope for associations and conjure up possible cues. His behavior may vary from one trial to another, and he may have used a different method of learning in each trial. After he has actually learned a number of lists, he tends to stick to whatever method he has found useful in the past, and so there is more internal consistency or reliability in his data.

Since this is a first exercise in learning nonsense syllables for you, we cannot hope to achieve much in the way of meaningful data. After you and your subject have learned your lists, the results will be analyzed to see if the data of the class as a whole illustrate any principles of nonsense-syllable learning.

Apparatus and Procedure. Your instructor will prepare a list of 10 nonsense syllables for you to arrange on a memory drum, or other exposure device, so that a new syllable will appear in an aperture every three seconds. It will take 30 seconds for a single run through the list. A 30-second rest period will take place between trials. Just before the first syllable is to appear, a figure, e.g., a star, will appear in the aperture. As soon as the star appears, the subject is to try to name the first syllable. The experimenter

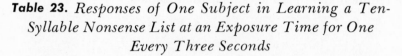

Table 23. *Responses of One Subject in Learning a Ten-Syllable Nonsense List at an Exposure Time for One Every Three Seconds*

Trials	Syllables									
1										
2										
3										
4										
5										
6										
7										
8										
9										
10										
11										
12										
13										
14										
15										
16										
17										
18										
19										
20										
21										
22										
23										
24										
25										
Trial learned										
Rank order										

notes whether the subject was able to "anticipate" the appearance of the first syllable. When the first syllable appears, the subject is to try to name the second, and so on through the list. This procedure is known as the "anticipation method."

FIGURE 21. *AN INEXPENSIVE MOTOR-DRIVEN MEMORY DRUM.* The motor is one of a type sold for driving advertising displays. Any slow-speed motor will do. Depending upon the speed of available motors (some can be slowed down with rheostats), one or more spokes are fitted into a sleeve which is then fastened to the motor shaft. As the motor rotates, the spokes strike against pegs protruding from the drum. The pegs are stove bolts covered with rubber tubing to deaden the sound of contact. The number of pegs depends on the number of syllables to be used. The drum itself is a No. 2 vegetable can with round sections of wood fitted into the ends. Circular metal disks are then fastened to the blocks. Tapered bolts serve as bearings. Nonsense syllables are printed on strips of paper at predetermined intervals, and the strips are pasted on the drum. When the spokes push against the pegs, the drum is thrown over a distance corresponding to one syllable. The drum rests there until the next spoke pushes against the next peg. A screen curved over the drum allows the subject to see only one syllable at a time through the window.

When the subject has been able to recite the list correctly twice in succession, we will say that he has "learned." Two errorless trials, are, therefore, our *criterion*. If the subject does not master the list in 25 trials, terminate the experiment.

After one subject learns his list, the experimenter changes places with him before the memory drum, and learns another list. Keep a record of performance in Table 23. In order to do this, the experimenter must be in position to see the drum aperture along with the subject. Do not score as correct anything but a clear anticipation. If the subject reports incorrect syllables either from his actual list or from other sources, write these in the proper spaces in Table 23. If the subject responds correctly, make a check mark. Use a line for no response.

Results

1. How many trials did it take your subject to learn to the criterion?
2. Indicate in Table 23 the number of the trial on which the subject first learned each syllable (learning means that he gave two successive correct responses and never missed again more than once). If, for example, your subject responded correctly for syllable 5 on the 12th and 13th trials, and did not miss again more than once before the experiment was over, record 12 as the trial on which this syllable was learned.
3. In the table, indicate the *order* in which the syllables were learned by finding the rank order of the numbers just recorded.
4. Group data: Report the results of 3 (above) for class tabulation. The class will average the rank orders of all students and determine the rank order for the groups. Both rank-order averages and rank orders will be plotted.
5. Which syllables were learned first? Last? Does this correspond to your expectation? Does this order of learning prevail in other types of learning, e.g., mazes?
6. What methods did you adopt for learning the material? Did you try to use a system?

7. What kinds of errors did your subject make? Do these have any meaning?
8. Does the first experimenter, when he becomes the subject, start at the same zero point as did the first subject?

Discussion

1. Did the memory drum you used affect the nature of the learning?
2. Would you accept your subject as now suitably trained for use in a regular learning experiment?
3. Do you think nonsense material is the best possible for use in human verbal-learning situations?
4. Does the way in which you learned nonsense syllables correspond to the way in which you learn meaningful material?
5. What was your subject's motivation in this experiment? Do you have to worry about the motivation variable in nonsense-learning experiments?

References

1. Postman, L., and Egan, J. P. *Experimental psychology*. New York: Harper and Brothers. 1949, chap. 15.
2. Underwood, B. J. *Experimental psychology*. New York: Appleton-Century-Crofts. 1949, chap. 12.
3. Woodworth, R. S. *Experimental psychology*. New York: Henry Holt. 1938.

Experiment 22. Learning V: Paired Associates.
Retroactive and Proactive Inhibition.
The Gibson Study

Introduction. The learning of a serial list is not always the most useful process by which to observe learning. It is not always easy to determine how much learning has taken place. A subject may learn all the syllables but not know the exact order, and it is difficult to evaluate position mistakes. If the subject cannot get started, he may be unable to proceed, even if he knows every syllable after the first. To "spot test" is difficult because of the varying efficiency with which the syllables are learned in different positions. Usually it is necessary to check the amount of learning by relearning trials and "saving" scores.

One technique which avoids some of these difficulties is the use of *paired associates*. In this method a subject is presented with items two at a time, and he is instructed to learn the second item as a *response* to the first. The first item will serve as a stimulus in future presentations. The experimenter can present as many pairs as he wishes. A trial is over when all of the pairs have been presented. The experimenter then usually varies the order of the pairs in the next and succeeding trials to *avoid* serial learning.

The pairs can be made up of any of a variety of items, e.g., numbers and letters, words, nonsense syllables, faces and names, etc. It is only necessary that the response be something in the capacity of the subject to do; usually the subject responds verbally. The paired-associates technique has numerous advantages over serial lists. You will be asked to discuss these later.

In the present experiment you will use paired associates in a partial repetition of an important study made by Gibson (1) in attempting to get at the factors underlying retroactive inhibition. In this experiment you will have a chance to observe both proactive and retroactive inhibition and the controls involved in the study of these phenomena. The procedure and apparatus will be essentially like Gibson's and are described below.

Apparatus and Procedure. In a retroactive inhibition experiment the subjects learn some material (*A*) then learn some "interpolated" material (*B*), and finally are tested for the retention of *A* by means of recall, recognition, or relearning techniques. If the learning of *B* has somehow reduced the efficiency of retention of *A,* we speak of "retroactive inhibition." The words need not be taken literally, as they have important and questionable connotations, but for our purposes *R.I.* refers to the decrement in retention as measured by the experimenter in the situation described.

Because the decrement might be due to the passage of time, a control group, matched for learning ability, does not learn *B,* but waits for the retention test while the experimental group learns the interpolated material. During this waiting period it is important that the control group neither practice *A* nor learn anything else. How can you arrange this state of affairs?

Our procedure will follow that of Gibson, and is in effect a repetition of one-fifth of her experiment. The materials to be learned consist of 13 nonsense figures paired with nonsense syllables. Each figure-syllable pair is drawn on a glass slide in India ink. Half of the slide is devoted to the figure, the other half to the syllable. The 13 slides of Set *A* are projected on a suitable screen for the entire class, one at a time, two seconds per slide. After this first presentation, the experimenter will expose only the figure side of each slide for three seconds. The subjects try to write down on slips of paper, with 13 blanks, the syllable that accompanied the figure. The slides are shuffled between learning presentations and "test trials." Four more learning and test trials are given.

The experimenter then divides the subjects into two groups, an experimental and a control group, on the basis of their learning scores, taking care to balance the groups. The experimental group now learns (five trials) 13 more figure-syllable combinations (Set *B*) in which the figures are similar to (but not identical with) those of Set *A*. The control-group subjects leave the experimental room and occupy themselves with *New Yorker* (or other) cartoons, each member trying to pick the funniest cartoon. When the experimental group is finished with *B,* both groups are tested by recall and relearning (2 trials for material *A*). Materials *A* and *B* are reproduced in Appendix 3.

Table 24. *Comparison of Local Data with Data Obtained by E. J. Gibson from 22 Smith College Students in an Experiment on Retroactive Inhibition* *

Results	Experimental Group		Control Group	
	Gibson N =	Local N =	Gibson N =	Local N =
Mean no. of correct responses on test 5 of original learning	7.86		7.91	
Mean no. correct responses on test 5 of interpolated learning	9.68			
Mean no. correct recall of original learning	3.00		7.57	
Mean no. of trials to relearning original	3.73		2.35	
Retroactive inhibition on Recall I	59.9%			

* "Retroactive inhibition" is calculated by comparing the percentage of retention in the experimental group with the percentage of retention in the control group. If the control group retains 90 percent and the experimental group retains 30 percent, then the experimental group retains only thirty-three percent of the amount retained by the control group. It has lost sixty-six percent. This loss is the "retroactive inhibition."

Results. Gibson found for her subjects the results listed in Table 24. Space has been provided for inserting the group data of this experiment in the same table for ready comparison. How much retroactive inhibition did the experimental group show? Were there any proactive effects? How could you test for these? Do you have any data which bear upon the factors responsible for proactive or retroactive inhibition?

Discussion

1. How do your experimental data compare with those of Gibson? Can you account for any discrepancies?
2. Why did she use such figures as she did for the stimulus side of the paired comparisons?
3. Why did she use 5 trials in the original learning and 2 in the relearning? Why 13 pairs?
4. Why was material *B* so much like *A* on the stimulus side? Did it confuse the members of the experimental group?
5. Why use figures at all? Why not nonsense-syllable pairs?
6. What sources of error do you detect in this experiment? How could they be controlled?

References

1. Gibson, E. J. Retroactive inhibition as a function of degree of generalization between tasks. *J. exp. Psychol.,* 1941, *28,* 93–115.
2. McGeoch, J. *The psychology of human learning.* New York: Longmans, Green. 1942.
3. Postman, L., and Egan, J. P. *Experimental psychology.* New York: Harper & Brothers. 1949, chap. 16.
4. Woodworth, R. S. *Experimental psychology.* New York: Henry Holt. 1938.

17

The Laboratory Study of Thinking

THE SUBJECT of "thinking" belongs to the psychologist by long tradition, although it cannot be claimed that he has distinguished himself in the analysis of the problems included under this term. Whenever the psychologist approaches the study of activities that are commonly considered in large measure "conscious," "mentalistic," "private," or "subjective," and leaves the security of the measurement of movement that he abstracts from "behavior," he seems to make little scientific progress in the sense of acquiring an agreed-upon body of knowledge which can be used for prediction of future events.

To add to the confusion, there have been those awkward philosophers, and even lesser mortals, who report on subconscious and unconscious "thoughts," and who tell us anecdotes about solving mathematical and other types of problems in their sleep. The study of such efficiency in sleep-states has not yet been attempted in the laboratory, although the dreams of deaf-mutes have been investigated in terms of finger movements. Judging by the patterns of brain waves in sleep, which differ markedly from those in waking states, it is highly unlikely that much organized activity goes on in sleep.

Although speculation has been vigorous for several thousand years about how we think, the speculative approach has not led to any great advances in our understanding of the "thought processes." Even such a phrase as "thought processes" has no ready

347

reference to anything beyond the words themselves, although we use the expression glibly enough and normally do not excite an agitated challenge as to "just what do you mean?" Everyone *knows* that thought processes have to do with "ideas," but there are precious few ideas as to what an idea is. We also "know" that we think with our heads, or, more properly, with our brains—some writers even talk about "cerebration"—but the evidence for such statements and for any other statements relating the nervous system to thinking is inconveniently lacking.

In spite of the lack of any empirical referents, there is no halt to popular discussions and writings about "how our minds work," "improving mental efficiency," and so on. It may, of course, turn out that someday someone will find a scientific answer to the problem of thinking on the mentalistic level. In the meantime, we can take a look at a more "behavioral" approach and see what satisfaction it offers. Before we do so, however, it is necessary to come to some agreement on the limits of our problem.

The subject of thinking is complicated for us by confusing what is more or less properly the business of the scientist, namely, the understanding and explanation of events and activities, with the *practical* problem of how "thinking" *should be* carried on for purposes of best, most efficient, or "true" results. The latter problem is the problem of logicians, the "reasoners," philosophers, moralists, and educators. It is concerned with the content of a problem and its solution. Values are placed upon the outcome of thinking. With such attempts to apply rules and evaluate results, the psychologist may or may not care to deal. At present he is hardly in a position to do so, and might well leave the task to others perhaps better equipped through training in logic, symbolic and otherwise. The principles of the syllogism are in the province of logic and not in that of today's psychology.

Another source of difficulty is the fact that, since the time of the early Greek philosophers, it has been recognized that "language (including a variety of written and unwritten symbols) is closely associated with what commonly passes as thinking. The recognition of the tremendous influence of language in problem solving has led many psychologists into a too-easy dismissal of the problem. Watson, for example, classified thinking as "subvocal speech," and thereby practically dismissed it from study. To acknowledge that speech and thinking are related merely opens the question of how the relationship comes into being and by what means it is mediated. Some psychologists are only now beginning to make studies of the relationship of words to thinking, and their work is just beginning to show results. Only recently attempts have been made to analyze the functions of signs and symbols in behavior. That signs and symbols can be treated on a behavior level has been demonstrated to some extent by Hull with his "pure stimulus acts," by Tolman with his "sign gestalts," and by Morris (3) in his translation of signs and symbols into behavioral terms. Such attacks on the problem of thinking are beyond the scope of our present interest, and we will not consider them further, leaving the matter for future inquiry by the interested reader.

The fact that in many problem situations such signs and symbols appear to be produced by the organism itself should be mentioned. In the double-alternation maze, the organism must supply the cues at the choice point, since the physical environment remains the same. In an interesting variation of this experiment Solomon (4) trained rats to enter the *fourth* of a series of alleys breaking off from a runway. Since the physical cues from the apparatus were presumably controlled, any success enjoyed by the rat was presumed to be due to internal or implicit cues which can be interpreted as symbols. How these cues were generated is, of course, the problem. Solomon found that when weights were attached to the rats, they tended to enter the earlier alleys. On the basis of this finding he assumed that the rats were being guided by proprioceptive stimuli resulting from exertion.

Such self-generated cues are presumably present in many problem situations, and their study and identification is a crying need. Until an adequate physiology is developed, it will be difficult to handle such cues except by assuming their presence on the basis of behavioral experimentation. Such an alternative may prove adequate for a psychology interested in prediction even if the physiology of the matter is never established.

To study thinking in the laboratory we must first come to some agreement as to terms. There is no necessity that we must define the term "thinking" itself, and there is little likelihood that any agreement would be reached if such an attempt were made. It will be enough, and probably more than enough, if we outline a problem area, i.e., select some aspects of behavior that might be commonly recognized as including "thinking," and pick out some of the variables for close scrutiny. In effect we can do this by asking ourselves: "When do people (or organisms, generally) think?"

When do *you* think? If you are asked to multiply "mentally" (that usually means without pencil and paper, an operational definition to some extent) 2 times 2, and you respond correctly, did you "think" in arriving at the answer? How about 9 times 6? or 2397 times 4856? The last one requires a bit of "thought," you would agree. Do chess players think? Does an expert chess player think *as much* when playing against a rank beginner as he does against a worthy opponent? Suppose you are asked to solve a puzzle in which you are to discover in *three* weighings on a balance scale which *one* of eight pennies is defective in weight (either too light or too heavy) and to tell the nature of the defect. Does this call for thinking? Do you have to think when you are asked to separate a pair of interlocked nails or other pieces of wire in a typical Chinese puzzle? Do you have to think as much in solving your twentieth Chinese puzzle as you did in your first?

Suppose a child is shown some candy placed under a red cup which is on a table alongside a blue cup; suppose further that a screen is interposed between child and cups for five seconds and then raised. Does the child "think" in picking out the correct cup? You will find that *with practice* the child makes fewer mistakes. Does it think as much in the later trials? Now suppose that, while the screen is between child and cups, you switch the candy to the blue cup. When the screen is removed, the child reaches for the red cup and finds nothing. He tries the blue and finds the candy. Suppose you continue this switching technique. How long will it be before the child reaches for the cup which is *not* the one in which the candy was placed? It took one two-year-old child 97 trials to go to the correct cup without error. Did the child "think" out the solution?

Harlow (1) trained monkeys in a similar problem situation. He used varied sizes, shapes, and colors of stimulus objects under which to hide the food. The monkeys made many errors in solving these problems. As soon as they had solved one problem, he gave them another. What happened was that the monkeys eventually learned to solve new problems in one trial. After solving hundreds of such problems, the monkeys were given the switching technique; again they had difficulty, but again they got to the point where they could solve a new problem in one trial. A visitor watching a monkey on his first trials might tend to regard him as stupid, as he made error after error. Another visitor watching an "experienced" or "educated" monkey solve a problem in one trial, if unfamiliar with his history, might regard him as a monkey "genius." According to Harlow, the monkeys learned "insight" by gradual stages. They slowly acquired habits of responding to internal cues which can be assumed to have been present, even though we cannot, as yet, identify them.

Suppose, for a last example, that you put a cat into a Thorndike "puzzle-box," and that he emerges in twenty minutes. On subsequent trials he takes less time, until on late trials it is only a matter of seconds before the cat is out of the box. Did the cat "think" its way out of this "puzzle box"? According to Thorndike, the cat *learns* to get out; and, furthermore, he learns in a "trial-and-error" fashion. If the means for getting out of the box consists of pulling a string, and if the string is moved to another place in the box, a new problem results for the animal, and for some time it continues to "pull" at the place where the string used to be.

Consider any of the illustrative problems described above. Does it appear that "learning" is involved to some extent in each of them? In some instances the learning may take place on one trial, or at least very rapidly; sometimes the learning is so rapid that the fact of learning is obscured. In several of the problems it is clear that "past experience" is being applied to a "new" situation. Without suitable past experience, "thinking" is quite impossible in the problems mentioned. If you don't know the rules of chess, you can't "think" effectively in chess. If you have no experience with the calculus, you have trouble "thinking" your way through a problem involving that technique.

Viewing the matter in another way, if you have suitable experience or habits, *you do not need to think.* You merely respond to the stimuli of the new situation as you did in the past to the same or similar stimuli (generalization of conditioned stimuli). This brings us to the question of what goes on when you do not have appropriate habits or past experience for meeting a new situation, if you can imagine such a situation. If the new situation can be described as a "problem" for the organism involved, and if there are stimuli affecting the organism, we can expect responses to occur. Some psychologists like to label such responses "attempted solutions." This wording is gratuitous and does not help us in appreciating what is going on. The behavioral facts of the matter are that one or another of the responses that is made may eliminate the problem situation. If such a response is not made, the organism either gives up the problem by default, or the problem eliminates the organism. Consider the problem of a rabbit caught in the coils of a constrictor. If his struggles are not successful, his problem is over in due course. This type of problem, however, does not seem to require thinking. It is a matter of trial and error.

What about the child who takes 97 trials to respond correctly to the problem of the switched cups? Is that a situation of less trial and error? What about the novice in chess who picks up a piece, places it on some square, retrieves it, tries some other move, and finally completes a move from social pressure and desperation? For the more advanced player the rules call for moving any piece that has been touched. This is a form of inhibitory pressure to prevent *overt* trial and error. A player functioning under such rules must not touch a piece until he is ready to move it. What goes on during the period of arriving at such readiness? We do not get too much help by asking a subject to tell us what goes on inside of him. He may report such things as "feelings of effort," images of various kinds, vague tendencies or attitudes (the "image-less" thought of the early German psychologists), and a variety of other activities depending upon his skill at verbalizing. Behavior-ially, we can describe some of his activity as incipient movements, hovering movements, eye movements, possibly some lip activity; and if we ask for it, we can get considerable "talking to myself" activity reported by the player. This "talking" typically follows the pattern: "If I move this here, he'll move there," etc.

The trial-and-error nature of the activity is obvious for the beginner. The expert shows less such activity because he has ac-quired the appropriate habits. The recent development of "think-ing machines" in the form of giant calculators, which can play a reasonably good game of chess based on mathematical probabili-ties, should at least illustrate the point of the usefulness of "hab-its" for thinking. In the "thinking machine," such habits are built into the device. A living organism must acquire its own.

From the above discussion we can approach the laboratory study of thinking as a matter of understanding the conditions under which problem situations come into being for an organism, and the conditions under which responses appear that are either appropriate or inappropriate in terms of eliminating the problem situation. By providing a suitable history for one group of ex-perimental subjects, in terms of experience or "habits," and by preventing a control group from acquiring such a history, we can approach the problem of the relationship of learning to problem solution. An illustration of such a procedure might illuminate the situation.

Suppose we arrange, as was done by Lumsdaine (2), to condi-tion an eyelid blink to a light which precedes a tap on the cheek.

After this conditioned response is established, we condition the subject to withdraw a finger from a shock plate by using the tap on the cheek as a conditioned stimulus. Now, if the subject has his finger on the shock plate, we find that he withdraws his finger when the light is presented even though the light was never associated directly with the shock. Whether this can be thought of as a problem situation or not, it does have some problem components: a new situation, appropriate and inappropriate "solution responses," and the possibility of putting "two and two" together, in terms of the use of previously unrelated items of past experience.

Such an experiment illustrates one of the laboratory types of approaches to "problem solving." The term "thinking" is so loaded with mentalistic connotations that its usefulness in laboratory study is highly questionable if we are to stick to operational definitions of terms. The approach through "problem solving" may not be too much better, but it provides at least a basis for an operational definition of the problem under study.

In recent years some psychologists have approached the study of problem solving through the use of hypothetical constructs, which they label "insight," "hypotheses," etc. Such terms must be handled with extreme care if they are not to raise more problems than they solve. Even though they have some possibility of operational definition, their connotations may overflow the operational meaning. To say that thinking takes place when insight occurs merely raises the question of what is "insight." To talk about "seeing relationships" likewise only raises questions instead of providing answers.

This is not to deny the possibility of accumulation of considerable information concerning problem solving through such approaches as those of Kohler and Lewin. Before problems are solved, they must be recognized, and various procedures may apply at different levels of discourse or with different approaches. The differences between Gestalt and behavioral approaches are largely terminological ones, and to some extent differences of emphasis. The approach of a behaviorist like Dashiell or of a Gestalt-ist like Lewin to problem solving is similar in many respects. Both conceive of a problem as consisting of some interference with goals of an organism. Such interferences are labeled "barriers" by each. The organism attempts to get through, over, or around the barrier by using the response repertoire available. Both writers in describing such a problem situation lean heavily on trial and error, on past experience, on the present stimuli, and on the nature of the organism. It is in interpreting this last feature, the nature of the organism, that differences develop. That these differences may eventually be eliminated by careful research is to be expected.

For our present purposes we can admit that there are no ready or easy answers to what goes on during thinking. We have already seen that many situations that are superficially described as problems or that appear to require thought are, to a large extent at least, *learning* problems and are susceptible of study through "learning" experiments. One can even entertain the question whether there is any such activity as thinking divorced from trial-and-error activity and subsequent learning of adjustive responses, which eliminate the need for "thinking" in future similar situations.

It may turn out that a successfully completed and adequate learning theory will be able to handle the matter of understanding "thinking," at least so far as the scientific aim of prediction is concerned. If that is the case, we might better concentrate on "learning" mechanisms for the time being, especially since the direct frontal attack on "thinking" is quite impossible in terms of a behavioral approach, and other approaches have failed to reveal the "thought processes" to us in anything but verbalisms which need study themselves.

While allowing learning theorists to work out their contribution to the problem of adjustment, we need not abandon all other possible approaches, for to gamble on learning theory alone for successful answers to our questions regarding thinking is to risk the possible loss of fruitful leads from researchers who prefer to emphasize the contribution of the organism. In laboratory investigations we should be guided by evidence and controlled experiments, and not by faith. In our own laboratory study we will examine the learning approach to two typical "thinking" problems: the solution of a form of puzzle, and the development of "concepts." In these experiments you will be asked to do some "self-observation," and after you have performed these experiments, you may be in a better position to think about thinking.

References

1. Harlow, H. The formation of learning sets. *Psychol. Rev.*, 1949, *56, 51*–65.
2. Lumsdaine, A. A. Conditioned eyelid responses as mediating generalized conditioned finger reactions. *Psychol. Bull.*, 1939, *36,* 650.
3. Morris, C. *Signs, language and behavior.* New York: Prentice-Hall. 1946.
4. Solomon, R. The role of effort in the performance of a distance discrimination. *J. exp. Psychol.*, 1949, *39,* 73–83.
5. Underwood, B. J. *Experimental psychology.* New York: Appleton-Century-Crofts. 1949, chap. 13.

Do not read until instructed to do so

Experiment 23. Problem Solving I: Concept Formation

Introduction. The term "concept" is defined as a universal idea of the meaning of a term, or as a mental image representing objects or events. Such is the dictionary definition. In common speech we use concepts like justice, honesty, or democracy. What is your "idea" of any of the above terms? What do you think of when someone says "democracy"? Do you think of the constitution, a hand at the ballot box, a New England town meeting? Do you have a "general idea," or do you think in terms of concrete and isolated items? Can you think of a chair, for example, without thinking of a *specific* chair?

In his *Essay on Human Understanding,* Bishop Berkeley went to considerable pain to prove that one cannot think of "chairness" or "horse-ness" or of any "general idea" without some specific reference. We are often told that children who are city-bred call cows and horses "dogs" when they first see them on a visit to the country. This is probably a well meant piece of fiction, since children see pictures of such animals in books before they visit the country. The suggestion that infants refer to all men as "daddy" is another overstrained illustration of the suggestion that our "ideas" or "concepts" develop slowly on the basis of experience by a process of abstracting essences from general instances or cases. The dictionary definition of a concept is hardly acceptable operationally, and we will attempt to get at a closer appreciation of the term in a simple experiment, first devised by Hull, who tried to discover the relationship between abstraction and generalization in "concept" formation.

Apparatus and Procedure. A problem situation is created for a subject by asking him to learn the names of 36 symbols. The symbols resemble Chinese ideographs * and are drawn on 3″ by 5″

* The ideographs are reproduced in Woodworth (2), p. 802.

filing cards, one to a card. The 36 cards on which the characters are printed are divided into six groups, or classes. Each class consists of six cards on which are printed ideographs based on the same "radical," or basic figure. The basic figure is obscured by additional lines and figures.

The experimenter shuffles the deck; then he exposes each card for three seconds and names it for the subject on the first run through the deck. He uses only six names (nonsense syllables of a Chinese flavor) for the 36 cards, since he names only the radical on each card. On the second and later trials, the subject is asked to anticipate the names of each card, and if he fails to do so within two seconds, he is prompted.

Trials are repeated, the deck being shuffled to prevent serial learning, until the subject names each card correctly. He is then asked to tell why he named the cards as he did, and is asked to draw the radicals if he mentions their existence. Any mistakes, additions, or omissions from his drawings and descriptions are noted by the experimenter.

Results. Indicate the subject's progress in Table 25 by writing in his responses. How many trials did he take to learn each radical? Which radicals were easy; which were difficult? Why? What kinds of errors did the subject make? Did he develop incorrect concepts? Did his behavior indicate any trial-and-error activity? Did he generalize first and abstract later, or vice versa? or both at the same time?

Discussion

1. What is a "concept"? Can you define the term operationally on the basis of this experiment?
2. Is this experiment a good one for the purpose of noting the processes of abstraction and generalization?
3. Did your subject's behavior illustrate the formation of "concepts" in everyday life?

4. Did your subject know that this was an experiment in "concept formation"?
5. Was he looking for elements to abstract?
6. Did he give the right answers before he knew the reasons?
7. Does the experimental procedure qualify as a "problem" situation for the subject? Does it illustrate "thinking" behavior?

Table 25. *The Progress in Identification of Ideographs in the Hull Concept-Formation Experiment*

Trials	Ideograph names					
	OO	YER	LI	TA	DEG	LING
1						
2						
3						
4						
5						
6						
7						
8						
9						
10						
11						
12						
13						
14						
15						

References

1. Underwood, B. J. *Experimental psychology*. New York: Appleton-Century-Crofts. 1949, chap. 13.
2. Woodworth, R. S. *Experimental psychology*. New York: Henry Holt. 1938, chaps. 29, 30.

Do not read until instructed to do so

Experiment 24. Problem Solving II: Flexibility in Thinking.
The "Insight" Learning Curve

Introduction. In experiments in which monkeys solved a series of problems involving the selection of one out of two containers differing in size, shape, color, etc., Harlow (2) found that successive solutions became easier and easier. The monkeys became "educated" and would solve problems in one trial; such solutions are ordinarily described as "insight." The animals could be educated to shift their selections and pick out the container under which the food reward had *not* been placed.

Esta Berg (1), a student of Harlow's, devised an experiment in which the problem situation faced by Harlow's monkeys could be elaborated for use on an adult human level. Her experiment consists in having subjects sort cards on which are printed symbols (cross, star, circle, and triangle) differing in number and color. An arbitrary base for sorting is selected by the experimenter, say color. When the subject discovers this base and makes five correct sortings, the base is arbitrarily changed to another variable, say form. The subject must now shift his criterion, and a record is kept of the number of errors made until he adjusts to the new problem, at which time another base is selected.

Harlow and Berg regard this situation as useful for the analysis of "shift of set," flexibility in thinking, and "abstract" or concept-forming behavior. The experiment offers an opportunity to observe conflict, ego-involvement, and levels of aspiration. In our own laboratory experiment we will attempt to observe all these phenomena and aspects of behavior. Since we are duplicating Berg's experiment, we have an opportunity of comparing our results with hers (Berg's data are reproduced in Table 26).

Apparatus and Procedure. The experimenter will set out on the table in front of the subject four cards: one red card with a

Table 26. *Number of Errors Made by Each Group of Berg's Subjects and by Subjects from the Experimental Psychology Class on Each Successive Sorting Category in a Three-Choice Sorting Task*

Subjects	N	Successive Sorting Categories								
		1	2	3	4	5	6	7	8	9
Berg's A	15	3.33	7.27	7.14	2.60	3.20	3.20	2.40	1.80	2.13
Berg's B	21	4.27	9.14	9.67	8.86	11.43	6.76	6.85	5.48	8.19
Berg's C		3.87	20.79	18.00	9.17	21.40	19.25	13.50	— *	— *
N in C		15	14	14	12	10	8	4		
Individual										
Group										

* Did not complete.

triangle, one green with two stars, one yellow with three crosses, and one blue with four circles. He will then hand the subject a pack of 60 cards consisting of fifteen each of blue, red, green, and yellow. Each card will have from one to four figures on it (either crosses, circles, triangles, or stars).* The subject is instructed to sort the cards into four groups corresponding to the four key cards. No further instructions are given.

The experimenter arbitrarily decides the basis for the first sorting (or the instructor will furnish a prearranged sorting order), and informs the subject, after each card is placed below one of the key cards, of his success or failure by saying "right" or "wrong." When the subject has sorted five successive cards correctly, the experimenter changes the basis for sorting. This continues until the subject has correctly solved nine categories of response (or until one hour has elapsed, whichever happens first). The experimenter counts the number of errors made per category.

* To prepare the cards, cut up colored cardboard into playing-card-size pieces. There should be 16 each of red, yellow, green, and blue. Taking one color at a time, draw a star on one card, 2 stars on the next, then 3, then 4. Then repeat with crosses; then with circles; and, finally, with triangles. Repeat the procedure with each color.

Results. Berg found three classes of subjects: (A) those who discovered that the experimenter was shifting the criterion and then solved the problems; (B) those who solved the problems but had only vague notions concerning shifts, and could not state when the shifts occurred; and (C) those who could not solve the problem. Berg's data are included in Table 26. Insert your subject's data and the group data of your class in the same table. Include in your results descriptions of your subject's behavior, signs of conflict, changes in assurance, reactions to failure, etc. Draw curves of Berg's results for her A group, for your individual subject, and for the group results.

Discussion

1. To what Berg group do your class and individual data correspond?
2. To what do you attribute failure to solve the problems quickly, or not at all?
3. How do you account for the trend of Berg's A group, which shows a general decline in errors after the second trial?
4. Why are the first trial scores so low for all groups?
5. Did your subject learn "insight"?
6. Can the term "shift of set" be reduced to an operational definition?
7. What observations did you make relative to the "abstraction" of concepts?

References

1. Berg, E. A simple objective technique for measuring flexibility in thinking. *J. gen. Psychol.,* 1948, *39,* 15–22.
2. Harlow, H. The formation of learning sets. *Psychol. Rev.,* 1949, *56,* 51–65.

18

The Laboratory Study of Emotional Behavior

THE EXPERIMENTAL APPROACH to the study of emotional behavior has been, thus far, a rather unrewarding one, except perhaps in a negative sense. We now know that a lot of wrong answers are wrong. The student who hopes that he can make an important research contribution of psychology has practically virgin territory in the area of emotional behavior. In no other aspect of behavior is there less agreement and more argument.

Far from being able to settle down to serious study, psychologists are not yet agreed on what the term "emotion" means. Any student can *name* a variety of "emotions." He usually starts off his list with "fear, anger, and love," and then begins to list what he might term "shades" of these, such as "joy, anxiety, terror, horror, jealousy, affection." Ask him to define any one of these, and the resulting verbal effort is not very satisfying to anyone, including the student doing the defining. He may have been "in love," but can't seem to tell us what it is that he has been "in." His verbalizing of a "fear" is equally personalized and non-communicable.

The same difficulties concerning definition and communication prevail in our attempts to study intelligence, thinking, motivation, and even learning. These difficulties are not insuperable obstacles, and serious studies can proceed even in the absence of unanimous agreement on terminology. There have been attempts to work with operational concepts in the field of emotion. Skinner's (5) suggestions about treating emotion as something which alters the rate of response might prove fruitful.

The student has learned by now that it is not likely that much valid information will be discovered through listening to personalized descriptions of alleged experiences, and he may wish to examine the results of the laboratory approach. With the warning that not too much should be expected, we may inspect the traditional experimental approach to emotional behavior. Such an inspection may help reveal the sources of error of such a study, and the basic reasons for the paucity of information and poor understanding of "emotion."

In general, there have been four types of investigation attempted (or, better, measures used) in the study of emotion: (1) the study of facial emotional expression, primarily by means of photographs, (2) the recording of action of the body as a whole, (3) the recording of reactions of the visceral organs and nervous activity, and (4) introspective accounts of "feelings" and "states" of subjects. To these four methods we might add a fifth category, that of attempting to relate emotional behavior to learning and motivation as exemplified by studies of conflict, conditioning, unconditioning, "free association," forgetting or "repressing" unpleasant learning material, etc. Each of the above categories illustrates some of the major difficulties in the laboratory study of emotions, and a more detailed analysis should be profitable.

1. *Facial expression.* The basic problem here has been to discover whether there are consistent and characteristic facial (and postural) patterns which would help to classify the alleged "types of emotions." There are three ways of approaching this problem:

   a. One might try to photograph some one individual in a variety of real-life situations wherein the subject runs the gamut of emotion. The fact that no such collection of photographs exists is the chief argument against the probability of learning anything about emotion in this fashion. If the emotion is to be genuine, our "candid photographer" must be on the spot when our subject is horrified, terrified, amused, bemused, confused, surprised, amazed, in grief, in joy, etc. Since our subject is not likely to care for company on the occasions when he is behaving in some of the above ways, our photographer might have to maintain a discrete distance and perhaps a bit of invisibility. If we permit the use of more than one subject, we run up against the difficulty of individual differences.

b. Because the real-life approach is impractical, recourse has been had to posed photographs, usually of actors or actresses (like the famous Feleky or Ruckmick pictures). This procedure raises the question as to the genuineness of the data. Do the actors actually have emotional experiences, or are they intellectually arranging their facial muscles in a stereotyped fashion? If the latter is the case, then we can learn something about culturally-produced stereotypes, but nothing about emotion.

c. A third method has been attempted by some experimenters who are not pleased with the other two. Why not create the emotion in the laboratory and photograph the subject on the spot? At first glance this appears to be the solution. The only difficulty is the creation of suitable emotions in the laboratory. A laboratory subject is basically prepared (he is "set") to co-operate with the experimenter, and usually he tries to please the psychologist. How can you make him angry, for instance? No matter what you do to him, he is not likely to react as he would outside the laboratory, and a grave error would result if any label were applied to the reactions exhibited. The writer once participated in an experiment in which his function was to anger forty individual subjects. The experiment was designed to create considerable frustration in the subjects. The writer did things to those subjects which he would never dare to try outside a laboratory (name-calling, insults, physical injury were some of the mild stimuli employed). Throughout an hour of personal abuse, the subjects nobly maintained a politeness and an ability to "take it" which was most discouraging. They knew they were there to act as subjects, and that knowledge altered them in the direction of permissiveness.

The subject in the laboratory can be stimulated in a variety of ways calculated to produce "fear," "embarrassment," "anger," etc. But the experimenter's expectations do not automatically ensure the occurrence of some unique patterns of behavior corresponding to alleged "emotions." The subject *knows* that no harm will come to him in the laboratory; he knows he is participating in an experiment, and that knowledge or "set" prevents his reacting in the way he would if his home were burning, if his parents were dying, or if he heard a series of slow thumps in his cellar when home alone at night lost in a murder story. Because of the "set" of the subject, laboratory emotions are more than likely to be artificial affairs, and even more complicated than their real-life originals as far as analysis is concerned.

When the photographs of laboratory-produced or posed "emotions" are presented to students for inspection and identification, a new problem, that of vocabulary, arises. Student judges find themselves at a loss for words and fail to identify photographs easily unless they are told the terms the experimenter wants used. When a vocabulary is furnished, they still do not do well unless some variation is allowed in the use of synonyms. Some alleged emotions like laughter, surprise, and scorn or contempt are usually identified without difficulty; others are not so readily named. Nothing much is learned from such exercises except some appreciation of cultural effects in stereotyping certain facial gestures and grimaces. Some useful negative information has been obtained through such studies; we know, for example, not only that the hero's eyes cannot "blaze with anger," but that the eyes play a minor, if any, role in emotional expression. The eyebrows and mouth play a more important one. The hope of deriving a basis for a classification of emotions has not been fulfilled by the photographic technique, and it is no longer seriously considered.

2. **Other forms of expression.** The face is not the only aspect of an individual that can be investigated for signs of emotional behavior. The behavior of an individual as a whole, for example, may be studied. Various studies of fear, anxiety, likes, and dislikes have made use of measurements of progress toward, or away from, stimuli which are assumed to evoke the desired reaction. Some of these will be described shortly. Movies or photographs of reactions of the whole body, or posture, have been attempted with some encouraging results.

The voice may prove to be a useful source of information. Studies of crying in infants have not been too successful in correlating type of crying with stimulus conditions, but there are possibilities of using the changes in pitch of vocalizations as indicators of emotional disturbance. Such reactions are subject to conditioning, and may become useful experimentally. Besides voice, posture, and behavior as a whole, we might find indications of experimental value in such measures as strength of grip and resistance to work decrement. The latter types of measurement might be difficult to use but should not be ignored as possibilities.

3. **Visceral reactions.** It is a well known fact that under conditions of strong or unusual stimulation a large amount of smooth-muscle activity (not readily controlled through self-instruction) occurs. The pounding heart, the rapid and shallow breathing, the hair "standing on end," the sweaty palms, etc., have been described by novelists and dramatists ever since the art of writing was invented. In general, strong changes appear to take place in the circulatory, breathing, digestive (including eliminative) and glandular functions under conditions of strong, unusual, or unexpected stimulation. Early investi-

gators of emotion believed that it might be possible to classify emotions on the basis of certain specific patterns of change in these functions. Accordingly, they set about measuring heart rates, blood pressure, blood volume, breathing changes, etc., but found, eventually, that no specific patterns could be described in terms of visceral change. Whereas psychologists used to argue that emotion was a primitive type of behavior, basically unorganized and based upon the lower neural functions, Leeper (2) now argues that emotion is highly organized behavior, an adjustment of great efficiency to the true needs of the organism. The visceral approach has been given up along with the facial-expression approach largely because the same kinds of changes seem to occur in a variety of similar stimulus situations; fear and anger, notably, seemed to be indistinguishable on a visceral level.

4. **Introspective accounts.** Wundt originally included "feelings" as one of his basic mental elements. The introspecter was supposed to describe his internal states in terms of Wundt's "tridimensional" theory. The dimensions were (a) pleasant-unpleasant, (b) excitement-calm, and (c) tension-relaxation. These characteristics or attributes of feeling were supposed to include all the possible basic processes involved in an emotional experience. Trained introspecters had no difficulty in describing their "feelings" in such terms, and even the untrained observers can do fairly well with "unpleasant-pleasant," although the other two dimensions might make him hesitate. The introspective analysis of emotions in terms of Wundt's theory did not contribute much to our understanding of emotion because of the obvious difficulty of our stopping to introspect while the lion is chasing us or the battle is on. With the decline of introspection as a standard laboratory technique, the analysis of emotion in terms of "dimensions" of feelings has quietly been set aside, along with sensations and images, as an unsuitable scientific technique.

Emotion as Response

The failures of the four approaches described above have forced the experimental student of emotion to a reorientation in his thinking about the subject. The search for basic emotional patterns has proved as fruitless as the search for the fountain of youth. The older psychologists are not ready to give up their search for individual and discrete emotions. It seems so obvious that we have such different states as anger, fear, and love. Even Watson was willing to accept these three as basic. Other psychologists have reached the point where they fail to see the value of perpetuating what, to them, amounts to a fiction, foisted upon a gullible public by poets and romantics. They do not deny that organisms behave "emotionally," but they are ready to deny that these organisms *have emotions.*

Although the view just mentioned might be startling to some students who are quite convinced that they have had an emotion or two, there is nothing especially new or outrageous about this position. In criticizing Watson, for example, Sherman (4) found that his observers (doctors, nurses, psychologists) were unable to identify the emotions exhibited by their infant subjects *unless they knew what stimulus* or conditions had been imposed on the subjects. If, for example, they saw a baby dropped, they described the subsequent agitation as "fear." The same behavior, with stimulus unknown, might be described as due to "colic," "anger," "hunger," "wet diaper," etc. Sherman suggested that Watson call his emotions *"x," "y,"* and *"z,"* instead of fear, anger, and love. We can go a step further and eliminate the *x, y,* and *z,* as of no special positive significance.

If we recall the stress placed by Sherman on the stimulus, we find ourselves in a familiar theoretical position. Why can we not look at "emotional behavior" in the same way that we look upon any other kind (unemotional behavior, for example, if there be such)? From our laboratory viewpoint we need make no assumptions about a variety of supposed "states"; we need only to go about the study of "emotional" behavior in stimulus-response terms, recording and describing as much of the stimulus side as possible (including an historical appreciation of the "stimulus-function") and concentrating as usual on the measurement of the time, amplitude, direction, and frequency factors of the responses involved. If our scientific aim is to remain that of prediction of behavior, there appears, indeed, no other method of proceeding. To conjure up special "emotions" which we are unable to define operationally has proved itself an unsatisfactory procedure. It is time to try another approach.

As a matter of fact, the implied approach has already been tried, and with some success, by numerous investigators. Behavior that might be labeled "emotional" has been observed in a variety of situations where the experimenter was not concerned with "emotions" as such, but with the *responses* made to stimuli. It was suggested by Sherman in the original criticism of Watson that behavior could profitably be broken down into "approaching responses" and "avoiding responses," with a presumed "indifference" category between the positive and negative varieties. A great many studies have been made of both the approaching and avoiding types of responses with no special reference to, or concern about, the organism's emotional life. The famous "goal-gradient" study of Hull illustrates the positive side. Any of a great number of "avoidance" conditioning studies could illustrate the negative aspect. In most such studies the use of animal subjects is a distinct experimental advantage. In the first place, you will not concern yourself with the animal's mental state or the type of emotion it is undergoing or "experiencing"—you know you are not going to find out what it is. In the second place, the laboratory rat, unlike the college student, does not *know* that the experimenter will not harm it; the behavior is likely to be at least less artificial.

Most current experiments involving behavior that could be called "emotional," if one observed the tradition, proceed in a very matter-of-fact way, with no mention of old concepts, but with a new language, new methods of describing responses in terms which have some operational security. An example of such research is the effort of a group of Yale psychologists to study frustration and aggression (1), both of which terms are operationally defined in behavioral terms. Another attempt to study "emotional" behavior is represented by a series of experiments and a theoretical treatment of conflict behavior presented by Miller (3). Miller expands the Sherman suggestion of positive and negative reactions into four basic behavioral patterns that might occur when two or more positive or negative stimuli or situations impinge upon an organism. Miller proposes that conflict be analyzed into the following categories:

1. Approach—approach conflicts (where two positive stimuli affect the organism at the same time).
2. Avoidance—avoidance conflicts (two negative stimuli present at the same time—the devil-and-the-deep-blue-sea situation).
3. Approach-avoidance conflicts (one positive and one negative stimulus affecting the organism at the same time, as, for instance, cheese in a mouse trap for a trap-wise mouse).
4. Double-approach avoidance conflicts (where two positive stimuli are present simultaneously, and responding to one of them automatically excludes a response to the other).

It will be noticed that the behavioral situations that can be encompassed by these conflict types are "loaded with emotion," yet no mention of emotion is made. Miller's approach represents the modern trend. It is no longer felt necessary to discover what "fear" or "love" *is*. Neither probably *is*. It is more useful and effective to study what organisms *do*. If at times certain kinds of responses, e.g., rapid pulse, shallow breathing, cessation of digestion, etc., occur along with positive or negative reactions, they too must be studied. The *visceral reinforcement* of responses to certain stimuli cannot be ignored, and deserves the fullest study; on the other hand, one cannot manufacture "fear" out of a pounding heart in the laboratory.

For purposes of general conversation, we can retain the term "emotional" to refer to those responses wherein visceral reinforcement is strongly noticeable. There is no need to get "emotional" about the matter; on the other hand no special purpose is served by attempting to retain the term in scientific discourse. In your reading of those modern studies where viscerally supported behavior is prominent, you will find little use for the classical "emotions." Older studies are likely to contain elements of confusion. The average student reading about Watson and little Albert is ready to believe that Watson conditioned little Albert to fear the rabbit. In modern language we might talk about the conditioning of an avoidance response, and ignore little Albert's "feeling." The student must be on his experimental guard in his reading of the classics and should be ready to question the masters who discourse learnedly on "repressed emotions," "inherited emotions," "learned emotions," etc.

References

1. Dollard, J. *Frustration and aggression*. New Haven: Yale University Press. 1939.
2. Leeper, R. W. A motivational theory of emotion to replace "emotion as disorganized response." *Psychol. Rev.*, 1948, *55*, 5–21.
3. Miller, N. Experimental studies of conflict. Chapter 14 in *Personality and the behavior disorders,* J. McV. Hunt, ed. New York: Ronald Press. 1944.
4. Sherman, M. The differentiation of emotional responses in infants. *J. comp. Psychol.*, 1927, *7*, 265–284.
5. Skinner, B. F. *The behavior of organisms*. New York: Appleton-Century. 1938.

Experiment 25. Emotional Behavior I:
Conditioning an Avoidance Response

Introduction. In recent years many psychologists have become interested in avoidance behavior because of its significance for abnormal behavior and its usefulness in providing a situation for testing clinical concepts. It is also of great interest for "learning" theorists, some of whom consider avoidance training a separate kind of learning. Some learning theorists have made use of avoidance situations to demonstrate secondary or "derived" drives, i.e., drives that depend on learning for their effectiveness in initiating responses.

Mowrer (2), for example, suggests that in avoidance behavior the following sequence of events occurs: (1) Some strong, natural (unconditioned) stimulus arouses a fear reaction. (2) This fear leads to some form of activity which reduces the fear. (3) If other stimuli are present at the time the fear is aroused, they can be associated, by Pavlovian learning (contiguity) with the fear, and later can arouse it in the absence of the original stimulus. (4) The learned fear then serves as a derived drive to activate the same activity which followed the naturally incited fear.

New responses, too, can be learned if the derived drive of fear is reduced. Mowrer and Dollard and Miller (1) use the term "anxiety" in referring to derived fears of this nature. In the present experiment you will have an opportunity to observe the formation of an avoidance response and to study emotional behavior in a real-life situation for an animal subject. When you complete your observations, consider the problems involved in using human subjects in an avoidance situation such as you will impose on your rat.

Apparatus and Procedure. A suitable apparatus for the study of avoidance behavior can be constructed by making a long narrow box, about 18 inches high, 40 inches long, and 5 inches wide.

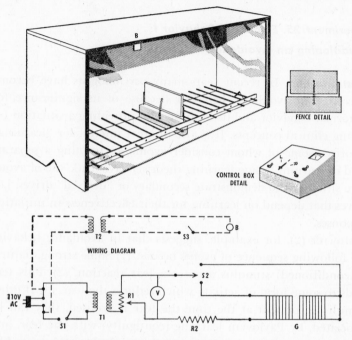

FIGURE 22. *MODIFIED MOWRER-MILLER DEMONSTRATION BOX*. This avoidance training apparatus is patterned after that describe by Mowrer and Miller † and can be used, with proper modification, for any of the purposes they mention. As represented here, it is

V – a 0–300 AC voltmeter (Emico) ; *
T 1 – a 110–300 volt step-up transformer (Utah Y240) ;
T 2 – a 110–8 step-down bell transformer
R 1 – a 50,000 ohm wire-wound potentiometer (Clarostat)
R 2 – a 350,000 ohm, 1 watt, fixed resistor
S 1 – a single-pole, double throw (off-on) switch
S 2 – a four pole selector switch (Clarostat 1465)
S 3 – a door-bell push button
G – grid floor
B – a 6–8 volt adjustable buzzer (Auth)

  * Manufacturer's names are given for parts used in this apparatus. Substitutions can be made freely depending upon local conditions of supply.
  † Mowrer, O. H., and Miller, N. E. A multi-purpose learning-demonstration apparatus. *J. exp. Psychol.*, 1942, 31, 163–170.

The front wall of the box is a sheet of window glass through which you can watch your animal. The floor of the box is a grid made of $\frac{1}{8}$-inch stainless steel bars (wire can be used if tightly stretched) through which a shock is administered to the animal's feet. The box is divided in the middle by a 6-inch grid fence, so that there are, in effect, two compartments in the box. The box shown in Figure 22 is modified from an original design by Mowrer and Miller (3). The various dimensions are not important. All that is essential is to provide the animals with running room.

---

ready for use in connection with Experiment 25. The apparatus consists of a long, narrow chamber with a grid floor and a glass front through which an animal can be observed. The box is divided across the middle by a small fence which tilts if the animal tries to sit on it. The animal can be shocked on either side of the fence. The box is 34 inches long, 22 inches high, and 5 inches wide. These dimensions are convenient but not essential and can be freely altered. In using the box, the experimenter gives the animal a signal (buzzer attached to back of box) for two seconds and then a shock through the grid floor. Buzzer and shock are maintained until the animal crosses the $5\frac{1}{2}$-inch fence to the "safe" area. After a suitable delay, e.g., 30 seconds, the buzzer is again sounded and the animal is again shocked until he jumps. The procedure is repeated until the animal jumps to the buzzer cue before the shock is applied. Other procedures depend upon the experimenter's purposes.

The details of construction are indicated in the figure. One important point is to make the fence flexible so that the animal cannot find it a place of refuge. The arrangement shown in the detail drawing has proved practical. The fence is mounted on pin bearings with compensating weak springs. Sitting is discouraged because of the tilting action of the fence.

The shock circuit is virtually the same as that of Mowrer and Miller and their description should be consulted in order to appreciate the merits of the arrangement. All wires are brought to a control box (see detail) where the experimenter can operate signals and shocks from a remote location. The grid floor consists of $\frac{1}{8}$ inch thick steel rods placed $\frac{1}{2}$ inch apart. The rods are connected to two leads, every other rod being "positive" with intervening rods "negative." The electrical parts can be purchased for about $10.00.

In order to shock the animal, you must so wire the bars that every other bar is connected with one wire. The intervening bars are then connected with another wire. Both wires then lead to a shocking device as shown in Figure 22. By suitable connections and switches you can arrange to shock animals on either side of the fence, leaving one side or the other unelectrified. Conditioning stimuli can be mounted on the box or in the near vicinity. Buzzers, bells, lights, etc., are commonly used, and any of these can be used in this experiment. Lights are preferred if you are working with others under conditions where your buzzer might stimulate some other rat in another box. The procedure described below will include a buzzer stimulus. If you use some other type, there need be no change in the procedure.

Your rat should be habituated to the box for 10 minutes, during which time you count the number of times he crosses the fence. This will serve as an indication of his "operant rate." After 10 minutes, sound the buzzer 5 times for periods of 5 seconds each at 30-second intervals to see if the CS evokes any crossings. Following this preliminary check, start the buzzer, and after 2 seconds turn on the shock. Keep the buzzer and shock on until the animal crosses the fence, then silence the buzzer and turn off the shock. Thirty seconds later, repeat this procedure, regardless of which side of the box the rat happens to be occupying. Continue the presentation of CS and Unc.S at 30-second intervals until the animal begins to cross the fence to the CS before the Unc.S is presented. Under ordinary conditions, a rat should begin to show conditioning in about 30 minutes, or after approximately 60 trials. Some rats develop habits which delay conditioning, and may "freeze" or huddle, and thereby fail to jump. If this occurs, and you are unable to make the rat jump by tapping his feet from below the grid, get another rat.

Your rat may begin to jump before it is time to present the CS. Note the number and time of such "spontaneous" jumps. Keep up the training until the animal meets a criterion of 5 successive jumps without a shock. Then start an extinction series by presenting the CS every 30 seconds until the animal fails to jump in 5 successive 30-second periods. If the animal continues to jump, record all the jumps in a half-hour period, and terminate the experiment.

Results. Make up a table like the sample below, and record all the jumps made during the training and extinction periods. Circle all the conditioned jumps, and identify all "spontaneous" jumps by writing S in the appropriate time interval.

Table 27. (The student should provide a suitable title for this table.)

Trials in 30-second periods	Time in 5-second periods					
	0–5	5–10	11–15	16–20	21–25	26–30
1	1					
2	1					
3	0				S	
.	0					S
.	0					

N	0					

How many times did you have to shock the rat before he made his first jump to the CS? How many additional shocks were required to meet the criterion? Did you note any spontaneous jumps? At what time intervals did they occur? Were you able to extinguish the response to the CS? In how many trials?

Discussion

1. Did you condition your animal to an external CS or to a time interval? What evidence can you cite? How could you demonstrate that it either was or was not a case of temporal conditioning?
2. Did you detect any signs of fear? of anxiety? How is "anxiety" defined in the current literature (see Dollard and Miller)?

3. Did you collect evidence for a "derived" drive? Is it possible that the animal was jumping to the *CS* without having a "drive" of any kind of fear operating?
4. What is the "intervening variable" in Mowrer's explanation of avoidance behavior?
5. On the basis of your observations, set up an operational definition of "fear."

References

1. Dollard, J., and Miller, N. *Personality and psychotherapy.* New York: McGraw-Hill. 1950.
2. Mowrer, O. H. Anxiety-reduction and learning. *J. exp. Psychol.,* 1940, *27,* 497–516.
3. Mowrer, O. H., and Miller, N. A multi-purpose learning-demonstration apparatus. *J. exp. Psychol.,* 1942, *31,* 163–171.

Experiment 26. Emotional Behavior II:
Conflict and Levels of Aspiration

Introduction. In the laboratory course we must be content with a rather mild form of conflict experiment, as vigorous stimuli cannot be used on student subjects without special precautions which would extend the time of experimentation well beyond any reasonable laboratory period. The most common current views of conflict emphasize the significance of competing stimuli, competing goals or choices, and competing tendencies. Sometimes the conflict situation is described as consisting of positive and negative goals, stimuli, tendencies, or habits.

In Miller's (1) analysis, approach and avoidance gradients are stressed as the basic mechanisms underlying conflict. In his view, an organism can be thought of as affected by two approach gradients (variations in the strength of stimulus-response tendencies) by two avoidance gradients, or by an approach and avoidance gradient at the same time. In Pavlov's "experimental neurosis," an animal was placed in a situation calling for fine discriminations between positive (excitatory) and negative (inhibitory) responses.

In our own experiment we will attempt to set up two competing habits by training, and observe how the habits affect each other. Woodworth (3) discussed this type of problem as "negative transfer." We have already worked in a related area (retroactive inhibition), but in this experiment our interest will be in the manifestations, or "symptoms," of conflict reactions. Because our procedure lends itself easily to an incidental observation on the "level of aspiration," we will attempt to collect some data on this interesting "personality" phenomenon.

Apparatus and Procedure. The students will first test each other for speed in the sorting of an ordinary deck of 52 playing cards. Two trials will be taken for each subject, and the best time (in seconds) of the two trials will be reported to the instructor, who will then select subjects to form two comparable groups. In this preliminary sorting, the shuffled deck will be sorted out into suits in the order Spades, Hearts, Diamonds, Clubs, forming four piles in a row on a table.

When the two groups are equated, they will be instructed to proceed as follows: members of Group A will sort the cards in cross-pattern I on the first trial. On the second trial they will sort the cards in cross-pattern II. They will continue alternating the patterns for a total of 20 trials, 10 in each pattern. Members of group B will sort the cards in pattern I for 10 successive trials, then take 10 trials with pattern II.

The patterns will be drawn out on the work table in chalk in the following forms: pattern I, H $\begin{smallmatrix} S \\ D \\ C \end{smallmatrix}$; pattern II, D $\begin{smallmatrix} C \\ S \\ H \end{smallmatrix}$. The time per trial will be recorded in seconds and noted in Table 28. No errors will be permitted; all cards must be placed correctly although the number of corrected errors per trial, if any, will be counted, and their nature noted. If the subject drops a card between two groups, or if he has a tendency to do so, the experimenter will note the cards and locations involved. If a card is incorrectly placed, the experimenter will note which suit it belonged to, where it was placed, and where it actually belonged on that trial.

For observations on the level of aspiration, the subjects *in each group* will be further subdivided. One half of the subjects in each group will be told their actual scores on each trial; the other half will not be told. *All* of the subjects will be asked to *estimate* the time in seconds that each trial will take. The estimate will be made and recorded just before each trial. The estimated and actual times will then be plotted for each subject and for the group as a whole, and the estimates and scores made by the group that has "knowledge of results" will be compared with those of the uninformed group. For efficiency in tabulating results, the instructor will appoint tabulators for each subgroup in A and B ("with knowledge" and "with no knowledge"). Report your data to the proper tabulators.

Results. The individual and group data are recorded in Table 28. The student will formulate a title for this table which will

Table 28

Trial No.	Own Subject		Mean Group A, N =				Mean Group B, N =			
			Knowledge		No Knowledge		Knowledge		No Knowledge	
	Time	Est.	Time	Est.	Time	Est.	Time	Est.	Time	Est.
1										
2										
3										
4										
5										
6										
7										
8										
9										
10										
11										
12										
13										
14										
15										
16										
17										
18										
19										
20										
Mean total time										

adequately describe its contents. Description of errors should be kept as pencil-draft records and included in your report. Before the experiment is started, the subject should attempt to guess which group will have the faster scores and this guess should be noted. The results of both groups should be plotted for ready examination. Did group B have more or less trouble on Trial 1, pattern II, than group A had on Trial 2? What technique revealed more conflict? More errors? Were there any differences in the forms of the curves of level of aspiration of the two groups (A and B)? At which trials were the differences most marked? Did the aspiration levels of the "with-knowledge" group vary from the "with-no-knowledge" group within either group A or group B?

Discussion

1. What signs of conflict did you observe in your subject or yourself?
2. What factors were responsible for this conflict?
3. Can you state the purpose of this experiment in the form of an hypothesis?
4. What justification can you suggest for treating "conflict" as a matter of habit interference?
5. Do you regard this type of conflict as having any bearing on serious personality disturbances?
6. Can you illustrate from case material (of friends or acquaintances) how mutually exclusive habits can be incited in a given stimulus situation and lead to difficulty?
7. What criticism can you offer of this experiment in either or both of its phases?

References

1. Miller, N. Experimental studies of conflict. In *Personality and the behavior disorders,* J. McV. Hunt, ed. New York: Ronald Press. 1944.
2. Underwood, B. J. *Experimental psychology.* New York: Appleton-Century-Crofts. 1949, chap. 8.
3. Woodworth, R. S. *Experimental psychology.* New York: Henry Holt. 1938, chap. 8.

Experiment 27. Emotional Behavior III: Attitudes, Group Preferences, Approach and Avoidance

Introduction. Thus far in our study of emotional behavior we have had occasion to note the difficulties involved in the traditional approaches, which generally make the assumption that there are a wide variety of emotions (each with its own variety of names, specific expressive features, and specific physiology). Before much experimental progress can be made in the study of emotional behavior, such assumptions must be strongly questioned, and new approaches tried out. In the classic criticism of Watson's three innate emotions (fear, anger, and love), Sherman suggested that, behaviorially speaking, it is preferable to talk about "going-toward" and "going-away-from" behavior. Such a suggestion has an operational merit, and it opened the way to an analysis of behavior in terms of "avoidance and approach."

We have already had an opportunity to study some of the features of approach behavior in our experiment on conflict (Experiment 25). In the present experiment we shall make some preliminary observations of approach and avoidance behavior in terms of attitudes or preferences and of likes and dislikes. Our experiment will not actually deal with emotional behavior as such, but may reveal some of the important theoretical and practical problems involved in an appreciation and understanding of "emotion."

Thurstone has defined an attitude somewhat loosely as "all that we think and feel about a person, place, or thing." We shall define an attitude for our purposes as a "set" (see chapter on "Motivation") to respond in an approach or avoidance manner toward stimuli in the behaviorial field. When no stimuli are present for a given attitude, we shall assume that no attitude exists except in the sense of a habit. This latter assumption frees us from the danger of endowing or burdening the "personality" with a variety of independent, autonomous, and dynamic attitudes which act as "causes" of behavior. For a suitable introduction to the study of attitudes we will analyze an "attitude scale," see how it is constructed and what assumptions underlie its development and use, and then we shall make a minor application of our findings to a simplified analysis of some interpersonal attitudes of the members of the class.

Apparatus and Procedure. The data for the second part of the experiment will be collected first to allow the instructor, who will be the only person to see the raw data, an opportunity to code and classify it. While the instructor is so occupied, the students will be busy with the first part of the experiment.

The data referred to will be obtained in this fashion: The instructor, after pledging complete secrecy of the information, will ask each person in the group to write his name on a slip of paper. Below his own name he will write the name of a person present *in the class* whom he prefers above all others as a laboratory partner. There may be a variety of reasons for this choice (because he gets help from him, or because he can boss him, or any other reason). He then writes the name of a member of the class whom he *least* prefers to have as a laboratory partner. Again a variety of reasons may underlie the choice. The slips of paper are collected by the instructor, who assigns each name a number.

After making a list of the positive and negative preferences in terms of the numbers which now stand for names, the instructor destroys the slips. His list is arranged to read like the following example:

No.	Prefers No.	Does not prefer No.
1	8	11
2	6	4
3	12	2
etc.	etc.	etc.

Part I. After the slips are collected, the students will receive a form sheet containing 21 statements which are quotations of opinions about the Germans as a national group. (An "opinion" is a verbal expression of an attitude.) The list of statements (see Appendix 3) was prepared by L. L. Thurstone and is labeled "An Attitude Scale Toward the Germans." The list contains statements that vary pro and con from high approval to great disapproval. Each statement has a numerical value from 0–11, and the strength of a person's attitude is allegedly measured by the most favorable statement he is willing to endorse. These statements were originally selected from a great number of similar statements. Many judges sorted out the statements into 12 groups, from least to most favorable.* In effect, the judges were using the psychophysical method of limits, or "equal-appearing intervals," in that they were forced to distinguish just noticeable differences in favorableness among the statements. The value of each statement represents its *average placement* in the twelve intervals or classes by the group of judges.

Each student will now, working backwards, attempt to place each statement into one of twelve groups. To do this most effectively, separate the statements (by tearing the form into strips) into two groups (favorable and unfavorable); then working in from each end, approach the middle value. Use twelve groups. Each group must have at least one statement, and may have two or more. In Table 29 indicate the value of each statement after you have made your arrangement.

Part II. While the students are busy with their arrangements, the instructor will plot a Moreno-type "sociogram" of the preferences of partners in the group, and another of the "least preferred" choices. These sociograms will be then made available for class discussion.

The sociograms are prepared by writing all of the numbers that represent class members on a sheet of paper and drawing arrows joining the numbers to indicate the choices. Thus, if No. 5 chose

---

* Statements placed in the first group have a value of 0, those in the second group, a value of 1, etc., so that statements in the last group have a value of 11. Using 12 groups provides 11 "equal-appearing intervals."

Table 29. *Rank Order Correlations of Ratings Made by Experimental Psychology Students and Thurstone's Judges of Statements Used in the Scale Measuring "Attitudes toward the Germans"*

Statement	Own Rating	Thurstone Rating	Class Mean Rating	Own Rank	Thurstone Rank	Class Rank
1						
2						
3						
4						
5						
6						
7						
8						
9						
10						
11						
12						
13						
14						
15						
16						
17						
18						
19						
20						
21						

ρ (self and Thurstone) =
ρ (self and group) =
ρ (group and Thurstone) =

No. 6, an arrow is drawn from No. 5 to No. 6. If they chose each other, a double-headed arrow can be drawn to show this relationship. It is probable that some people will be chosen by quite a number of others and when all the arrows are drawn connecting the choosers with the chosen the resulting diagram will consist of a maze of criss-crossing lines. This chaotic condition can be made more intelligible by redrawing the diagram after the most popular individuals are separated widely to represent focal points of popularity. In the new diagram much of the criss-crossing can be avoided by proper planning of the positions to be assigned to each number. A similar diagram is prepared for the negative choices. If desired, the two diagrams can be combined by using different colors for the types of preferences.

Discussion

1. Compare the relative merits of the 12-point Thurstone scale and the 2-point Moreno scale.
2. Is the psychophysical method justified?
3. Are there 12 shades of "attitude" toward the Germans or anything else? Are there perhaps more?
4. What does any given scale value, say, 8.3, mean; that is, how would you interpret it in describing someone's attitude?
5. Discuss your findings with the Moreno technique.
6. What suggestions for other uses of this procedure can you make?
7. Could you pick out "leaders," "followers," "cliques," etc.?
8. How do you interpret a Morenogram in which a person chooses someone who definitely does not want him?
9. Does the Moreno technique open the way to an experimental social psychology?
10. What relationships do you infer for the study of emotion from your investigation of attitude-scaling techniques?
11. Considering attitudes as "sets," and "sets" as equivalent to motivation, what relationships do you consider to hold between emotion and motivation features of behavior? (See Skinner, 3, pp. 408–410, and Leeper, 1.)

References

1. Leeper, R. A motivational theory of emotion to replace "emotion as disorganized responses." *Psychol. Rev.*, 1948, *55*, 5–21.

388   THE STUDY OF RESPONSES IN EXPERIMENTATION

2. Moreno, J. L. *Who shall survive?* Washington, D. C.: Nervous and Mental Disease Publishing Co. 1934.
3. Skinner, B. F. *The behavior of organisms.* New York: Appleton-Century. 1938.
4. Thurstone, L. L., and Chave, E. J. *The measurement of attitude.* Chicago: University of Chicago Press. 1929.

19

Psychology and Experimentation:

A Backward Glance and a Forward Look

THE STUDENT who has toiled his way through the experiments included in this volume recognizes how complex are even the simplest behavioral phenomena and how difficult it is to acquire reliable and valid information about them. Our experiments were short and simple because of the restrictions of educational timetables. Assuming that boredom could have been controlled, we might, perhaps, have learned as much from one long experiment lasting throughout the year.

There should be little danger that any student regards an experiment as some affair that is done and over with in a two- or three-hour laboratory interval. That may be time enough to run one subject through a test, but not enough to take care of the variables of apparatus, procedure, stimuli, and responses as they appear in different guises for different subjects.

The elementary statistics involved in this book are truly elementary, and the student will soon learn, if he continues the study of psychology, that statistics, the handmaid of the sciences, must be assiduously courted if the data collected in research are to be properly and *fully* appraised. Individual differences have time and again prevented a clean-cut demonstration of the worth of some hypothesis. The failure to obtain critical and significant differences may have discouraged some students about the experimental approach to psychology. Such students often turn to one

389

form or another of nonexperimental study where "results" are rapidly obtained.

Some students turn to studying one "personality as a whole," hoping to find out some valid information about at least *one* person. Such an approach may have value for some purposes, especially for guidance, counselling, or therapy; it may be fruitful in terms of suggestions and may result in "insights," but the variables determining human behavior will, if history repeats itself at all, call for a modification and tempering of the suggestions and insights, possibly to the point of vague generalizations. Such is the case with various wonder drugs and panaceas in medicine, and also with a host of personality psychologies. Some principles of behavior can, no doubt, be studied by the case method, but the scientific psychologist is not especially interested in any one person or rat, any more than a physicist is interested in any one cannon ball. In the search for principles or laws descriptive of behavior, case studies without controls are valueless. The introduction of controls brings back the experimental method, which may have been denied as a suitable means for study in the first place.

We are left with a dilemma: (a) Either we study individual cases, as such, and acquire information about individuals (there is no objection to this procedure unless the student describes his findings as "the new science of the mind" or "the scientific study of personality" and begins to generalize to all humanity); or (b) We attempt to study behavior in its various aspects under the constant government of operational principles and controls, taking account of individual differences, of course, but searching for information *about behavior,* and not about individuals. From the general viewpoint of science, we are interested, for example, in how learning occurs, and not how Individual A learns. When the answer is found, the principles involved will take care of Individuals A to Z. The correct principle will account for deviations and individual differences, either in itself, or in conjunction with other principles whose relations to the first are known.

There is no intention in the above to endorse one procedure

because it is "scientific" and to decry another because it is an art, or "common sense," practical, or "applied." It is simply a matter of recognizing the limitations of various procedures and of acknowledging their functions. Whatever procedure is followed, one must take account of the rules of the game. The general aims of science are to produce theories which will account for the phenomena of the world in such a way as to explain them or make them understood to the point where predictions of consequences from antecedents can be made. Science cannot proceed without problems which will intrigue scientists. By and large, such problems come from the practical needs of society as such needs are recognized. It is rare indeed that a scientific discovery is already available and waiting for society to develop a problem which can make use of the scientist's discovery. The case-study approach often locates the problems, and sometimes it is used to solve them. If suitable controls are introduced, there is no objection whatever from any side. It is only when controls have not been introduced that the argument arises.

Some psychologists are impatient with the experimental method because the problems which preoccupy laboratory researches seem trivial and refined out of all semblance to "real" human situations. Psychologists working with "lower" animals are, occasionally with scorn, sometimes with condescension, referred to as "rat psychologists" and ivory-tower tenants. They are censured for not tackling the problems of the clinic, the nursery, the schoolroom, and the factory. The reluctance to work in these areas is not a matter of choice, however, but one of the necessities of the scientific method. Until the problem is presented in terms which the experimental method is capable of handling, there is no point in working on it just because it is "real." How can one experiment, with anything like a semblance of scientific method, with such assumed mechanisms, or behavior aspects, as *ego involvement, unconscious desires, the higher processes, schizophrenia,* or even fear, prejudice, anxiety, etc. The last three words are not italicized because we think we know what they mean, even if we do not. This is not to say that some experimenters have not *reported* experiments about these alleged types of behavior. It hardly needs to be pointed out that they were probably studying something. What they studied and what they reported are not necessarily equivalent.

In some experimental studies of "ego involvement" for example, a subject is asked to report about the "subjective" or apparent movement of a tiny light stimulus in a dark room. The light, although stationary, seems to move. The frequency and amount of movement reported varies with the subject and with different conditions. If another "subject" is introduced who deliberately reports more or greater movement, his reports sometimes influence the first subject. Such findings are interesting. To jump from such data to "ego involvement," and then to use "ego involvement" as an explanatory principle, seems injudicious at best.

Such a procedure is essentially equivalent to the long practice of certain physiologists, like Pavlov and Sherrington, who study, measure, and record responses of animals (in terms of salivation or leg reflexes) and thereupon *devise* a nervous system which will accommodate itself to their findings. This "conceptual nervous system," as Skinner calls it, is then utilized to explain the same behavior and other phenomena which it happens to fit. When it does not fit, a new principle is added to the system. Thus, Pavlov, for example, insisted that conditioned reflexes were formed by certain hypothetical processes in the cerebral cortex. When it was demonstrated that conditioning could take place in the absence of cortex, Pavlov just said that it could not, since obviously the hypothetical processes could not take place; later he denied that the behavior was actually conditioning, even though his own specifications were met. Still later, Pavlovians *invented* new principles by which subcortical centers could accommodate the data. The same story is true, as Kantor (1) insists, of most functional localization experiments and of the convenient principle of "vicarious functioning."

If one is going to study the nervous system, a good place to start appears to be the nervous system, and not behavior. If one is studying "ego involvement," it likewise seems wise to study "ego involvement," and not autokinesis. Since the factors underlying autokinesis are themselves not too well understood, it might be wise to acquire some plain, ordinary facts about the phenomenon before adding "ego involvement" to it.

The experimental method is ready, and experimentalists are willing and eager to study the complex and important, sometimes crucial, problems of society as they are discovered and described by psychologists working in the areas of personality, abnormal behavior, and social behavior. All that is necessary is to describe these problems in such language that the factors in the problem can be reduced to operational terms.

There are four reasons, at best, why some problems are neither studied nor solved: (1) If an operational reduction cannot be made, no solution is possible. (2) If the problem is presented in a form which can be charitably described as unrealistic, no answer can be found. (3) If no answer is really wanted, there is little likelihood that one will be forthcoming. (4) If the problem is not amenable to the psychologist's technique, the psychologists cannot solve it. Let us illustrate these reasons by samples of illegitimate questions that might be asked by laymen of a psychologist:

1. **The nonoperational question.** How does the mind work? Why do people go crazy? What's the best way to bring up a child? How does schizophrenia arise, and how can it be cured? Are people careless by nature or by training? These will do.

2. **The unrealistic question.** (These are questions which assume a state of affairs for which there is no factual basis, and challenge a theory to explain, or an experiment to study, the imaginary events. Failure to present a ready answer is taken as an indication of the weakness of the experimental method.) The illustrations might be considered outrageous, but they

are not more so than questions often asked by students: If a person were brought up by apes on a jungle island, would he have any morals? would he like classical music? What would happen if you put a man in a man-sized Skinner box? If you connected the auditory nerve with the occipital lobe, would you see with your ears, or see sound? etc. If you could quick-freeze a person into suspended animation and later thaw him out, would he pick up the threads of a conversation held at the time of the frost? If a child of some race other than white were raised as a white child, etc. If a dog did solve the double-alternation problem, then what? The answer to all these questions, of course, is to request the questioner to arrange the necessary conditions, and then call in the experimental theorist for an accounting.

4. ***The questions for which no answers are genuinely desired or for which the price of answers is too high.*** Why does man fight? The question might more properly be arranged in the form: Why do nations go to war? but somehow "man" has been handed the burden. The results of a poll of draftees might be interesting in this regard, but we can judge from budget appropriations for the scientific study of the causes of war as compared with military budgets throughout the world, how much "society" cares for the answer. The causes and cures of psychotic disorders represent another question in this group, if we take society as a whole. Such questions require the concentrated strength of at least as many highly skilled scientists as produced the atomic bomb, but "society" has not demanded it with the same energy. What are the most efficient educational techniques? The answer to this question demands a degree of control over education that the scientist himself would hesitate to request, and which society is in no present mood to grant, with possibly good argument on its side. But, then, why ask the question and complain that the answers are slow in coming from picayune attempts by isolated students?

4. The nonpsychological question which is asked of psychologists (sometimes by psychologists): What are the causes and cures of nervous disorders? What are the causes and cures of "functional" disorders? This question is included in this group because it may turn out that biological factors have been neglected and unrecognized in the conditions classified as "functional." This is certainly no place to argue the point, but it can be pointed out, at least, that psychiatrists and psychologists do not in all cases see eye to eye on such matters as schizophrenia, manic-depressive psychosis, and alcoholism, among others. Can feeble-mindedness be cured? The complications in this question are so obvious as to require no comment. How can you cure laziness, accident proneness, nervousness, and similar states, all of which *may* have *essential* biological bases, and never submit to the psychologist's probing beyond a peripheral description?

It is unfair to require an experimental answer to questions that are not subject to experimentation. A proper appreciation of scientific method will result in a more efficient science. It will not and should not be asked to answer questions of metaphysics, theology, ethics, logic, politics, or of any other pursuit which is not subject to the tools and procedures of scientific method. When questions are asked that are within the legitimate scope of science, someone will attempt to find the answers. Questions in abnormal and social psychology plague the experimentalist as much as any other citizen. When these questions are reduced to workable form, some progress is made; when they are phrased in vague terminology, little can be done. As a matter of fact, the experimenter is often taken to task, as was McGranahan (2), for example, who attempted to study the Freudian mechanism of "repression." When his results were published, he was told by critics that, after all, he was not observing what Freud *really* meant. Until we find out what Freud and many other writers really mean, there is little hope for progress.

The few attempts made in this text to study some problems in the field of social and personality psychology should not be taken as typical. There are many experimental inquiries in these areas which are as "scientific" as can be desired. The advancing student will come to them in his future studies. With an appreciation of experimental procedure, he will realize the necessities of control and the limitations in the analysis of complex phenomena. He will realize the difference between a stimulus and a "stimulus complex" or "stimulus situation" or "behavioral field." He will realize, further, that a movement recorded on a laboratory tape is not the equivalent of a response or "behavior pattern" such as is exemplified by a voter dropping his ballot or a baby crying. Skinner (4) has attempted to show how a psychologist might help to arrange human social life on a scientific basis in a fictitious community that permits experimentation. The socially interested student will find this challenging book worthy of his attention.

A final comment is added with some hesitation, but from a compulsive feeling of necessity. The average student has an extraordinary ability to learn specific details or specific habits (just as some learning theorists say they do). The failure of the student to *generalize* his knowledge is on the appalling side when we consider the generally cited benefits of education. The student persistently sticks to his specific experiences. If he learned how to attack some problem by using nonsense syllables, it remains forever a nonsense-syllable problem. If he once used a kymograph for a certain type of investigation, he must use it again in a similar problem. The examples that could be cited are unhappily numerous.

The greatest fault and danger, however, of our laboratory study is to confuse an experiment with a laboratory room, with apparatus, with animals, or with college-student subjects. An experiment, be it noted for the last time in these pages, is a *controlled observation*. The observation can be made anywhere, any time, by anyone capable of controlled observation, on any type of event susceptible of controlled observation. It can be made on a street corner or in a grocery store. All that is required in an experiment is that when you make your observation you *know* what you are observing, and that you *know that nothing of consequence* is occurring outside the scope of observation. This comment is probably superfluous, but it is a final plea to dissociate the experimenter from his white coat, his cellar, or his attic, and to place him where he belongs, at the observing end of a controlled situation.

References

1. Kantor, J. R. *Problems of physiological psychology.* Bloomington, Ind.: Principia Press. 1947.
2. McGranahan, D. V. A critical and experimental study of repression. *J. abnorm. soc. Psychol.,* 1940, *35,* 212–225.
3. Skinner, B. F. *The Behavior of Organisms.* New York: Appleton-Century. 1938.
4. Skinner, B. F. *Walden two.* New York: Macmillan. 1948.

Appendixes

Appendix 1

How to Prepare a Laboratory Report

A LABORATORY REPORT is a piece of scientific literature with the specific objective of describing research in such a manner that the work can be repeated readily by anyone having access to similar materials, subjects, and conditions. If a reader could not repeat your experiment from your description, assuming appropriate facilities, your report is inadequate. If someone is to repeat your experiment *exactly,* you are obliged to report it *exactly.*

To facilitate accurate reporting, certain commonly followed customs relating to the format of reports have developed and, although they are not compulsory, the customary practices have advantages which can hardly be ignored. Readers expect to find certain specific features in a report, and should not be asked to dig them out of a highly personalized document. Reports, such as are to be described below, can be used profitably in any situation calling for objective writing, and should not be identified with psychology alone. They are equally suitable for reporting the functions of a bank, a hospital, or any form of enterprise. Practice in preparing such reports should greatly improve the student's comprehension of the actual business of science. The common practices in the preparation of formal reports have been described by Anderson and Valentine (1).

It is customary to describe an experiment or other research in a series of sections, each of which has its own specific function. These functions will be described for the following parts and sec-

401

tions of a formal report: Title, Author's name (and address), Introduction, Apparatus and Procedure, Results, Discussion, Conclusions or Summary, and References. It is customary to separate the several sections by appropriate headings, which are centered on the page.

1. *Title.* The title should be informative. Its length is unimportant. It should contain sufficient information to distinguish your report from *any* other report dealing with similar problems. Such a title as "Fatigue," for instance, is not only useless, it is irritating. A title like " 'Rehearsal' and Guessing Habits as Sources of the 'Spread of Effect' " has obvious superiority.

2. *Name and address.* The full name and location of the writer is to be included in case of need for additional information, or for purposes of correspondence, criticism, discussion, etc.

3. *The Introduction.* In the introduction state the purpose of your experiment, possibly the reason for doing it, and describe the current status of the problem based on your reading concerning the subject. In a serious report you are expected to show familiarity with the basic background of your problem as well as with all of the specific literature pertaining to the experimental hypothesis itself. If you are testing some hypothesis, state this clearly, and indicate the theoretical consequences of positive *or* negative results.

4. *Apparatus and procedure.* (These can be described separately.) Name your apparatus if it has a recognized technical name; if not, describe it as accurately as possible, using diagrams if necessary. There is no need to give elaborate descriptions of *standardized* apparatus. In describing your procedure, tell *exactly what you did,* not what is mentioned or recommended in the laboratory manuals. Report by full quotation any instruction given the subjects. Confusion will be avoided if the procedure is described step by step, exactly as it was followed. Always use the past tense. Remember, you are writing an historical account, not an instruction booklet.

5. *Subjects.* Mention prior laboratory experience, age, sex, edu-

cation, race, and other *pertinent* factors concerning your human subjects. Remarks concerning the suitability of the subjects are often necessary. Indicate how subjects were obtained, that is, whether they were volunteers, etc. For animal subjects, describe species, sex, age, strain, prior laboratory experience, habituation procedures, feeding schedules, etc.

6. *Results*. In this section of your report present *all* the data that you have obtained from your experiment. Summarize this data as clearly as possible in tables and graphs. Be sure all columns of figures and all graphs are labeled fully and accurately. Assign numbers to graphs and tables (Roman numerals for tables). Provide explanatory titles for figures and tables so that a reader can study the data with intelligence and be able to form his own conclusions. *If results are properly labeled and titled, it should be possible for any reader to know what was found out about the topic without reading the rest of the report.* All graphs and pictures should be labeled as "figures," not as "graphs" or "charts," thus: Fig. 1. (with appropriate caption). Captions for figures should appear *below* the figure. Titles for tables should appear *above* the table.

7. *Discussion*. In this section, discuss *your results* in relation to your hypothesis, the results of others studying the same problem (if data are available), and explain any unusual deviations in the results. Describe factors influencing the results which you were unable to eliminate or hold constant. If your results do not correspond with expectations, it is necessary to explain this lack of correspondence. Suggest ways in which future experimenters may save time and trouble. Indicate problems arising from your experiment which require study.

8. *Conclusions*. In this section summarize the general findings of your experiment in relation to your purpose. Has your purpose been fulfilled? What have you proved or disproved? Be careful that your conclusions follow from *your own* data, and not from some other source. Keep in mind your discussion of the data, as you may have listed therein some factors which invalidate your

conclusions or make conclusions impossible. It is customary to number the specific conclusions and to state these succinctly.

9. *References*. In the body of the text identify all references by a number enclosed in parentheses, e.g., (9). At the end of your report list alphabetically all the writers to whom you have referred. Consult the latest issues of journals cited for current practices in abbreviating names of journals and the order of items such as title, author, publisher, volume number, pages involved, and date. The current practice in psychological writings is to give the complete reference as follows: Name and initials of writer (last name first). Period. Title of book or article. Period. *Book titles* and *names of journals* are underlined. Only the first word (and proper names) in a title of a book or journal article are capitalized. Address of publisher, colon; Name of the publisher, period. Year of publication in the case of books. Thus: New York: Henry Holt. 1949. In the case of journal articles, the procedure is to list an abbreviated name of the journal, the year, the volume number, and, finally, the page numbers. Thus: (1) Sheffield, F. D. "Spread of effect" without reward or learning. *J. exp. Psychol.,* 1949, *39,* 575–579. The volume number is underlined.

The following outline illustrates a suitable format.

SAMPLE REPORT OUTLINE

An experimental test of Thorndike's proposals
relative to place vs. response learning.

by

Joyce James
University of Erewhon

Introduction
Apparatus and Procedure
Results
Discussion
Summary and Conclusions
References

Reference

1. Anderson, J. E., and Valentine, W. L. The preparation of articles for publication in the journals of the American Psychological Association. *Psychol. Bull.*, 1944, *43*, 345–376.

Appendix 2

Anagram Lists for Experiment 16

Experimental List	Control List
1. elunc	1. enluc
2. klcha	2. khalc
3. ensce	3. ehyno
4. tsgho	4. erspa
5. lecam	5. bushr
6. yehon	6. ohgst
7. dlchi	7. dlchi
8. neque	8. nolem
9. frsca	9. kaste
10. peshe	10. nquee
11. nitra	11. hsfle
12. macre	12. afscr
13. elwha	13. phsee
14. ytpar	14. naorg
15. htmou	15. maste
16. bushr	16. ritna
17. nolem	17. egbul
18. kaste	18. camre
19. hsfle	19. tslea
20. naorg	20. hawel
21. maste	21. tnsai
22. egbul	22. tesle
23. tnsai	23. umhto

Experimental List	*Control List*
24. tslea	24. naoce
25. tesle	25. reang
26. nrtho	26. cnees
27. reang	27. nrtho
28. ersho	28. ersho
29. erspa	29. tarpy
30. naoce	30. macle

Appendix 3

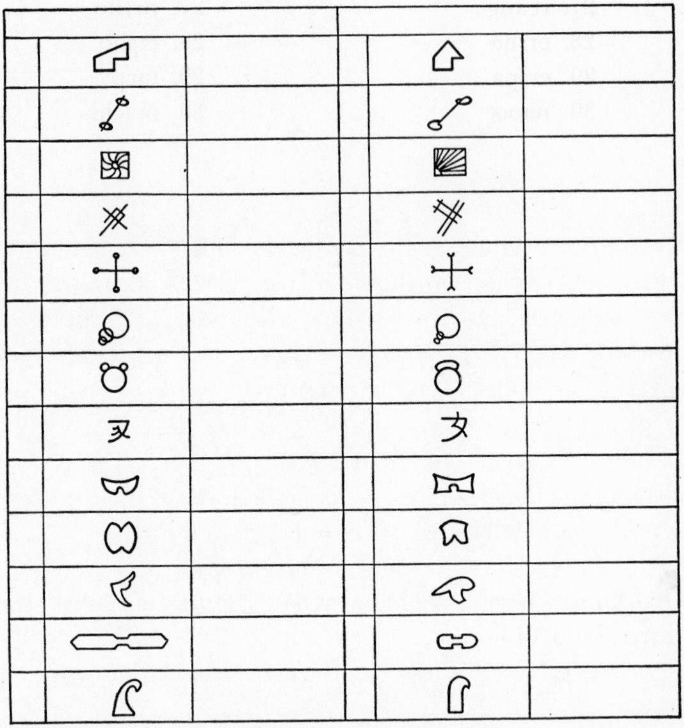

FIGURE 23. *THE GIBSON PAIRED ASSOCIATES.* Two sets of 13 slides are prepared on glass slides (size depending on projector to be used). Slides are prepared in India ink on one surface. This surface is then covered with a plain glass cover slide and the two sheets bound with tape. Each slide contains one of the diagrams shown above, drawn on the left half of the slide and followed by a dash-line, and then by a nonsense syllable. When the slide is exposed, it is possible to show the diagram alone or the diagram plus syllable. The figures have been copied from Gibson's groups I and II, which are supposed to be relatively similar and to produce a high degree of retroactive inhibition when used as described in the procedure for Experiment 22.

408

Appendix 4

Attitude Scale for Experiment 27

INSTRUCTIONS: Indicate the degree to which you believe each statement is favorable to the Germans. Rate a statement "0" if it is most unfavorable. Rate it 11 if it is most favorable. Try not to give the same rating to more than two statements. Also, try to use each value from 0–11 at least once.

1. The Germans are excellent workers.
2. I don't see how anyone can really be fond of the Germans.
3. On the whole, the Germans are pretty decent.
4. The Germans are slow and unimaginative.
5. If I know a person is of German descent, I am slightly prejudiced in favor of him.
6. The more I know about the German people, the better I like them.
7. The German respects only brute force.
8. I have no particular love or hate for the Germans.
9. German parents are harsh to their children.
10. German people have a refinement and depth of feeling you don't find anywhere else.
11. I think some German traits are admirable, but, on the whole, I don't like Germans.
12. German people are no different from other people.
13. German home life is ideal.
14. The Germans are very fond of showing off.

15. I can't see how any intelligent person can help being pro-German.
16. The Germans are the most despicable people in the world.
17. German art is superior to that of any other nationality.
18. Few countries are as progressive as Germany.
19. We must not let our national hatred of Germany die.
20. German culture is unequaled in the world.
21. There is nothing about the Germans that I could ever like.

Do not examine this table until after you have rated the statements.

Thurstone Values for the Attitude Scale Used in Experiment 27 (Attitudes toward the Germans).

Statement	Value	Statement	Value
1	7.8	11	4.5
2	2.6	12	5.5
3	6.6	13	9.0
4	3.6	14	3.9
5	7.3	15	9.4
6	8.3	16	0.0
7	1.7	17	11.0
8	5.5	18	8.6
9	3.0	19	0.5
10	9.8	20	10.6
		21	1.0

Index

Index

ABBA method of presenting variables, 20
absolute judgment, method of, 211
act, and movement, 241
adaptation, 123
in olfaction, 215
in reflexes, 255
in vision, 169
aims,
of psychology, 39
of science, 48
alleys, runways, 291
Anderson, J. E., 401
Andrews, T. G., 138
animals, use of, in experiments, 110 ff.
anticipation error, 137
anticipation method, 329, 341
apparatus, purpose of, 99–101
artificial pupil, 166
attention, 280
span of, 86
attitude scale, 383
audition, 191 ff.
acuity, 197
apparatus, 197
physics of, 192
range of stimuli, 198
stimuli, 192

audition (*Continued*)
variables in study of, 202–203
average deviation, 27
average error, method of, 131, 132, 139
avoidance training, 305
experiment and apparatus, 373–374

backlash, in apparatus, 112
Bartley, S. H., 152
Beach, F., 112
Beck, L., 122, 209
behavior,
analysis of, 193
experimenting with, 16
recording, 239
thinking, 354
voluntary, 249
Bell Telephone Company, 193, 199
Berg, E., 360
Bills, A. G., 258
biting board, 177
blind spot, 176
Boring, E. G.,
on color, 172
on history of psychology, 4, 10

413